# Hiding in Plain Sight

## The Story Behind Megilat Esther

Rabbi David Shabtai, MD

Targum Press

First published 2020


ISBN: 978-1-56871-675-6



Published by
**Targum Publishers**
Shlomo ben Yosef 131a/1
Jerusalem 9380581
editor@targumpublishers.com

Distributed by
**Ktav Publishers & Distributors Inc.**
527 Empire Blvd.
Brooklyn, NY 11225-3121
Tel: 718-972-5449, 201-963-9524
Fax: 718-972-6307, 201-963-0102
*www.ktav.com*

*Printed in Israel*

Rabbi Hershel Schachter
24 Bennett Avenue
New York, New York 10033
(212) 795-0630

הרב צבי שכטר
ראש ישיבה וראש כולל
ישיבת רבינו יצחק אלחנן

מכתב ברכה

ידידי - יקירי הרה"ג דוד נ"י כבר
הי' מוכר בעולם הישיבה כת"ח גדול
וחזקה על חבר וכו', אלא כידוע מהש"ס
ריש יבמות ובעוד מקומות, היכא
דאפשר למבדק בדקינן ולא סמכינן
אחזקה, ולכן עברתי בעצמי על כמה
פרקים מן הספר, ומאוד נהניתי, ולא רק
מתוך הדקדוקים (המלאכה הספרותית
אותה ופרשנות נראה על פי עמודה)
אלא אף מסגנון הרב אותו. ובודאי ימצא
את יקירי, שיחי', שגם ספרו זה ימצא
חן בעיני הקהל, וממנו ילמדו להבין
ביותר עמקות את ספר אסתר בפרט, ועוד
יותר מזה - לפתח גישה נכונה
ללימוד כתבי הקודש בכלל
בכבוד,
צבי שכטר
חנוכה תשפ"א

HAHN JUDAIC CAMPUS ■ 7900 MONTOYA CIRCLE NORTH ■ BOCA RATON, FL 33433-4912
TEL 561.394.0394 ■ FAX 561.750.2451 ■ OFFICE@BRSONLINE.ORG ■ WWW.BRSONLINE.ORG



בס״ד

Kislev 5781

In his new book, "Hiding in Plain Sight," Rabbi Dr. Shabtai's brilliance, erudition, and penetrating insight are on display for all to see. Although God's name doesn't appear in the text of *Megillas Esther*, Rabbi Dr. Shabtai skillfully demonstrates how it jumps out from between nearly all words and lines. If our mission when reading *Megillas Esther* is to be *megaleh* the *nistar*, to reveal that which is hidden, Rabbi Dr. Shabtai provides us with the tools, the vocabulary, the evidence and, most importantly, the inspiration needed to accomplish this task. This wonderful work will not only enlighten your Purim but will inspire your quest to find and feel Hashem's presence throughout the year.

Rabbi Efrem Goldberg
Marah D'Asrah
Boca Raton Synagogue

# Dedications

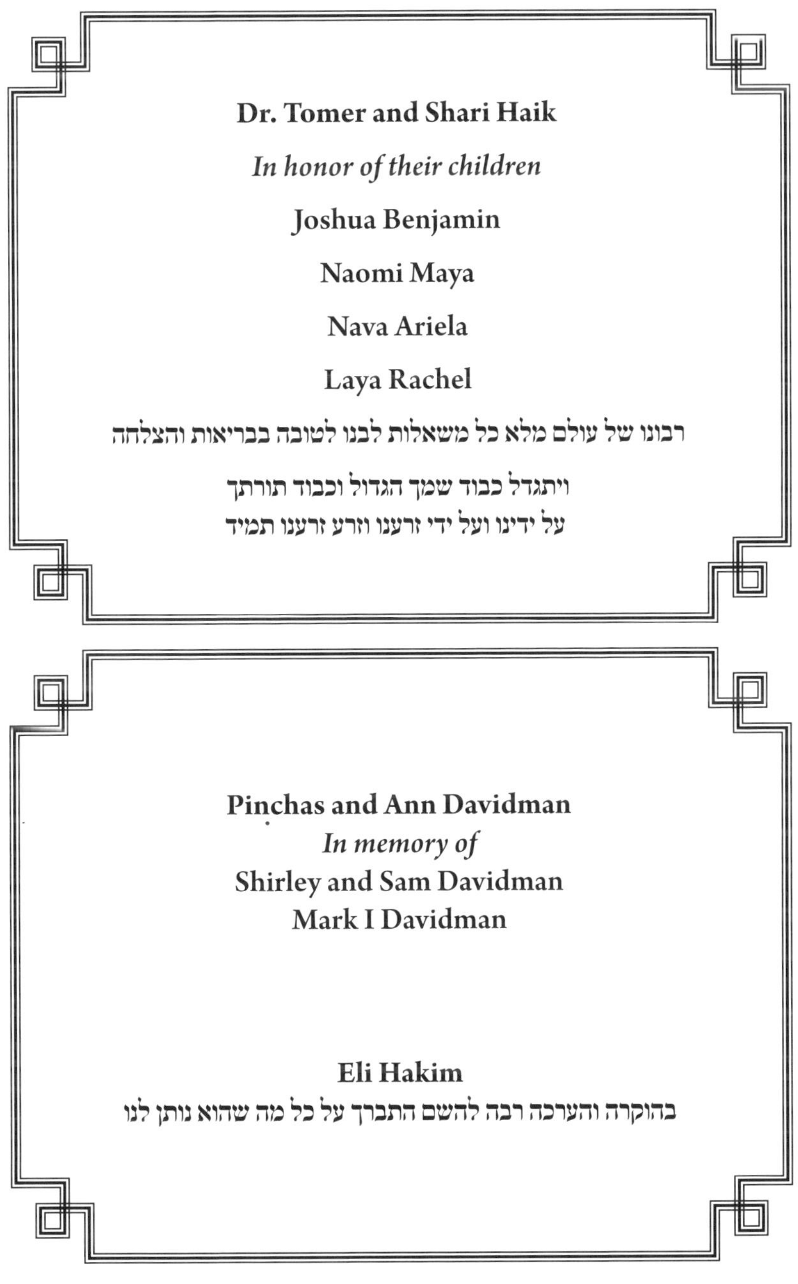

**Dr. Tomer and Shari Haik**

*In honor of their children*

**Joshua Benjamin**

**Naomi Maya**

**Nava Ariela**

**Laya Rachel**

רבונו של עולם מלא כל משאלות לבנו לטובה בבריאות והצלחה

ויתגדל כבוד שמך הגדול וכבוד תורתך
על ידינו ועל ידי זרענו וזרע זרענו תמיד

**Pinchas and Ann Davidman**
*In memory of*
**Shirley and Sam Davidman**
**Mark I Davidman**

**Eli Hakim**
בהוקרה והערכה רבה להשם התברך על כל מה שהוא נותן לנו

# Dedications

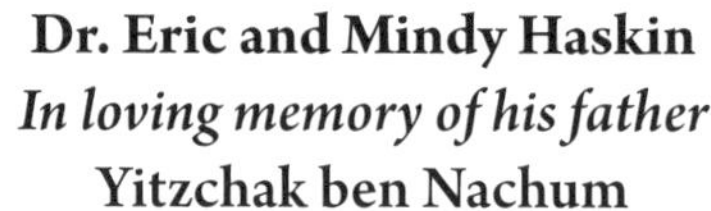

**Dr. Eric and Mindy Haskin**
*In loving memory of his father*
Yitzchak ben Nachum

**Dr. David and Marissa Levenson**
*In loving memory of their parents*
Lana Ditchek Goldberg
Harold Levenson
Mildred Pallas Levenson

**Isaac and Dr. Veronica Mizrahi**
לעילוי נשמת
דוד בן רבי אבא
ויקטוריה בת אירן

# Preface

I can't quite put my finger on when exactly Purim became my favorite holiday.

For most children, Purim is indeed among the most fun holidays. Dressing up in costume, eating lots of candy, and being encouraged to make noise in shul were sure to spice up our day off from school. And even as we grow up, the festivities and revelry may change in form, but are indeed highlights of the adult Jewish calendar as well. But at some point, at least for me, the amusement and enjoyment transformed into something far more meaningful and elevating.

A number of years ago, our shul hosted Rabbi Eli Mansour for Shabbat. While we often host Friday night Onegs and shiurim in people's homes, we planned a talk for Rabbi Mansour in the shul itself. And even though we were a bit nervous about attendance, in retrospect it was definitely the right decision as the large sanctuary was filled with people. As I walked in and saw the room filling, I was pretty grateful for our fortuitous choice of venue.

Rabbi Mansour's title for the shiur was pretty generic, *Developing an Attitude of Gratitude*. No one would debate the centrality of being grateful as a prime Jewish value, but it didn't give much in the way of hinting at the content of his talk. I can't remember many of the details, except for one idea, which admittedly, may not have been his prime focus: recognizing Hashem's role in our lives. Rabbi Mansour pointed out that it's often hard to see the *yad Hashem* in the world, but the more we look for it, the better we get at seeing it. It's a skill that needs development and practice. But it's also something that requires more than just thinking about it. He encouraged us to talk about it, openly.

As a society, even in the more devoutly religious groups, we seem to have a hard time talking about Hashem, even more so as He relates to the intricacies of our daily lives. But if we want to truly appreciate and understand the *yad Hashem* in this world, it needs practice. And if we want to ensure that it remains a Jewish value, then we need to teach it to our children. But Rabbi Mansour went further than that. It's not enough to simply teach the value of recognizing the yad Hashem in the world, as parents, we need to model it.

He recounted how in his home, every Shabbat, each person takes turns describing how they saw the *yad Hashem* in their lives during that past week. Not necessarily something earth shattering or miracle-worthy, but something nonetheless. Having just enough change for the supermarket; leaving the house just in time to avoid traffic; getting to shul a moment earlier than usual and avoiding a downpour in the parking lot. Little things indeed and from a big-picture perspective large scale of things, perhaps not terribly noteworthy, but important in building our skill of seeing the yad Hashem all around us – such as in choosing a large enough venue to accommodate the unanticipated large Friday night crowd.

This message strongly resonated with me, and in our family, it's become part of our Shabbat table ritual. Our entire family plays this 'game' each week. Truth be told, it was somewhat awkward the first Friday night that we had guests over and our kids asked us if we were going to play the game. We indeed did, and from then on, we invite any of our guests to participate as well.

As things would have it, I also 'just happened' to be teaching Megilat Esther in school that year. It was one of the first times that I read the text of the Megilah that carefully and was beginning to appreciate how the entire story is crafted around the notion of Hashem, hidden behind the scenes, orchestrating all of the events. It's about that time that I became interested to learn some of the Maharal's thought and since I was teaching Megilat Esther, purchased a set of his Ohr Chadash commentary to the Megilah. His depth of thought and development of ideas within the Purim story strongly resonated with the message of seeing the yad Hashem everywhere that I was trying to put more into action in my own life. Every page (and in the Rabbi Hartman edition of the Maharal that I use, that means a few lines of Maharal and tons of enriching commentary) of the Ohr Chadash was a journey deeper and deeper into the richness that lay just beneath the surface of the Megilah's text. It's then that I became hooked – both on the Maharal (and since then have learned many more of his sefarim, and always the Rabbi Hartman edition) and also on Purim.

Purim became more than just about festivities and gratitude to Hashem for our survival. It was about man's existential need to see God in world events and in small events. For me, it became a holiday that was about recognizing our place in God's world and His ever-present place in ours. It's perhaps the reason that Purim is a holiday when we are enjoined to fully immerse ourselves in the very physical pursuits of food and drink because in so doing, we can more fully come to appreciate how infused our world is with yad Hashem. And this notion permeates everything about Purim – from the various halachot and minhagim to the theme, underlying message, and explanation for so much of what happens in the Megilah. It's the key to the entire holiday and what this book is all about.

Indeed, publishing this book also seems to be the result of many fortuitous circumstances, which clearly, were anything but coincidental or random.

I'm blessed to have the support of my wife Monica, in pretty much everything I do. (When she's opposed, it's usually because it's not a good idea and doesn't work out anyway.) She has not only stood by me through every twist and turn that we've faced, but has always pushed me to be my best. Her care and concern for me, our children, and our family are behind everything that any of us accomplish and we are all forever grateful.

I'm tremendously grateful to members of our community who are steadfast in their commitment to the spread and teaching of Torah and have sponsored this book. Dr. Tomer and Shari Haik are true stalwarts of living and loving Torah Judaism and are an inspiration to all of us. Eli Hakim is always a reliable resource for anything pertaining to supporting Torah. Pinni and Ann Davidman can always be counted on for Torah and chesed projects and endeavors. I am similarly indebted to Dr. Eric and Mindy Haskin, Dr. David and Marissa Levenson, and Isaac and Dr. Veronica Mizrahi. It's through their commitment and generosity of spirit that this book is being published. May Hashem repay each of them with tremendous berachah and hatzlachah in everything that they do and may the zechut of Talmud Torah forever remain in their merit. Hashem has brought us together as a community from all different places and walks of life and recognizing how only through yad Hashem could any of this had taken place is not only appropriate given the book's theme, but something that resonates deeply with each of them.

Nothing about any of this is coincidental, it's all a demonstration of yad Hashem. Recognizing the yad Hashem in the world should and does lead to a deep sense of appreciation and gratitude. I'm tremendously grateful to be able to share and teach Torah. It's not only one of the most rewarding endeavors but also a deeply spiritually inspiring adventure. אשרי חלקי שזכיתי.

It's my tefilah that Hashem continue to enable me to share and teach Torah, להגדיל תורה ולהאדירה, and to be able to continually feel His guiding Hand in all areas of life.

David Shabtai
Kislev 5781

# Introduction

*Megilat Esther,* its story, and the Purim holiday stand out in many regards.

From a literary perspective, the Megilah stands out among all other books of Tanakh in completely omitting any mention of Hashem. He doesn't seem to play a direct role and His name is simply not recorded at all. On some level this makes sense, as *Chazal* describe the era of the Purim story after the destruction of the *Beit ha-Mikdash* as one bereft of public, ostentatious miracles. Prophecy was scarce and it wouldn't be surprising to not find a direct interaction between Hashem and some individual in the story. But aside from not directly communicating with any of the characters, there isn't even any explicit reference to Him whatsoever throughout the entire story. Nobody throughout the entire Megilah discusses God or anything He may have done or might do. And while as a mostly secular history of the Jews in Persia this may not seem very striking, even those aspects of the Megilah that are more religious in nature – Esther's exhorting the Jews of Shushan to fast on her behalf – make no direct mention of Hashem's assistance or appeal to Him for success. It's almost as if the Megilah is trying to show that He is hiding.

*Chazal* saw this notion of hiddenness as relevant to a crucial aspect of the Megilah's status – it's role in Tanakh. While familiar to us as part of Ketuvim, the Tanna'im debate whether or not *Megilat Esther* has a place in the official canon of Tanakh. The Gemara concludes that it indeed should be included as it was written ברוח הקודש. But thinking about it more broadly, the other side of the debate – excluding *Megilat Esther* from Tanakh – seems to make a lot of sense.

Not only is it the only book that does not mention Hashem's name even once, it doesn't even describe very much religious activity at all. Only toward the end do the Jews accept upon themselves to remember the miracles that occurred and agree to annually celebrate Purim. It's a story of palace intrigue, deception, gluttony, and debauchery. It contains no direct Divine message, features no prophets, nor explicitly offers any religious guidance or words of wisdom. There are plenty of reasons to think that it should not count among the official biblical canon.

And yet, as *Chazal* have a tradition that Mordekhai and Esther were infused with a special Divine gift, the message of the Megilah was declared worthy of inclusion.

This is possibly the background for a strange comment in the Gemara (*Chullin* 139b) searching for a "source" for Esther in the Torah. Clearly, *Chazal* do not expect to find any mention of a story that will only take place about 1,000 years after the Torah being recorded. Instead, they are looking for some hint, some lesson in the Torah that relates or gives context to the Purim story. The reference found is a *pasuk* in *Parshat Va-Yelekh* that mentions הַסְתֵּר אַסְתִּיר – a play on words that appears to have the same root as the name Esther. Digging a bit deeper, it's clearly not just a play on words, but relates to the larger context of those *pesukim* - וְאָנֹכִי הַסְתֵּר אַסְתִּיר פָּנַי בַּיּוֹם הַהוּא – And I shall certainly hide My face at that time. If the Torah is hinting at the Purim story with a simple play on words, it's 'coincidentally' fitting that it does so in referencing Hashem "hiding His face" – or keeping Himself hidden. This is perhaps a reference to Hashem's name being absent from the entire Megilah.

But the truth is that it's most certainly not a coincidence. It's precisely because He is practicing הסתר פנים – a time of hiding – and so His name is not mentioned.

An even closer look reveals an even more important lesson, perhaps the defining lesson, goal, and motivation of writing *Megilat Esther* in the first place. The *pesukim* in *Parshat Va-Yelekh* don't just mention Hashem hiding His face, but also its context:

> וַיֹּאמֶר ה׳ אֶל מֹשֶׁה הִנְּךָ שֹׁכֵב עִם אֲבֹתֶיךָ וְקָם הָעָם הַזֶּה וְזָנָה אַחֲרֵי אֱלֹהֵי נֵכַר הָאָרֶץ אֲשֶׁר הוּא בָא שָׁמָּה בְּקִרְבּוֹ וַעֲזָבַנִי וְהֵפֵר אֶת בְּרִיתִי אֲשֶׁר כָּרַתִּי אִתּוֹ. וְחָרָה אַפִּי בוֹ בַיּוֹם הַהוּא וַעֲזַבְתִּים וְהִסְתַּרְתִּי פָנַי מֵהֶם וְהָיָה לֶאֱכֹל וּמְצָאֻהוּ רָעוֹת רַבּוֹת וְצָרוֹת וְאָמַר בַּיּוֹם הַהוּא הֲלֹא עַל כִּי אֵין אֱלֹקַי בְּקִרְבִּי מְצָאוּנִי הָרָעוֹת הָאֵלֶּה. וְאָנֹכִי הַסְתֵּר אַסְתִּיר פָּנַי בַּיּוֹם הַהוּא עַל כָּל הָרָעָה אֲשֶׁר עָשָׂה כִּי פָנָה אֶל אֱלֹהִים אֲחֵרִים.
>
> Hashem said to Moshe: You will soon die and this people will rise up and go astray after the foreign gods in their

> midst, in the land that they are about to enter; they will forsake Me and break My covenant that I made with them. Then My anger will flare up against them and I will abandon them and hide My countenance from them. They shall be ready prey and many evils and troubles shall befall them. And they shall say on that day, "Surely it is because our God is not in our midst that these evils have befallen us." Yet I will keep My countenance hidden on that day, because of all the evil they have done in turning to other gods.

The simple reading of this warning is that the promise / prediction of אָנֹכִי הַסְתֵּר אַסְתִּיר פָּנַי בַּיּוֹם הַהוּא is a punishment for *Bnei Yisrael* having וְהֵפֵר אֶת בְּרִיתִי אֲשֶׁר כָּרַתִּי אִתּוֹ. The two go hand in hand. If *Bnei Yisrael* will not faithfully uphold their end of the covenant and stray after false gods, then it appears that Hashem is warning that He too will no longer "shine His countenance upon them." If they are going to act as if they no longer need Him, behave as if they can find solace, certainty, and salvation in other gods, then He will no longer make Himself available to them. Practically speaking, if *Bnei Yisrael* don't think He is necessary in their lives, then He will not take an interest in them.

From these *pesukim,* hiding His face seems to be Hashem's way of saying that He will not care about what might happen to them, won't protect them, or watch over them. The abandonment seems both real and warranted. If *Bnei Yisrael* don't recognize their need and appreciation of His involvement in their lives, both communal and private, then Hashem, for his part, won't be interested in involving Himself in them.

The problem, however, is that although His name appears nowhere in the Megilah, His hand is implicitly evident throughout the story.

# Chapter One

For a short story, the number of 'coincidences' therein is simply astounding.

Even while Hashem's name is never mentioned, twice in the story – by both Mordekhai and of all people, Zeresh – there is a conscious awareness that a larger plan is taking place, one that is above the control of any of the story's characters. Additionally, as will be described throughout this book, the sheer number of coincidences rises almost to the point of absurdity. One chance event is compounded by another, and then another, and yet another all coming together to bring about the salvation of the Jews. Highlighting these numerous improbabilities one after another seems to be trying to get the reader to recognize that they may not be occurring simply out of random chance. Instead, there is a larger plan – one which the characters are unable to control or manipulate, but one which, when they pay close enough attention, can experience and understand.

The story of the Megilah is a story of recognizing the *yad Hashem* in the world. There is no such thing as chance or coincidence; everything is part of a plan, we just aren't always privy to see or understand all of its details.

In fact, the very name of the holiday perfectly captures this point. Of all names to choose for a holiday celebrating the events of *Megilat Esther*, Purim is likely the least appropriate.

It's not without meaning, as the Megilah itself explains the naming of the holiday – עַל שֵׁם הַפּוּר. It commemorates the lots that Haman drew when calculating when best to execute his plan of destruction upon the Jews. Many questions abound, but perhaps the most basic is why name a holiday after the instrument through which the story's villain tried and failed to annihilate the protagonists?

Many will argue that even in victory, it's important to remember what led to the challenge in the first place. This is reminiscent of *Chazal*'s insistence that at the *Pesach Seder*, we מתחיל בגנות ומסיים בשבח – we begin the story with the negative and transition to praise. We cannot truly be grateful for overcoming adversity without first appreciating and understanding the hardships, dangers, and misfortunes that brought about the need for a victory. But even granting that approach, the holiday should then reflect something about Haman or perhaps about his accusation against the Jews to Achashverosh. What sense is there in focusing specifically on the פור – the method by which Haman chose the date for his plan and not something about the plan itself?

If the main message of the entire Megilah is recognizing the *yad Hashem* in the world, then perhaps the naming choice is understandable. Certainly in an ironic or satiric way.

In retrospect, it's somewhat strange that Haman looks for a way to select a date to destroy the Jews. Why not promulgate the ruling and get it over with as soon as possible? It's understandable that it might take some time for word of the edict to reach each of the 127 provinces, but once it did, wouldn't it make more sense to execute the plan immediately? Instead of expediency, Haman chooses to leave the matter to chance and draws lots to select the execution date of his plan.

Haman specifically wants to leave it up to chance and let randomness run the day. He is ready and willing to go along with whatever his lottery will turn up, seemingly without any concern for efficiency and expediency or taking any military, social, or other factors into consideration. It's almost as if Haman is effectively declaring that only through pure chance can he succeed.

Understanding that the underlying theme of the Megilah is recognizing the *yad Hashem* in the world, Haman serves as the chief villain who fails to understand this fundamental lesson. [Interestingly, the Megilah's most explicit acknowledgment of *yad Hashem* in history is by Haman's wife Zeresh, who, after watching her husband parade Mordekhai around the streets of Shushan, recognizes that there is a larger plan in place in which Haman's downfall plays prominently.]

As the foil to the heroes of the Megilah, it's perhaps fitting that Haman chooses random chance as his best ally in bringing about the death of the Jews and it's specifically through the Jews recognizing the *yad Hashem* in the world (וּמִי יוֹדֵעַ אִם לְעֵת כָּזֹאת הִגַּעַתְּ לַמַּלְכוּת) that they secure their salvation. Effectively, the story of the Megilah is one of the recognition of *yad Hashem* overcoming a perspective of the world as happenstance and randomness. That which Haman does not or cannot grasp is his downfall and is specifically how Esther and Mordekhai properly relate to and understand the events that are unfolding before them that brings the redemption.

It is this idea that the name Purim highlights. Considering that the message of Purim is recognizing the *yad Hashem* when it isn't always obvious to see, to look past the superficial and 'dig a little deeper' to see the truth, it would be hard to capture that idea in a name. Because it's specifically that which is not seen that is the focus of the story, it would be strange to name the celebration after such an idea. It would bring that which was beneath the surface to the forefront of people's consciousness and perhaps weaken the message of looking for the hidden *yad Hashem* in history.

Since they were unable to directly or explicitly reference the idea of the hidden plan behind everything that happens, Mordekhai and Esther chose a different name that would cleverly hint at or at least get people thinking along these lines.

Purim is the perfect name because it perfectly satirizes the point of the story. By naming the holiday celebrating our victory over Haman after the method which Haman chose to develop his plan to exterminate the Jews, the name itself ironically highlights our triumph over randomness and chance. The name Purim is most certainly not a celebration of Haman's lots, but of the defeat of the false conviction that Haman invested in them. It fits the Megilah's message because it's what the lots represent – their symbolism or hidden meaning – that the name references. The lots reflect an approach to the world that everything is random and coincidental; there is no particular meaning or order to how events unfold or why they occur.

The Megilah is the story of the victory of divine Providence and recognition of the *yad Hashem* over experiencing the world as chance and randomness. Its message is that we must not look at the world through a Purim-lots lens, but rather through one that sees beyond those lots, that sees Purim for what it really is – a recognition that Hashem runs history.

# Chapter Two

The lesson of the Megilah is not only recognizing that *yad Hashem* is everywhere so long as you know how to look for and see it, but also that the protagonists of the story itself responded by recognizing the *yad Hashem* in the world. The Megilah's story is not only intended to teach us about Divine providence in an abstract sense, but also to describe a paradigm and active examples of modeling appropriate responses and reaction to recognizing it.

It's only because Mordekhai persuaded Esther that וּמִי יוֹדֵעַ אִם לְעֵת כָּזֹאת הִגַּעַתְּ לַמַּלְכוּת that she agreed to risk her life in an attempt to save her people. She not only realized that her position on the throne of Persia was part of Hashem's plan, but once recognizing that she might be an active part of His plan she acted on it.

When Esther saw the complete reversal of fates between Mordekhai and Haman as they marched through the streets of Shushan, coming directly on the heels of Haman's plotting to kill Mordekhai that very day, she recognized that the *yad Hashem* was at play. Recognizing that Hashem was clearly planning for Haman's downfall, Esther reacts and changes her plan.

She comes to understand that convincing Achashverosh that she and Haman are having an affair (her original plan, see chapter 25) is not the only way that she can bring about Haman's demise. Since Hashem's plan for Haman's downfall is already set into motion, to properly respond she needs to switch tactics and use that to her advantage.

And while the final third of the Megilah seems to be an overly belabored and technical description of the battle, victory, and subsequent Jewish celebration, in reality it's vital to the story since it's the way the Jewish people responded to seeing the *yad Hashem* in the world in vanquishing their previously considered to be insurmountable enemies. They didn't just fight and win, but recognizing that their success was part of Hashem's plan for the world they established a new holiday, to forever remember and concretize this important lesson in the collective Jewish experience and memory.

But if all this is true, then *Chazal's* reference to the story of the Megilah as one of Hashem abandoning His people is difficult to understand.

But perhaps in finding this reference and making this identification, *Chazal* are teaching something vital to understanding our relationship with Hashem. The Torah doesn't mean that Hashem will abandon *Bnei Yisrael*, that He will no longer involve Himself in their struggles and save them from their troubles. He will never abandon His people; several covenants throughout the Torah and Tanakh guarantee that end. Instead, the הסתר פנים that the Torah foretells is not that He will no longer be involved, but that His involvement will be hidden.

The *yad Hashem* guiding world, communal, and personal events will certainly still be present, although no longer obvious. Instead of explicit and open miracles, changing and deviating from the laws of nature, Hashem will now interact and guide the world and world events in a more subtle and hidden manner. He is still very much there, it's just harder for us to see His guiding hand. And perhaps that's the symbolism of Hashem's name missing from the Megilah.

It's clear to the reader as well as to the characters in the story themselves that there is some larger plan going on, that *yad Hashem* is guiding the political and social comings and goings of Shushan, but it's not obvious. Looking only at the superficial events themselves, it can easily be missed. It requires reflection and looking somewhat 'beneath the surface' to see, understand, and realize that events are connected and guided by the *yad Hashem*. If so, these *pesukim*, far from describing the opposite of the reality of the Megilah, capture its essence and most important message.

The Torah is predicting that there will be a time of הסתר פנים, where the *yad Hashem* will not be obvious in the world, when it will take effort to 'see' it functioning in world, communal, and personal happenings. What's most telling is that the Torah describes this as a punishment. Ideally, recognizing the *yad Hashem* in the world should be obvious; nobody should ever be confused or mistaken about the fundamental fact that Hashem runs the world.

While perhaps at first counterintuitive, the Torah is not saying that a failure to recognize the *yad Hashem* in the world will inevitably lead the Jews down the road to exile and punishment, but that a failure to follow His rules and commandments will result in הסתר פנים. Our inability to see how *Hashem* runs the world can make us feel abandoned, even when we actually are not. It can make us feel as if Hashem doesn't care or involve Himself in our lives, even though it is simply not the case. It's these thoughts of doubt and uncertainty that are the focus of this punishment. The punitive measure is not in Hashem changing the way in which He interacts with or involves Himself with the world, but instead how we **perceive** that interaction and involvement.

* * *

THIS APPROACH MAY help provide a deeper meaning to the ubiquitous practice of wearing costumes on Purim. Widely quoted in halakhic literature, it's often described as an additional way to achieve *simchah,* by wearing funny clothes and just acting silly overall. But out of the myriad ways to increase *simchah,* dressing up in costume is an almost universal practice and seemingly limited specifically to Purim. Perhaps a deeper understanding relates to the central message of the Megilah.

If the main message of the Megilah is that *yad Hashem* is sometimes hidden then we must look 'deeper' to understand the meaning and connections between events; it also means that that which appears on the surface doesn't represent the whole story. If the *yad Hashem* is hidden, it means that a superficial view of only that which is visible or exterior misses the point. Looking for the *yad Hashem* in the world requires looking beyond the exterior.

Perhaps that is the message of dressing up in costumes. Very few people are fooled by costumes. We know very well that there is a person hiding underneath the giraffe outfit and that there wasn't a sudden influx of tuxedo clad penguins into our synagogues on Purim night. And yet we wear them anyway.

Costumes exaggerate and highlight the superficial and exterior aspects of a person to such a degree that we immediately recognize that that is not who they truly are. A person's true identity and what really matters, is what is hiding underneath the costume. That is the lesson of Purim.

Natural and historical events are just the exterior, superficial covering for the *yad Hashem* in the world. What really matters is what lies beneath.

Whether or not we can accurately detect or infer the *yad Hashem* at work is slightly irrelevant. Even when we cannot accurately identify the person wearing the costume, we are still fairly certain that there is a person hiding beneath the façade and we aren't being confronted by a life-sized Snoopy. So too with world events. Even when we cannot discern the intricacies, details, and precise effects of the *yad Hashem* in the world, the message is that we should still be confident that beneath everything, the *yad Hashem* is indeed running the show.

# Chapter Three

The story of the Megilah opens in the tumultuous political climate of the nascent Persian Empire. Only five years earlier, the Babylonians ruled the vast land with an iron fist. During the second year of Belshatzar, the last Babylonian monarch, the king experiences a vision of indecipherable script that nobody can understand or interpret for him. Only Daniel, the Jewish prophet, can read the proverbial "writing on the wall" and explains it to be a message from God foretelling the imminent demise of the Babylonian Empire. Indeed, that very night Belshatzar is killed and his vast Empire is taken down (*Daniel* 5:1-4). Daryavesh of Madai takes over and rules for a brief two years, after which Koresh, the leader of the Persians, takes command. Four kings in five years is not a recipe for political stability.

Koresh was sympathetic to the Jewish cause and granted permission to the exiled Jews to rebuild the *Beit ha-Mikdash*. He was inspired by recognizing that Hashem granted him dominion over such a vast Empire so that he could grant the Jews the right of return to Israel. He encouraged the *Aliyah* to Israel and even pushed those who didn't or couldn't make the trek by financially supporting those that did. He even gifted the Jews many of the sacred *keilim* from the first *Beit ha-Mikdash* that Nevukhadnetzar had taken. But out of the entire nation of potentially millions, only 42,360 Jews followed through.

For this small group, it was not easy to get started with the building. It took them a bit of time to get organized and only once they all joined together in Yerushalayim for the *Tishrei* holidays were they able to start building the foundations for the *Beit ha-Mikdash*. This effort did not go unnoticed by the local population. Throughout their building campaign, there were local non-Jews who continually tried to thwart their efforts. The

Jews were so frightened, that it was only when they were all together for Yom Tov that they garnered the necessary courage to build the *mizbe'ah* – כִּי בְּאֵימָה עֲלֵיהֶם מֵעַמֵּי הָאֲרָצוֹת. Once they started building, it didn't get any easier – וַיְהִי עַם הָאָרֶץ מְרַפִּים יְדֵי עַם יְהוּדָה, וּמְבַהֲלִים אוֹתָם לִבְנוֹת.

But their fear tactics didn't stop there. Even while this local opposition was fierce, employing schoolyard bully tactics, they also tried their hand at political avenues as well – וְסֹכְרִים עֲלֵיהֶם יוֹעֲצִים לְהָפֵר עֲצָתָם – they bribing the Persian ministers to thwart the Jews' efforts. It's somewhat unclear as to whether or not they were successful as their next step, as described in Ezra was to appeal directly to the King himself. וּבְמַלְכוּת אֲחַשְׁוֵרוֹשׁ בִּתְחִלַּת מַלְכוּתוֹ, כָּתְבוּ שִׂטְנָה עַל יֹשְׁבֵי יְהוּדָה וִירוּשָׁלָ‍ִם – during the beginning of the reign of Achashverosh, they drew up an accusation against the inhabitants of Yehudah and Yerushalayim.

They told Achashverosh that the Jews were indeed rebuilding the rebellious and wicked city of Yerushalayim (קִרְיְתָא מָרָדְתָּא וּבִאישְׁתָּא). Beyond childish name calling, they made a prediction and backed it up with some history.

With extreme confidence, they asserted that:

> כְּעַן יְדִיעַ לֶהֱוֵא לְמַלְכָּא דִּי הֵן קִרְיְתָא דָךְ תִּתְבְּנֵא וְשׁוּרַיָּה יִשְׁתַּכְלְלוּן מִנְדָּה בְלוֹ וַהֲלָךְ לָא יִנְתְּנוּן וְאַפְּתֹם מַלְכִים תְּהַנְזִק.
>
> Let it be known to the king that if this city is built and its walls complete, they will not pay tribute or tax to the kingdom and it will eventually harm the kingdom.

And this wasn't without historical precedent.

> דִּי יְבַקַּר בִּסְפַר דָּכְרָנַיָּא דִּי אֲבָהָתָךְ וּתְהַשְׁכַּח בִּסְפַר דָּכְרָנַיָּא וְתִנְדַּע דִּי קִרְיְתָא דָךְ קִרְיָא מָרָדָא וּמְהַנְזְקַת מַלְכִין וּמְדִנָן וְאֶשְׁתַּדּוּר עָבְדִין בְּגַוַּהּ מִן יוֹמָת עָלְמָא עַל דְּנָה קִרְיְתָא דָךְ הָחָרְבַת.
>
> If you will check in the history books of your forefathers you will find that this city was always rebellious and caused harm and damage to kings and nations; it is filled with violence and for that it was destroyed.

And just to make sure that Achashverosh reached the 'proper' conclusion, they said that they were

> מְהוֹדְעִין אֲנַחְנָה לְמַלְכָּא דִּי הֵן קִרְיְתָא דָךְ תִּתְבְּנֵא וְשׁוּרַיָּה יִשְׁתַּכְלְלוּן לָקֳבֵל דְּנָה חֲלָק בַּעֲבַר נַהֲרָא לָא אִיתַי לָךְ.
>
> Making the king aware that if Yerushalayim is built and

> its walls established, the king will no longer have any stake in this land!

Achashverosh quickly dispatched a message back to them that he took their advice and consulted the history books. Yerushalayim was indeed always causing problems and difficulties for its rulers, full of violence and rebellion. He therefore commanded them to immediately and vigilantly stop the Jews' efforts, to protect the integrity of the kingdom. The locals were all too happy to comply and used their strength and military might to physically stop the massive construction.

This stalled situation continued throughout Achashverosh's lifetime, ending only when Achashverosh's son, Daryavesh, finally granted the Jews permission to continue the rebuilding effort. The story of the Megilah takes place in the interim, opening during Achashverosh's third year and closely following on the heels of this political drama.

# Chapter Four

The Book of Ezra doesn't provide much detail about Achashverosh or his attitude toward the Jewish people in describing this episode. On the face of it, Achashverosh makes the politically expedient call. Why should he risk a potential rebellion? That would certainly not serve his or his nation's interests. It's not that Achashverosh necessarily buys the local non-Jews' argument at face value; he acknowledges that he came to his conclusion based on his own historical research. To him, the argument made sense. But moreover, even if the risk of revolt was indeed small – and it's hard to know how Achashverosh would have made that assessment – what benefit would he accrue from allowing the rebuilding of Yerushalayim and the *Beit ha-Mikdash*, particularly in light of the local Yerushalmi non-Jews who were opposed? Even from a broader political perspective that recognizes that a successful monarch needs the support of multiple constituencies, would refusing the request of the Yerushalmi non-Jews so as to appease the Jews grain him any support among the Jewish people?

From Achashverosh's perspective, rebuilding the *Beit ha-Mikdash* was something that affected only a very small population of Jews. The vast majority of the Jews didn't go to Israel even when Koresh encouraged them, choosing instead to live in the exilic comfort of the Persian Empire. Did these Jews of Shushan and its environs even care about what was happening in Yerushalayim? To the politically calculating Achashverosh, stopping the rebuilding effort just made a lot of sense – it appeased the local non-Jews, it reduced the potential risk of rebellion, and didn't seem to present all that much downside from whatever Jewish political support he may have previously had.

But from the opposite perspective, Achashverosh was clearly aware that it was Koresh, the first great Persian king to rule over the entire Empire, who had granted this right to the Jews. It's important to remember that Koresh didn't simply give in to continued requests and pestering on the part of Jewish lobbyists and advocates. The Book of Ezra is quite clear that it was Hashem who inspired Koresh to promulgate this idea. Koresh was very much aware of this Divine guidance, as he makes clear in his royal proclamation: כֹּה אָמַר כֹּרֶשׁ מֶלֶךְ פָּרַס: כֹּל מַמְלְכוֹת הָאָרֶץ נָתַן לִי ה׳ אֱלֹקֵי הַשָּׁמַיִם, וְהוּא פָקַד עָלַי לִבְנוֹת לוֹ בַיִת בִּירוּשָׁלַיִם אֲשֶׁר בִּיהוּדָה – "So said Koresh, king of Persia: Hashem, the God of the Heavens and earth gave me rule over all the lands, and He commanded me to build Him a home in Yerushalayim that is in Yehudah." – he knows that it is Hashem who placed him as the ruler of "the kingdoms of the entire land" and it is Hashem who commanded / inspired him to rebuild the *Beit ha-Mikdash*. Rebuilding Yerushalayim was part of a spiritual mission, with the *Beit ha-Mikdash* functioning as a physical manifestation of Hashem's presence in this world.

Historically speaking, Yerushalayim served as both the spiritual as well as political center of Jewish life. However, it wouldn't make much sense for Koresh to encourage the Jews – his subjects – to aspire to too much political independence. Maintaining the integrity of the Persian Empire was certainly of prime importance, which is why Koresh consistently focuses on the religious aspects of Yerushalayim and the *Beit ha-Mikdash*, going so far as to provide the Jews with various *keilim* that were plundered from them close to seventy years earlier.

That said, it's hard to imagine that Achashverosh was unaware of the significance that the Jews – no matter where they lived – ascribed to rebuilding the *Beit ha-Mikdash*. He may have even been aware of the history of how the Jewish people ended up living in his kingdom, having their land conquered once the *Beit ha-Mikdash* was destroyed. He may have wondered why more Jews didn't move back to Israel once they were given the chance. But as the leader of the Persian Empire, he was possibly proud that they were so happy and comfortable under his rule that they wouldn't want to take the risks or face the challenges of the long distance travel and resettling a land that presented too many unknowns to offset their relative comfort.

But even with this background, why did Achashverosh not consult any Jews to ask them about the current situation in Yerushalyim before stopping the rebuilding effort? Was he really concerned that the Jews would try to establish independence? Alternatively, they might be so grateful for the opportunity of religious freedom that they would wholeheartedly support

Achashverosh. Why was he so quick to acquiesce to the local non-Jews' request? Was it perhaps because he also harbored anti-Semitic feelings and tendencies?

This tension in understanding Achashverosh's character plays out in multiple episodes and is evident in various interpretations and *Midrashim* of the Megilah. What was Achashverosh's attitude toward the Jews? While he is quick to stop the rebuilding of the *Beit ha-Mikdash* and eventually grant Haman's request to annihilate the Jews, neither is described as being out of hatred or resentment.

Instead, both the Book of Ezra and the Megilah provide political contexts for these decisions – Achashverosh's fear of rebellion (admittedly at the insistence of the local non-Jewish population of Yerushalayim) and his desire to appease and ingratiate Haman, a rising star in Achashverosh's palace (possibly even while completely unaware that it was in fact the Jews who were the target of Haman's plot). Mordekhai, an outspoken Jew (one of the only people ever described as הַיְּהוּדִי), was a member of Achashverosh's court and according to *Chazal*, the Jews of Shushan were invited to Achashverosh's famous parties. And yet, even when the episode with Haman resolves, the Jews triumph, establish the holiday of Purim, and are clearly grateful for Achashverosh's kindness and leadership, he still does not grant them permission to continue rebuilding the *Beit ha-Mikdash*.

As much of the story of the Megilah is the story of Achashverosh, this question and tension as to understanding of his character is a theme that recurs throughout the story and its layered commentary.

# Chapter Five

The Megilah opens and ends with descriptions of Achashverosh's rule. It frames the entire story with his ruling over his kingdom, highlighting that the story of the Megilah is the story of Achashverosh's governance and his attempts to solidify his vast empire under this rule.

In introducing Achashverosh, the Megilah appears unnecessarily verbose – וַיְהִי בִּימֵי אֲחַשְׁוֵרוֹשׁ הוּא אֲחַשְׁוֵרוֹשׁ הַמֹּלֵךְ מֵהֹדּוּ וְעַד כּוּשׁ. The repetition and the need to emphasize his ruling over the entire Empire seems to be highlighting something that we may not have known or an element that we should be attuned to. *Chazal* point out that in fact, Achashverosh was not Koresh's (the previous king) son. Nonetheless, he was a continuation of the Persian Empire, having been established a mere five years earlier. Achashverosh does not represent a direct continuation of the previous dynasty, but rather something slightly different. As a successful leader in battle, fighting for the Persian army, Achashverosh rose through the ranks of leadership.

Cementing his role, he married Vashti, princess and daughter of a previous king, Belshatzar. But this was a far more shrewd and complicated move than a new son-in-law seemingly starting off his own royal dynasty. Achashverosh is Persian and Belshatzar was Babylonian. It's hard to guess the political climate at the time, but far beyond the 'usual' challenges present during a period of royal transition, particularly when it doesn't follow a straight dynastic path, transitioning to a whole new culture must have caused quite the political upheaval. The story of the Megilah then begins with the transition of the vast Babylonian Empire into Persian hands.

Achashverosh is cautious and realizes that the nascent Persian Empire, while vast, is still in its infancy. His concern is not just ruling over as many people as possible, but uniting them together. While a dictatorial monarchy, Achashverosh is still concerned with revolt and rebellion and needs to constantly work to maintain that fine balance between insuring overall compliance, paying taxes, and general submission to authority with giving people what they want. It's precisely these political challenges that Achashverosh tries to navigate through the lavish parties that open the Megilah.

While at first blush appearing as raucous, drunken festivities, celebrating nothing in particular, they are actually part of his political strategy.

* * *

THE VERY FIRST scene opens with an elaborate party. No particular reason is offered, although the Megilah is quick to point out that Achashverosh uses the opportunity to display and emphasize his vast treasure trove and largess. Over the top with its description of fine linens, gold and silver utensils and trays, beautifully adorned couches, and an overabundance of gemstones, it gives the impression that this display is actually the party's very purpose – showing off his wealth and establishing himself as a benevolent dictator.

Although the Megilah gives no context for the party, it mentions Achashverosh's 'kingship' four times in the span of the first few *pesukim*. There is repeated reference to his established authority: הַמֶּלֶךְ [indicating his current role as ruler], כְּשֶׁבֶת הַמֶּלֶךְ אֲחַשְׁוֵרוֹשׁ עַל כִּסֵּא מַלְכוּתוֹ, בִּשְׁנַת שָׁלוֹשׁ לְמָלְכוֹ [seemingly in the midst of his established reign], and his ability and indulgence to cater to the whim and desire of every guest (לַעֲשׂוֹת כִּרְצוֹן אִישׁ וָאִישׁ). Taken together, the Megilah is trying to emphasize how important it was for him to have his reign acknowledged, respected, and even desired.

Everybody is invited – חֵיל פָּרַס וּמָדַי הַפַּרְתְּמִים וְשָׂרֵי הַמְּדִינוֹת לְפָנָיו – the leadership from throughout his kingdom, all 127 provinces under his rule. As a newly minted king, he is looking to consolidate power and garner allegiances. Understanding that political turmoil could undermine the nascent royal dynasty, what better way to bring everybody together than over an abundance of good food and fine wine?

Malbim adds an additional nuanced historical perspective. The party take place during the third year of Achashverosh's reign. During those first three years, Achashverosh was still establishing himself as a military leader, quashing small rebellions, and establishing the Persian Empire and army as a force to be reckoned with. Picking up on grammatical cues, the Gemara (*Megilah* 11a) explains that he wasn't part of the royal family but rather מלך מעצמו – came to rule on his own accord – and had to justify his right to do so to his subjects. Even while he was of Persian extraction, his kingship represented a new period of the Persian Empire.

Officially, he is celebrating his success in battle and inviting his allies to share in the festivities. Achashverosh's idea was to bring all the heads of state, ministers, and military leaders together to celebrate the Persian Empire with him at its helm. It not only solidifies Achashverosh's place as the recognized political and military leader but also promotes friendships, solidifies alliances, and establishes the Achashverosh-led-Shushan as the Empire's capital.

* * *

BUT THE JOYFUL festivities didn't end there. After partying for 180 days with leadership of the entire kingdom, he makes a separate seven day party for the citizens of Shushan. While once again no explicit reason or motivation is provided, it seems that he is just providing a separate venue for this smaller, more intimate contingent. This is not simply an excuse to continue the Bacchanalian festivities for yet one more week, but part of Achashverosh's calculated political agenda.

To demonstrate the transition of the Empire from Babylonian to Persian hands, Achashverosh also moves the capital city to someplace more Persian. And so aside from establishing himself as the undisputed ruler, he is also establishing Shushan as the undisputed capital. That may be the reason that he insists on inviting all the dignitaries to his palace – so that they may pay both homage to him as well as to their new capital. As a Persian city, the Shushanites were likely quite excited about this development. As natural supporters of Achashverosh's rule, they could now play important and significant role in Empire-wide geopolitics. So to show his appreciation, gratitude, and affinity for his own countrymen, he makes a separate party just for them.

In fact, it's this precise sequence of events that leads to one of the most popular misconceptions about the Megilah story. Many of us were taught back in preschool that Achashverosh was a foolish king, a boor who could not control his own wife or ministers and as a rash and petulant man who wasn't sufficiently confident to make decisions without repeatedly consulting experts. But reflecting on the opening scene of the Megilah, a different perspective on Achashverosh emerges. He comes off as thoughtful, nuanced, and politically savvy. Describing Achashverosh as a clown might make the story more understandable when we are first taught it in preschool, but a careful reading of the text and the Talmudic traditional commentary offers a more nuanced perspective of Achashverosh as a keen (if somewhat self-absorbed) political politician.

It's not even unanimously agreed that Achashverosh should be described as a fool to begin with. Rav and Shmuel (*Megilah* 11a) debate this very point, one indicating מלך טפש היה (he was a foolish king) while the other arguing the opposite extreme, מלך פיקח היה (he was a wise king). But even the one who argues מלך טפש היה (the Gemara doesn't attribute the different perspectives to Rav or Shmuel) doesn't base his analysis on an overall picture or understanding of Achashverosh's character. Instead, they argue about the wisdom of a technical detail: should Achashverosh have made the party for the citizens of Shushan before or after the party for the leadership of the rest of the extensive Persian Empire?

On the one hand, he shares a natural affinity with the Shushanites and is confident of their support. It makes sense that they can wait a bit since they will either understand the need to prioritize those without such strong bonds or because of their already existing allegiance, he may have calculated that he wouldn't be risking much by potentially offending them by celebrating with them second. Alternatively however, since the citizens of Shushan are the most influential among the Empire's people and are those who, practically speaking, would have the easiest job in fomenting a successful rebellion, perhaps their party should have been prioritized as a means of both showing them how important they are to Achashverosh or simply trying to solidify his local support. Both sides appear to have some merit, leading to the Talmudic debate.

The argument that Achashverosh was a טפש is not because he constantly acts like a buffoon – because he doesn't. Throughout the Megilah, Achashverosh behaves in a politically aware and astute manner. And even while he may seem to waver and even give in to random individual requests, this isn't because of any lack of confidence or gullibility. Instead, his decisions and actions throughout the entire story have just one goal and purpose – to promote, support, and prop himself up as the Supreme Leader of the Persian Empire. Even the debate as to whether he was טפש or פיקח is really just a matter of choosing sides in a political science argument. The jester-like image we might have of Achashverosh simply isn't supported by the text or even by the Talmudic opinion declaring him a טפש. The opposite perspective in fact, seems to be more accurate.

# Chapter Six

The first actual episode in the Megilah's story further cements Achashverosh's persona as a shrewd politician.

On the face of it, the whole back and forth regarding Vashti attending Achashverosh's party seems pretty straightforward, simplistic, and rather demeaning. Achashverosh demands that Vashti come to his party, she refuses, he gets angry, and punishes her.

As a point on the plot line, this story is necessary to explain why Achashverosh is without a wife, which leads him to select Esther, which eventually brings about the salvation of the Jews. But why all the detail? If the Megilah would have simply started off with Achashverosh looking for a wife, the story itself wouldn't be lacking in any meaningful way. Including these details means that the Megilah feels that Vashti's story is necessary, or at least plays a role in the reader's understanding of what is taking place.

Even before inviting Vashti to Achashverosh's party, the Megilah describes how she "also" held a party – for women – but seemingly in different location, in the בֵּית הַמַּלְכוּת. Whatever it is they were celebrating – and, as noted earlier, the Megilah leaves out this important detail – why couldn't they celebrate together?

And lest one think that the king and queen held gender segregated parties out of concerns of modesty, the story continues with Achashverosh inviting Vashti to his party לְהַרְאוֹת הָעַמִּים וְהַשָּׂרִים אֶת יָפְיָהּ (to show the nations and the ministers her beauty), since after all, טוֹבַת מַרְאֶה הִיא (she was very good looking). Clearly modesty was not on anybody's mind. What then is going on?

Understanding that the Megilah begins with Achashverosh working on establishing his authority and the shift to a Persian-dominated government, culture, and capital city frames Vashti in a very different light. Although not described in the Megilah, if the rest of the story is any indication as to Achashverosh's character, it seems fair to assume that his marriage to Vashti was also part of his larger political scheming.

In a world where social and class status were essential parts of a person's identity, Achashverosh was a blank slate. He had no place on the throne and many likely viewed him as a commoner who thinks too highly of himself being in a place that he simply doesn't belong. He could try to rule by force, overpowering any and all who try to undermine his authority, and while under normal circumstances that option is paved with political, military, economic, and social challenges, each of these would only be exponentially exacerbated by the sheer size of Achashverosh's Empire. He might find more sympathy to his militaristically-imposed reign in one area and less in another; support for his government and style of governing would span the spectrum of variability throughout his kingdom.

Achashverosh preferred a more politically calculated approach.

Even though not in line to inherit the throne from Koresh, Achashverosh is Persian and hopes to, at the very least, garner the support of his own countrymen. But even that wasn't a sure thing. Some Persians must have been wondering that if Achashverosh, who was not of royal extraction, managed to ascend to the throne, what's to stop them from trying to do so as well? So even while familial and communal bonds tied Achashverosh to his Persian comrades, their unwavering support was not guaranteed. This wavering potential base of support also needed to be part of Achashverosh's calculations and provides some of the backdrop for the Megilah's opening scene. Aside from the Persians, Achashverosh also needs to worry about the other nations under his vast rule, one of the largest and most powerful of which were the Babylonians. They were the previous ruling class and it was likely somewhat of an adjustment for them to accommodate to their new governmental realities as no longer the unchallenged leaders. After the native Persians, they were his most populous constituency. The challenge was how to win them over.

*  *  *

Vashti's father, Belshatzar, was the last of the Babylonian kings.

Achashverosh, of the rapidly expanding and rising Persian Empire, seems to follow the historically tried and true method of political alliances – through marriage.

While Achashverosh may in fact be interested in the Persian Empire swallowing up, taking over, and completely absorbing the declining Babylonian government – it's far more politically expedient and militarily cost effective to do so with a wedding than through force. Because even with a new king at the helm, shifting actual allegiances of the vast empire is a far more complicated task than a military victory. One way to show that he intends to be 'everybody's king' and win the hearts and minds of the Babylonians is by marrying their former princess. It's a sign of friendship, camaraderie, and a demonstration that Achashverosh cares for them and, on some level, represents a continuation of the governing structure that they are used to.

We can only imagine what the political climate was in Shushan at the time that such shrewd politicking and marriage was deemed expedient and worthwhile. Because even while Achashverosh was trying to win over the hearts and minds of the Babylonians, ultimately he was a dictator. Meaning, even though it might be easier to convince the Babylonians to support his new authority through seemingly respecting their heritage and embracing their ruling class as part of his own, at the end of the day Achashverosh needed to assert his authority as the new king in town.

The very fact that Achashverosh married Vashti, the former princess, instead of taking over in a more forceful (and likely violent) manner, would seem to indicate that Achashverosh was unwilling, or perhaps more likely, unable to do so. He was left walking a fine balance between asserting himself as the undisputed sovereign while making sure his regime wasn't too overly oppressive, which could lead to mass distrust, malcontent, and possible revolt. It's this balance that Achashverosh was pushing with the multiple parties.

# Chapter Seven

The political climate of Shushan is tense, and even though Achashverosh moved the Empire's official capital to the Persian city of Shushan there are still clearly elements still present from the previous Babylonian regime. The Jewish people, who were originally exiled by and then subject to Babylonian rule, appear to be long time citizens of Shushan and play a prominent role in its new governance. As with many political transitions throughout history, there were people supportive of the new regime (loyal to Achashverosh) and those whose opposition ranged from simple lack of support to outright attempts at reversing the political order (Reactionaries).

The Reactionaries, supportive of the *status quo ante* Babylonian regime, saw in Vashti everything that was right and good about the regime they supported and used to be part of. In fact, Malbim explains that this was Vashti's motivation in hosting her own party. She was doing far more than just celebrating; she was trying to establish herself as the rightful heir to the Empire's throne. After all, Achashverosh chose her precisely because of her royal pedigree. Her party was as much a statement of purpose as it was a challenge to Achashverosh's celebratory search for and solidifying allies and allegiances.

While the Megilah does not describe Vashti's party in anywhere near as much details as Achashverosh's, it notes that גַּם וַשְׁתִּי הַמַּלְכָּה עָשְׂתָה מִשְׁתֵּה נָשִׁים – she too made a party, which at the very least hints at some comparison between the two. If not in over the top decorations and culinary treats, perhaps the Megilah is drawing the similarity more in terms of the two parties' purposes and goals.

Just as Achashverosh strategically invited all governmental functionaries from far and wide to draw support, form alliances, and solidify his authority, Vashti may have been vying for something similar. If the Reactionary movement was going to survive, it needed to bring like-minded people together from which to draw support and strength. At the very least, that's how Achashverosh seems to have viewed it. Vashti's festivities might even be viewed as a challenge to Achashverosh – just as he was vying for political allies and supporters, so was Vashti.

* * *

ACHASHVEROSH WAS LIKELY somewhat concerned about what Vashti might accomplish and conceives of a plan to 'put her in her place.' His goal was to show his visiting revelers that he is the established ruler and Vashti is his subservient queen – clearly demonstrating that he is sitting on the throne by his own doing, not because he married a former princess. In solidifying his authority, he needs to show the various states and provinces that he indeed is in charge and deserves to be in charge. It's important to Achashverosh that this point be made, first and foremost to Vashti herself, but also to the representatives of the various states and provinces celebrating with him.

In fact, it's only after the Megilah describes how Vashti made her own party that Achashverosh invites her to his. While Achashverosh's party is 180 days long, there is no mention of the details of Vashti's. Nonetheless, the Megilah juxtaposes the relatively meager description of Vashti's party with Achashverosh's invitation / demand that she come to his, subtly indicating that it was Vashti's hosting a party in the first place that led Achashverosh to invite her to his. It was not her partying that bothered Achashverosh, but her veiled assertion of authority and leadership that he could not allow to go uncontested; it needed to be stopped before too strongly invigorating her base.

But at the same time, Achashverosh also had to consider the impression that would be left on Vashti's party attendees. Forcefully stopping her party would be considered a direct affront to Vashti's Reactionary supporters – whom Achashverosh doesn't particularly care for, but also represent a powerful group that he'd prefer, if possible, not to unnecessarily offend. Achashverosh needed to find a way to quietly quash Vashti's party / political rally-in-disguise, without it seeming like he was actually doing so. He needed a cover story such that it would only be natural for either her to leave the party or for her party to prematurely end, all while both managing to 'teach Vashti a lesson' while simultaneously not violently confronting or openly and directly confronting her Reactionary base. All of which led to inviting Vashti to join Achashverosh at his party.

Considering the rapid transition between the description of her party and Achashverosh's invitation / demand that she attend his, the Megilah is giving the distinct impression that Achashverosh is deliberately trying to pull her away from her party. It's almost as if he is looking for a plausible angle to shut her party down without resorting to force. This also explains why Achashverosh doesn't merely send for Vashti, but rather tasks seven of his advisors with this invitation. Showing off his wife's beauty should not require seven trusted cabinet level members. Perhaps Achashverosh was trying to frame the invitation less as what might seem as a favor for her husband and more as an official royal request – demanding that she show the monarchy its due honor and as such, sends an official contingency to request / demand her attendance.

This scheme ticks off all the boxes to accomplish all of Achashverosh's necessary goals: As an official royal request to join the king's party, Vashti would not be in a position to refuse. Her guests would understand why she is leaving and why their party had to be shut down. At the same time, even if Vashti would realize what was actually going on given the general tension in the palace, Achashverosh surmised that she would still acquiesce so as not to directly offend and oppose the king's official royal edict. In doing so, he would be able to quickly put an end to Vashti's party – which he viewed as a political rally – before anybody got too excited and did anything that 'they might later regret' (from Achashverosh's perspective).

From the perspective of Achashverosh's guests, Vashti's presence was clearly filling a different role. In describing the invitation, the Megilah makes it quite clear that he did not merely want her companionship during his drunken celebration, but rather specifically, לְהַרְאוֹת הָעַמִּים וְהַשָּׂרִים אֶת יָפְיָהּ כִּי טוֹבַת מַרְאֶה הִיא (to show all the visitors her beauty, since after all, she was an attractive woman). More than just 'mere' chauvinism, this was a calculated political move. Beyond just trying to show her off to his guests, it's almost as if the Megilah is telling us that Vashti's entire worth as a queen was because "after all, she was attractive." Achashverosh was demonstrating to everyone who cared to know – and particularly, those who might think of supporting a Reactionary agenda with Vashti at the helm – that Vashti was only there just for her "good looks." It wasn't her royal lineage that mattered anymore. She was the former princess, with an emphasis on the past tense, but now has no political role to play other than doing Achashverosh's bidding. She was to appear with her כֶּתֶר מַלְכוּת, the one that she was wearing as Achashverosh's queen, not as the daughter of a previous vanquished king.

In his public relations and marketing agenda to those present and to all who would be made aware of his party, Achashverosh was framing Vashti as the subservient wife and nothing more. The message would be clear, not only to Vashti, but more importantly also to Achashverosh's guests, and even those guests of Vashti's party who still lingered around the palace.

Adding a more specific historical context to this story, *Ya'arot Devash* (1:17) employs some technically derived calculations, demonstrating that Achashverosh's invitation was sent on the 15th of Nisan. And while that date is significant on the Jewish calendar as the first day of Pesach, it also has particular significant for Vashti as well, as *Chazal* have a tradition (based on the *piyut* ובן ויהי בחצי הלילה) that it's also the date that her late father, Belshatzar, was killed. If indeed correct, it is certainly not merely coincidental and gives added significance to the invitation and Achashverosh's overall agenda.

Taking the *Ya'arot Devash*'s calculation at face value, Vashti specifically planned her party to coincide with the anniversary of her father's death. What better day for Vashti to host her own party to invigorate her Reactionary base and search for ways to continue her father's legacy than on the very day he was killed. More importantly, it would have been difficult and likely unwise to otherwise gather so many like-minded Reactionary leaders, particularly in the palace itself. Achashverosh and his people would likely see that as too much of an affront to his authority, bordering on rebellious behavior that would be met with severe consequences. Perhaps it was precisely under the pretext of memorializing her late father that Vashti was able to bring together supporters of the former Babylonian regime and of Belshatzar in particular. It's hard to imagine any other opportunity where former Belshatzar supporters could swarm the palace without raising eyebrows or concerns among Achashverosh's people. If Vashti was as politically shrewd as her husband, this party was no mere celebration or even a *yahrtzeit* commemoration, but rather Vashti taking advantage of the unique opportunity to create a mini-Reactionary forum, without any of the otherwise attendant risks of doing so.

But the same is also true of Achashverosh's perspective. What better day to demonstrate his absolute authority and solidify his leadership than on the day commemorating the Persian takeover of the kingdom? If he was going to show that he can put Vashti in her place, doing so on the very day that her father lost his reign to the Persians makes the move all the more poignant.* Reading the simple text of the Megilah and understanding that Achashverosh wanted to quash Vashti's party as soon as possible, it would appear that it was on the very same day that Vashti started her own party that Achashverosh invites / demands her to parade herself in front of his.

Understanding the background to this invitation / demand, it makes Vashti's refusal all the more forceful. True, leaving the political overtones aside, Achashverosh's request was horribly demeaning to Vashti and to women in general. But perhaps that is too much of an anachronistic perspective, reading modern sensitivities into a historical culture. Leaving these aside, if indeed Vashti's intention in hosting her own party was to at least partially assert her own independence and solidify her position as the rightful heir to the throne, her refusal to do Achashverosh's petty bidding is even more understandable.

Her refusal is far more than simply a protest out of modesty or feminine pride. It has far less to do with Vashti as a woman than Vashti as the daughter of the former king. She most certainly understood the import of her actions, as she was keenly aware of the nature of Achashverosh's request. Her refusal is framed not only as a personal affront to Achashverosh but specifically

---

* The *Ya'arot Devash* actually uses this calculation to make a different point. He argues that Achashverosh could not understand Vashti's refusal to attend. He considered that it might be understandable if in fact she was 'coincidentally' commemorating the *yarhtzeit* of her father Belshatzar on that very day and was understandably, not in the most festive of moods. Admittedly, *Ya'arot Devash* argues that in the end, it turned out not to actually be Belshatzar's *yahrtzeit*, but Achashverosh only figured that out after consulting with experts. In fact, this is how R. Eibeschutz explains the Gemara that describes the חֲכָמִים יֹדְעֵי הָעִתִּים, with whom Achashverosh consulted after Vashti's refusal as Jewish Sages who were familiar with the intricacies of the calendar. Achashverosh reasoned that by his calculation, he did figure the dates correctly and it in fact was Belshatzar's *yahrtzeit*. The question he posed to this particular group of Sages was whether perhaps it was a leap year, meaning that his calculations were off by a full month.

As it turns out, *Ya'arot Devash* argues that these חֲכָמִים responded that it was in fact a leap year, but this was something that Achashverosh was unaware of until after her refusal. When he initially sent the invitation, he was under the [mis]impression that it was the 15th of Nisan and if Vashti was trying to plan something under the cover of memorializing her father, it makes sense that she planned for the date that Achashverosh thought was Belshatzar's *yarhtzeit*.

to the message he sent through his advisors – once again highlighting the invitation's political overtones.

Given what we know of her husband's temperament, it's likely that she was acutely aware of the risks raised by her refusal, but nonetheless felt it to be worthwhile. She wasn't just refusing a simple invitation. In the then-current political climate, she was taking a stand on an important matter of policy. Vashti, the dynasty from which she hails and now represents, and the (in her opinion hopefully burgeoning) Reactionary movement will not simply sit quietly and allow Achashverosh do with them as he wishes. More than just defending her personal dignity, she was standing up for her father, her people, and against what she saw as a corrupting governmental influence headed by Achashverosh. Achashverosh, understandably, was far from pleased.

# Chapter Eight

Taking all that in, Achashverosh should be understandably more than simply disturbed, which is precisely how the Megilah describes his reaction – וַיִּקְצֹף הַמֶּלֶךְ מְאֹד וַחֲמָתוֹ בָּעֲרָה בוֹ (extreme anger with a fire burning within him). From his perspective, Vashti didn't just refuse her husband's request, but was very openly and publicly opposing his authority as the rightful king. Given the pretext for inviting her in the first place, it's clear that he could absolutely not allow this to pass without a response.

In fact, the nature of Achashverosh's reaction is further evidence that this whole episode was merely thinly veiled political posturing and not just some pompous desire of to flaunt his wife's beauty.

Despite his understandable anger and rising resentment burning within, Achashverosh does not lash out at Vashti. He does not scold her or even publicly repudiate her. Even with his likely injured ego, Achashverosh realizes that Vashti's refusal was more than just a personal insult and therefore demands a politically appropriate response. Importantly, Achashverosh must weigh multiple political considerations in his response. Vashti's direct refusal demands repudiation, if just for personally insulting the monarch. Additionally, given the powerful political statement echoed by her very public refusal, it could not go unchallenged.

But he also had to consider Vashti's guests and the multitudes of potential Reactionary supporters throughout the kingdom, leading Achashverosh to hold back on his natural visceral reaction. Instead, as seems to be his style throughout the Megilah, Achashverosh takes counsel from a group of political advisors, rarely making political decisions on his own. The Megilah in fact highlights this particular tendency precisely at this time – כִּי כֵן דְּבַר הַמֶּלֶךְ לִפְנֵי כָּל יֹדְעֵי דָּת וָדִין – such was the manner of Achashverosh's decision making, to consult the wisdom of his advisors.

These are a second group of advisors, different than the first group he sent to issue the initial invitation. The Megilah describes this second group not only as חֲכָמִים יֹדְעֵי הָעִתִּים, but also as being הַקָּרֹב אֵלָיו – those who were close to Achashverosh, seemingly in contrast or in comparison to the first group. While the first group was tasked with the actual invitation and perhaps even helped come up with the plan to invite Vashti in the first place, her refusal threw Achashverosh into a political thorn bush.

The entire invitation was a political stunt to put Vashti and her Reactionary supporters in their place, demonstrating and solidifying Achashverosh's sovereign reign. But from the very fact that this was the plan, it's clear that Achashverosh was still somewhat hesitant and nervous about dealing with his political foes. His entire intention was to keep Vashti around and demonstrate to her supporters that they should and must now align with and pay homage to Achashverosh.

He therefore specifically did not choose to 'merely' get rid of Vashti – whether violently or by simply 'making her disappear,' since that would not advance his agenda. Eliminating her from the picture would simply force the Reactionaries to find a new figurehead, but would have minimal impact on quashing their political hopes and dreams. On the other hand, a more public and violent end to Vashti might invigorate her base and spark protests or even a revolt.

Achashverosh's ideal outcome would be to have Vashti quite publicly – in front of representatives of all 127 provinces – effectively demonstrate that she recognizes his right to the throne and bows to his authority by doing his petty bidding. When that plan went awry, Achashverosh needed guidance on how to proceed.

# Chapter Nine

While the original plan was quite straightforward, dealing with the current situation was far more complicated and required a keener sense of wisdom and insight, from those who were חֲכָמִים יֹדְעֵי הָעִתִּים and, particularly, those who he could intimately trust and those whom he could count as הַקָּרֹב אֵלָיו. This group wasn't merely convened to mete out a punishment, but to brainstorm the most appropriate and politically expedient response – one that would best promote his personal goals.

Many readers may instinctively recall that Achashverosh ignominiously puts Vashti to death, which is in fact what the Gemara (*Megilah* 19a) relates, but isn't actually mentioned in the Megilah itself. The only clear and explicit consequence to befall her is וּמַלְכוּתָהּ יִתֵּן הַמֶּלֶךְ לִרְעוּתָהּ הַטּוֹבָה מִמֶּנָּה – Vashti's queen-ship should be given to somebody more worthy. It seems intentionally vague and, interestingly, the Megilah is more interested in the seemingly less essential details of how this information will be publicized than the actual punishment itself.

The Megilah describes that it was Memukhan (whom the Gemara identifies with Haman), one of Achashverosh's close advisors, who suggests stripping Vashti of her queenship. But instead of detailing what should happen to her, his presentation is highly focused on the public relations aspect of the whole affair. Memukhan is worried – and from the number of *pesukim* dedicated to his description, perhaps excessively so – with what the public might think and do if they were to find out about Vashti's refusal without a strong reaction from Achashverosh.

He has to explain to Achashverosh that

לֹא עַל הַמֶּלֶךְ לְבַדּוֹ עָוְתָה וַשְׁתִּי הַמַּלְכָּה

her actions are far more than a personal affront to Achashverosh,

but rather

כִּי עַל כָּל הַשָּׂרִים וְעַל כָּל הָעַמִּים אֲשֶׁר בְּכָל מְדִינוֹת הַמֶּלֶךְ אֲחַשְׁוֵרוֹשׁ

to all the ministers and nation that are part of his vast Empire.

Explaining himself in painstaking detail, Memukhan continues,

כִּי יֵצֵא דְבַר הַמַּלְכָּה עַל כָּל הַנָּשִׁים לְהַבְזוֹת בַּעְלֵיהֶן בְּעֵינֵיהֶן

if the news of Vashti's refusal will spread, it will lead to *all* women refusing and disrespecting their husbands.

And just to make sure that there is no misunderstanding about what he means, he continues,

בְּאָמְרָם הַמֶּלֶךְ אֲחַשְׁוֵרוֹשׁ אָמַר לְהָבִיא אֶת וַשְׁתִּי הַמַּלְכָּה לְפָנָיו וְלֹא בָאָה

[these women] will say that Achashverosh requested Vashti to appear before him and she did not come!

And what of the ramifications? If it wasn't obvious enough yet, Memukhan continues to elaborate,

וְהַיּוֹם הַזֶּה תֹּאמַרְנָה שָׂרוֹת פָּרַס וּמָדַי אֲשֶׁר שָׁמְעוּ אֶת דְּבַר הַמַּלְכָּה לְכֹל שָׂרֵי הַמֶּלֶךְ וּכְדַי בִּזָּיוֹן וָקָצֶף

and this very day, the wives of the ministers throughout Persia and Media who will hear about Vashti's refusal and cause much disrespect and anger.

And just to make sure that Achashverosh got the point, Memukhan details how letters should be sent far and wide throughout the kingdom to insure that

וְכָל הַנָּשִׁים יִתְּנוּ יְקָר לְבַעְלֵיהֶן לְמִגָּדוֹל וְעַד קָטָן

and all women, from young to old, will give honor / glory to their husbands.

Considering that Achashverosh seems to be a politically astute leader and Memukhan's suggestion not being all that earth-shatteringly complex, this disproportionate level of detail seems unnecessary. It almost seems like Memukhan is playing up every detail so as to convince Achashverosh of his plan.

And perhaps that is precisely the idea.

# Chapter Ten

From a political perspective, Achashverosh cannot accept Vashti's refusal – it represents an affront to his sovereignty and would only strengthen and enliven those Reactionaries among his subjects. But for political reasons, he also can't ostensibly punish or publicly reprimand Vashti. As he was still working to strengthen his own base, his undisputed authority was not yet an accepted reality and he had to balance political sensitivities and sensibilities. And so, while Vashti's standing up to him demanded a reaction, if his response were too overtly political, it would actually hurt Achashverosh's agenda.

Up until this point the entire political back and forth was 'under the radar' – clearly part of Achashverosh's calculations, but never made explicit. Such is often the nature of effective politicking – some of the most effective political maneuvering works when people don't realize that they are being manipulated or swayed. That's the context for the Megilah's opening episode.

Achashverosh invites the ministers and leaders of all his provinces under the pretext of celebrating his kingship, while clearly trying to build alliances and solidify his base. He makes a big deal of his new palace in Shushan, seemingly to show off his vast treasure (recognizing that money equals power), while pushing to establish the Persian city of Shushan as the new political center of the Empire. So too Vashti, planned her own party, either as a commemoration of her father's *yahrtzeit* or even just as a women's complimentary party to Achashverosh's, but with the intention of solidifying her late father's supporters and invigorating the Reactionaries in the kingdom. This was a game of political showmanship, vying for favors and alliances without being too explicit or too obviously intentional about it.

Taking too harsh a stance against Vashti with an overt political motivation would destroy the balance that Achashverosh was trying so carefully to maintain. He needed to find a way to accomplish his goal while seemingly maintaining the façade of political correctness. This is exactly the solution that Memukhan was offering.

Memukhan suggests framing Vashti's punishment as lesson in maintaining a proper sense of marital respect and authority. If anybody were to ask, Vashti's punishment had nothing at all to do with politics – who could argue, after all, that Achashverosh simply couldn't simply tolerate this level of disrespect from his wife. He makes it clear that if the women of the Empire got word of Vashti's refusal and getting away with it, they too might be tempted to stand up to their husband's petty demands and threaten the (clearly fragile, if this is all it takes to shake it up) submissive nature of marital relationships throughout the land! Taking a proactive and preemptive stance against such a potential proto-feminist threat, Achashverosh had to insure that לִהְיוֹת כׇּל אִישׁ שֹׂרֵר בְּבֵיתוֹ וּמְדַבֵּר כִּלְשׁוֹן עַמּוֹ – each man should rule over his home and speak his native language.

All of this bluster strongly favors reading this suggestion as merely a pretext for Achashverosh's proclamation. Aside from Memukhan's long winded description of the intricacies in which Vashti's actions might lead to social disaster, the whole concern seems so unnecessary, perhaps even to the point of ridicule. Given what we know about ancient culture, was it even remotely reasonable for any Persian king to worry about a feminist revolt in the fifth century before the Common Era? From the excruciating detail of his explanation, it sounds as if Memukhan is trying to convince Achashverosh that there is a chance, albeit rather remote, that some woman somewhere might get the wrong idea about the 'culturally proper' balance in her marriage and it's up to Achashverosh to prevent this 'travesty.' The potential consequences of inaction, Memukhan tries to convince him, are simply too horrible to bear.

The detail is not the only excess in Memukhan's soliloquy. Even his argument itself is framed in an over-the-top way. Instead of simply explaining that there might be some women who might learn from Vashti's example and come to disrespect their husbands, Memukhan argues that כׇּל הַנָּשִׁים will come to לְהַבְזוֹת בַּעְלֵיהֶן בְּעֵינֵיהֶן. And it won't just be the common folk peasants who may not know better, but will also even infect the aristocratic שָׂרוֹת פָּרַס וּמָדַי. It's so overly broad and larger than life that it seems as if the Megilah is trying to convince the reader that it's not meant to be taken literally. Is is possible that one or two women who hear about Vashti's refusal start to think that they might stand up to their husbands as well? Certainly. Would they actually do it? Far less likely. Vashti, at least, was royalty, the daughter of the previous king. In a world where women were treated as second class citizens (and often even that is an overstatement), Vashti was at the very top of that second tier food chain. Given the culture, no other woman would dare outwardly disrespect her husband in a similar way.

Clearly, that's not what Memukhan was actually concerned with. He was merely using this as a pretext for Achashverosh to forcefully respond to Vashti, without making it too overtly political. Memukhan's concern for a feminist uprising was enough cover to deal with Vashti in powerful manner that would both accomplish his goal of establishing and solidifying his authority, without making it seem that this was his intention in doing so. It was the perfect plan.

# Chapter Eleven

And so Achashverosh goes along with Memukhan's plan. He sends elaborate letters to all the provinces, making sure to specify each in their own language and dialect to make sure they get the message loud and clear.

But as mentioned earlier, the details of the actual punishment are somewhat lacking. What Memukhan actually says is that

> אִם עַל הַמֶּלֶךְ טוֹב יֵצֵא דְבַר מַלְכוּת מִלְּפָנָיו
>
> if it's acceptable in the eyes of the king, he should issue a proclamation,

and the proclamation should be recorded

> וְיִכָּתֵב בְּדָתֵי פָרַס וּמָדַי וְלֹא יַעֲבוֹר אֲשֶׁר לֹא תָבוֹא וַשְׁתִּי לִפְנֵי הַמֶּלֶךְ אֲחַשְׁוֵרוֹשׁ
>
> Vashti did not appear in front of Achashverosh when she was summoned,

and therefore,

> וּמַלְכוּתָהּ יִתֵּן הַמֶּלֶךְ לִרְעוּתָהּ הַטּוֹבָה מִמֶּנָּה
>
> he will grant her queen-ship to somebody more worthy than she.

However, the language is not quite as straightforward as might appear. The phrase אֲשֶׁר לֹא תָבוֹא וַשְׁתִּי לִפְנֵי הַמֶּלֶךְ אֲחַשְׁוֵרוֹשׁ literally means, "that Vashti shall never come again before the king" – not that she had not, but that she may no longer do so. Alsheikh interprets that this is simply a polite way of saying that she will be put to death (which is why she will never come again before the king). The problem is that the Megilah isn't shy about talking about death and destruction and does so later in some detail, so why skimp on the details to imply something that isn't necessarily obvious?

Malbim argues that the Megilah doesn't mention Vashti's death because Achashverosh didn't kill her. Killing Vashti could have been seen as a sign of weakness that Achashverosh couldn't follow through or accomplish that which he wanted. Vashti stood up to him and if put to death, she would be forever portrayed as a martyr for the Reactionary cause. If Achashverosh had "real" power, people might think, he'd be able to control both his wife and the political factions backing her. She would be killed only because Achashverosh wasn't able to deal with her or her cause more effectively and it might actually invigorate her base to realize that Achashverosh is indeed frightened of them gaining power.

What seems more effective, Malbim argues, is to banish Vashti; to send her off in disgrace and never be allowed back into the palace or to politics. On the one hand, it's forceful and powerful, and on the other, she doesn't go out as a martyr. Achashverosh is showing that he isn't afraid, since he's willing to let her live, but also marginalizes her as a woman who didn't recognize her proper place in society. Banishing Vashti from the palace seems to accomplish the best of both worlds. It quashes any hopes she might have about revitalizing her father's legacy from within the palace and having a Babylonian influence to the throne while keeping this motivation and purpose hidden. For the politically motivated Achashverosh, Memukhan's suggestion not only makes a lot of sense, but speaks to Achashverosh's inner ambitions as well – something that will serve Memukhan well as the story unfolds.

* * *

WITH THIS DEEPER understanding of the political underpinnings of the beginning episodes in the Megilah, the assassination plot by Bigtan and Teresh takes on increased significance. We know very little about Achashverosh's life, his reign, or much about what people thought of him outside of this short episode. A superficial reading of the Megilah would argue that out of a myriad of details of Achashverosh's reign, this particular episode is included because it helps set up Mordekhai as somebody deserving of Achashverosh's gratitude.

However, given the backdrop to the story and the political tensions between the Reactionaries and the Loyalists, it does more than simply placing Mordekhai in Achashverosh's good favor.

It foremost highlights how tense the political situation has become – leading to an assassination attempt on the king. If at first the Reactionaries were trying to influence governmental policy in more subtle ways, if they were satisfied with perhaps attending Vashti's party and celebrating her father's legacy, they have since journeyed far from that more civilized level of political discourse.

The Megilah records the assassination plot right after describing Esther's ascent to the throne. If Achashverosh thought that banishing Vashti from the palace would have quieted any bubbling Reactionary rumblings, he has now come to learn that even if effective, they have not disappeared. While a precise timeline is not offered, the assassination attempt is described immediately after Esther is chosen as the new queen. The episode is introduced as בַּיָּמִים הָהֵם – the days surrounding Esther's ascension to royalty, highlighting the connection between Esther's selection and the assassination plot.

It seems as if finally replacing Vashti was a tipping point for the Reactionary movement, who now escalated from quiet grumbling and small protests to a more violent path. But adding insult to injury, Achashverosh didn't just replace Vashti and thereby eliminate any continuing Babylonian connection to the royal throne and senior level of government. It was the particular way in which he did it that really made the Reactionaries' blood boil.

In choosing Esther, Achashverosh chose a commoner, someone whose lineage was so unimportant to him, that he actually knew nothing about it and it didn't seem to bother him one bit. The Megilah is quite clear that the only virtue Achashverosh was interested in selecting for was a woman's "feminine" attributes. The Megilah spends an inordinate amount of 'textual real estate' on the details of how each woman physically prepared for her encounter with Achashverosh, emphasizing over and over again that while Vashti may have thought she played some political role in Achashverosh's kingdom, this new queen would certainly not. Her role was to be clear to her from her initial selection process – she is there to service the king; nothing else about her mattered.

In fact, Achashverosh used this to his advantage. Anybody and everybody from any of the 127 provinces had a shot at the throne. Achashverosh's Empire was an equal opportunity employer, even at the highest level of government. This may have been the greatest insult to Belshatzar's heritage. Vashti was Achashverosh's initial connection to the former Babylonian empire. From the Reactionary perspective, she was really behind his ascension to the throne; he only belonged there because of Vashti. Replacing her was bad enough, but choosing some random woman to fill her royal shoes emphasized to them how very little Achashverosh thought that he needed their support or backing.

Esther was the straw that broke the proverbial camel's back. Achashverosh needed to be stopped at all costs and Bigtan and Teresh were tasked with the deed.

* * *

BIGTAN AND TERESH's failure to execute their assassination attempt was not only a means by which Achashverosh eventually feels indebted to Mordekhai – a relationship that will present a particular advantage to Achashverosh later on in the story – but it also frames Mordekhai as a Loyalist to Achashverosh.

As a prominent Jew – he is described as אִישׁ יְהוּדִי indicating that he was both defined by and identified by his religious affiliation – his loyalties may have been somewhat suspect. Under the previous Babylonian regime the Jewish situation was somewhat tenuous. While there were certainly a number of Jews in prominent positions in the king's court, in everybody's recent memory the Babylonians had not so long ago destroyed the *Beit ha-Mikdash* and exiled the Jews from their land.

While many Jews harbored strong negative emotions and associations with the Babylonian monarchy, some likely welcomed the recent Persian takeover, perhaps offering a glimmer of hope from their previous oppressors. By this point, most Jews have lived through several rulers: the Babylonian Belshatzar, Daryavesh of Maday, and then Koresh of Persia, all before Achashverosh took over. All this political turnover took place over less than a decade. Belshatzar ruled for three years, Daryavesh for a year, and Koresh for only three years.

Koresh was particularly good for the Jews, allowing them to return to Israel, rebuild the *Beit ha-Mikdash*, and even releasing some of the seized *Mikdash* furniture and vessels for them to use. Even though only a small fraction of the Jewish population actually returned, the image of Koresh as a benevolent dictator likely loomed large in their eyes.

Koresh represented a new Empire, one that overtook the Babylonians who had destroyed the *Beit ha-Mikdash* and exiled the Jews. Even before issuing their 'right of return' proclamation, many Jews were likely at least cautiously optimistic as to what this new regime would bring. And so when he granted them the right to return and rebuild the *Beit ha-Mikdash*, particularly because, in his own words ה׳ אֱלֹקֵי הַשָּׁמַיִם ... פָּקַד עָלַי לִבְנוֹת לוֹ בַיִת בִּירוּשָׁלַיִם אֲשֶׁר בִּיהוּדָה – he saw this as a unique mission from Hashem – their optimism turned into gratitude and a positive outlook toward their new Persian rulers. And even while the situation in Israel itself was never certain, constantly being challenged by the local non-Jews, the Tanakh does not indicate whether or not the Persian Jews were aware of these efforts and if they were, how they reacted.

# Chapter Twelve

When the *Beit ha-Mikdash* construction project came crashing down with Achashverosh's reversal of Koresh's edict, the Jews of Israel were devastated. The official proclamation came from the king himself and word of it likely spread quickly throughout the Empire. Neither the Book of Ezra nor the Megilah describe the Persian Jews' reaction to the news, but it's reasonable to assume that they weren't all too thrilled, to say the least. Any optimism that peaked just five short years earlier with Koresh's proclamation was now seriously dampened. But this went beyond simply changing the rules on who is permitted to do what.

Achashverosh's reversal was predicated on recognizing the rebellious threat that the *Beit ha-Mikdash* and a Jewish presence in Israel meant to his kingdom. He is quite clear in his letter back to Israel that Yerushalayim and a Jewish presence therein presents and historically has always presented a danger to the foreign kings who ruled over it.

That said, Achashverosh's response specifically refers to the rebuilding of the *Beit ha-Mikdash* and establishing a Jewish presence in Yerushalayim in particular and makes no mention of any threat presented by any of the other many Jews scattered throughout his vast Empire. Technically speaking, they hadn't done anything wrong and practically weren't directly impacted by Achashverosh's reversal. But it's hard to believe that they felt very secure.

The Jews were well aware that they were in exile and certainly knew of Yirmiyahu's prophecy that it would soon come to an end. They likely saw such a glimmering of hope in Koresh's initial proclamation. Whether or not they chose to move to Israel, Achashverosh's reversal was a serious step backwards for the overall Jewish historical narrative.

Taking this idea only a little bit further, it stands to reason that the Persian Jews thought to themselves that if Achashverosh saw their Yerushalmi brethren as such a potential source of revolt and sedition, why should he view them all that differently? Admittedly, they chose to stay in exile instead of return to Israel, but, fundamentally, they were all part of the same people, sharing a common culture and belief system (even if this group was less willing to act on those beliefs and return to Israel). After all, it wasn't the actual walls of Yerushalayim or the edifice of the *Beit ha-Mikdash* that historically was, and according to Achashverosh will soon pose, a risk of rebellion and sedition. Rather, it's the Jewish people themselves that lived within those walls and ritually worshiped within the *Mikdash* that posed a threat. Leaving aside the age old anti-Semitic trope that holds all Jews responsible for the actions of a few, in this situation there seems to have been ample reason for the Jews of Shushan and throughout the Persian Empire to wonder if Achashverosh thought that they too were suspected of rebellion and violent sedition.

* * *

WHEN MORDEKHAI, SOMEONE who was clearly identifiable as and proudly presented himself as a Jew, saved Achashverosh's life, he helped stem those suspicions. Although the plot had ostensibly nothing to do with him or his Jewish people, Mordekhai intervened, showing Achashverosh that Mordekhai's commitment to doing that which is right trumps any resentment he might harbor toward Achashverosh for reversing Koresh's decree.

The fact that it was specifically Mordekhai who intervened might take on even greater significance according to *Chazal's* tradition (*Megilah* 16b, *Menachot* 65a) that the Mordekhai of the Megilah is the same Mordekhai who is counted among the leaders of the people joining Ezra in returning to Israel (*Ezra* 2:2; *Nechemiah* 7:6). *Chazal* do not appear to give much in the way of reasoning for identification, although, on the simplest level, this instance of mentioning Mordekhai in *Sefer Ezra* (and when the same story is repeated in *Nechemiah*) is the only usage of this name outside of *Megilat Esther*. Additionally, Ezra describes how this Mordekhai was exiled from Yerushalayim during the destruction of the *Beit ha-Mikdash*, much as Mordekhai of the Megilah is described similarly.

The only challenge to this identification is that if Mordekhai returned to Yerushalayim with Ezra, what was he doing in Shushan only a few years later? The Megilah seems to describe Mordekhai as a resident of Shushan and not merely a visitor (אִישׁ יְהוּדִי הָיָה בְּשׁוּשַׁן הַבִּירָה). It's certainly possible that after Achashverosh reversed Koresh's decree that Mordekhai, who may have previously returned to Israel, returned to Shushan. In fact, there is a whole line of thinking among the *Midrashei Chazal* that specifically adopt this approach, arguing that Mordekhai came to Shushan to try to convince Achashverosh to allow the continuing building of the *Beit ha-Mikdash*.

If indeed these are one and the same person, the goodwill Mordekhai garnered by his intervention was certainly politically well played. As somebody who felt the full brunt of Achashverosh's reversal of Koresh's decree and given the overall tense political situation in Shushan, Achashverosh may have pegged Mordekhai as sympathetic to those opposing his rule. Even though Mordekhai may have had some reservation in supporting Vashti, as a continual reminder of the Babylonian dynasty which originally exiled the Jews and destroyed the *Beit ha-Mikdash*, he may still have longed for the political realities of less than a decade earlier, under Koresh's rule. Mordekhai, more than anybody, would understand that not having Achashverosh around could be a positive development for the Jews and for the rebuilding of the *Beit ha-Mikdash*. And because, despite all of this, Mordekhai stands up to do the right thing, Achashverosh takes notice.

# Chapter Thirteen

Mordekhai is not the only one in whom Achashverosh takes a special interest.

The Megilah does not give much context or reasoning for Haman's promotion, only its consequences. The fact that Haman's position of power plays such an important role in the plot line and yet the background to his rise to power isn't even mentioned is likely because the Megilah is indicating that this background isn't necessary for the reader to follow the plot. However, from the story itself, both as hinted at up until now and from the ensuing episodes, it's possible to discern some understanding and explanation.

Famously, *Chazal* (*Megilah* 12b) identify Haman with Memukhan who had previously advised Achashverosh regarding Vashti in the opening scene of the Megilah. It's possible that *Chazal* possessed an oral tradition that Haman and Memukhan are two names for the same person, leading the Gemara and other commentators to offer various explanations for why Haman is called Memukhan in the opening story. *Chazal* often identify two characters as being one and the same, although sometimes it's clear that it's not meant to be taken literally at face value (perhaps indicating a spiritual similarity, similar personalities, or other mystical connections between the two). More often than not, it's hard to tell. In this case, there seem to be several reasons, aside from a possible Tradition on the matter, prompting *Chazal* to connect the two characters.

In introducing Haman's promotion, the Megilah seems to take it for granted that the reader is aware of who Haman is. It's אַחַר הַדְּבָרִים הָאֵלֶּה – following these previous events – seemingly indicating that this is simply the next link in the story line, almost something that the reader might expect.

If so, it's referring to somebody previously mentioned in the Megilah.

It clearly cannot refer to Achashverosh or Mordekhai (since Haman interacts with both of them) and as a married man, clearly cannot refer to Esther or Vashti (he also interacts with Esther later and it would make no sense for Achashverosh to bring Vashti back to the palace only to promote her). Bigtan and Teresh are dead and so are also disqualified. The only named characters left are Hegai (the שֹׁמֵר הַנָּשִׁים – guard of the wives), Sha'ashgaz (the שֹׁמֵר הַפִּילַגְשִׁים – guard of the concubines), and the thirteen advisors from the opening chapter. Out of all of those characters, the only one who plays any significant role or takes any initiative on their own is Memukhan.

While the Megilah describes Hegai's and Sha'ashgaz's roles in Achashverosh's palace, so little is told about them that there would be no reason for the Megilah to assume that the reader would understand why Achashverosh is promoting them. If the Megilah indeed intends to indicate that Haman is just another name for a previously introduced character, then by process of elimination alone, it must be Memukhan.

Additionally, the language itself may lend a key to making this identification as well. In promoting Haman, Achashverosh does so at the expense of others, וַיְנַשְּׂאֵהוּ וַיָּשֶׂם אֶת כִּסְאוֹ מֵעַל כָּל הַשָּׂרִים אֲשֶׁר אִתּוֹ (he elevated him and placed his chair above all the ministers that were with him). Once again, the Megilah seems to assume that the reader is familiar not only with Haman, but also with his colleagues over whom he now has some measure of authority.

Up to this point in the story, there are only two groups of people who are identified together, both in the opening scene. The first group consists of the seven servants whom Achashverosh tasks with bringing Vashti to his party. The second group consists of those advisors with whom Achashverosh consults to figure out how to deal with Vashti's refusal to participate. This second group is described as רֹאֵי פְּנֵי הַמֶּלֶךְ הַיֹּשְׁבִים רִאשֹׁנָה בַּמַּלְכוּת (those who greeted the king and sat at the most prominent place in the kingdom) – the most senior of his innermost cabinet members.

When promoting Haman, Achashverosh not only is גִּדַּל ... אֶת הָמָן בֶּן הַמְּדָתָא הָאֲגָגִי, but also goes a bit farther in וַיָּשֶׂם אֶת כִּסְאוֹ מֵעַל כָּל הַשָּׂרִים אֲשֶׁר אִתּוֹ. In other words, Achashverosh promotes Haman to the highest position in his government. But the language itself is telling.It's not just that Achashverosh elevates him מֵעַל כָּל הַשָּׂרִים אֲשֶׁר אִתּוֹ, but more specifically וַיָּשֶׂם

אֶת כִּסְאוֹ. Aside from the indication that Haman is an already familiar figure who was introduced as a member of a group, it's the language describing Memukhan and Haman that is revealing. The group of seven ministers among which Memukhan is listed aren't just described as רֹאֵי פְּנֵי הַמֶּלֶךְ and serving in the highest echelons of government but specifically as הַיֹּשְׁבִים רִאשֹׁנָה בַּמַּלְכוּת – who sit foremost in the kingdom. And so, when Haman's כִּסְאוֹ – his chair – is placed מֵעַל כָּל הַשָּׂרִים אֲשֶׁר אִתּוֹ, it seemingly refers to those previously described as sitting – the seven ministers of the opening scene.

It's interesting that of that list, it's Memukhan, the last on the list, who speaks up. Given their extensive description and focusing particularly on how they are הַיֹּשְׁבִים רִאשֹׁנָה בַּמַּלְכוּת, it would seem (and indeed *Chazal* read it this way) that they are listed in order of seniority or rank.

Considering that he is the lowest ranking minister of the list and is the only one to play any active role, *Chazal* criticize him for not according respect to those more senior than he. In identifying Memukhan with Haman, *Chazal* see in him a pervasive character flaw of not recognizing his place and jumping ahead of those who should naturally come before him.

Flaw or not, it clearly serves him well as Achashverosh values the advice and appreciates Haman's counsel.

# Chapter Fourteen

The connection between the two runs even deeper. Both Memukhan and Haman present similar arguments in similar styles and with similar takeaways. Memukhan explains that Vashti's personal slight to Achashverosh was actually something far greater – לֹא עַל הַמֶּלֶךְ לְבַדּוֹ עָוְתָה וַשְׁתִּי הַמַּלְכָּה (not only did Queen Vashti sin against the king). Leaving aside any political motivations she may have had, the very fact that she refused the king's request is an offense to כָּל הַשָּׂרִים וְעַל כָּל הָעַמִּים אֲשֶׁר בְּכָל מְדִינוֹת הַמֶּלֶךְ אֲחַשְׁוֵרוֹשׁ (all of the ministers and the nations throughout King Achashverosh's empire). Even while he cannot respond to the political undertones of her refusal, it was not just Achashverosh that she disrespected, but the entire Empire. So too Haman. When a single individual, Mordekhai, refuses to bow to him, וַיִּבֶז בְּעֵינָיו לִשְׁלֹחַ יָד בְּמָרְדֳּכַי לְבַדּוֹ (it was too simple / degrading in his eyes to strike out only against Mordekhai) – it wasn't just about Mordekhai refusing to acknowledge Haman's superiority in the royal food chain but something that Haman believes is infectious far and wide throughout the entire Jewish people, who must therefore be killed.

Both make an appeal to the health and well being of the kingdom. Memukhan points out that if word of Vashti's refusal to appear before Achashverosh gets out, the social and cultural consequences throughout the kingdom will be disastrous. כִּי יֵצֵא דְבַר הַמַּלְכָּה עַל כָּל הַנָּשִׁים לְהַבְזוֹת בַּעְלֵיהֶן בְּעֵינֵיהֶן (if word of the Queen's actions became known, all the women will degrade their husbands in their eyes). Haman appeals to the same line of reasoning. The Jews have their own rules and וְאֶת דָּתֵי הַמֶּלֶךְ אֵינָם עֹשִׂים (they not follow the dictates of the king) – they cannot be trusted. But most importantly, וְלַמֶּלֶךְ אֵין שֹׁוֶה לְהַנִּיחָם (it is not worth it for the king to let them be) – it doesn't make sense for the king to allow them to continue to live. What's best for the Empire is to get rid of the Jews.

Additionally, as a technical matter, both Memukhan and Haman suggest that Achashverosh issue a written proclamation to document and insure that the king's will be swiftly done.

But perhaps the most persuasive argument in favor of *Chazal*'s identification is the way in which Achashverosh treats and responds to Haman's actual request.

*   *   *

Before delving into their dialogue and interaction, it's important to understand the significance and ramifications of Haman's promotion.

The nature of Haman's promotion makes a lot of sense, given the background just explained, even if somewhat excessively described in the text (גִּדַּל ... וַיְנַשְּׂאֵהוּ וַיָּשֶׂם אֶת כִּסְאוֹ מֵעַל כָּל הַשָּׂרִים אֲשֶׁר אִתּוֹ, Raised him up ... He elevated him and placed his chair above all the ministers that were with him). But the promotion entails far more than just a change in name, rank, and likely responsibilities. It also seems to demand widespread recognition of Haman's new status.

Acknowledging Haman was now taken to the extreme. וְכָל עַבְדֵי הַמֶּלֶךְ אֲשֶׁר בְּשַׁעַר הַמֶּלֶךְ כֹּרְעִים וּמִשְׁתַּחֲוִים לְהָמָן (And all the servants of the king who sat at the entrance to the palace would kneel and bow to Haman). Lest a reader think this to be a result of sudden adoration for Haman's accomplishments or character, the Megilah is quick to note, כִּי כֵן צִוָּה לוֹ הַמֶּלֶךְ (For that is what the king commanded to him). Prostrating and bowing were not optional, but rather demanded by royal fiat.

It's interesting to explore why Achashverosh would institute such a rule. What does the king gain by having his subjects bow down to one of his ministers? While his ministers – and certainly the most senior ranking among them – are supposed to represent the king and sometimes even appear on his behalf, it would seemingly be important to the king that his people don't confuse these representatives with the king himself. Bowing down – and not just a mere curtsy or ceremonial tipping of the head, but כֹּרְעִים וּמִשְׁתַּחֲוִים, bowing and prostrating oneself on the ground – should be reserved exclusively for the monarch. If all Achashverosh wanted was for the people and lower ministers to show some respect to Haman, there are a myriad of other ways accomplish this same goal that could easily avoid all of these problem.

Perhaps, in fact, this is what the Megilah has in mind when it describes Achashverosh's instruction – כִּי כֵן צִוָּה לוֹ הַמֶּלֶךְ. It's possible to read this phrase as "this is what Achashverosh commanded regarding Haman," meaning that the king issued a proclamation that everybody should bow down to Haman.

Alternatively however, it's also possible that Achashverosh צִוָּה לוֹ – commanded, or more accurately, authorized Haman to issue whatever he'd like as part of his promotion. Accordingly, it was Haman who demanded that everybody bow before him and the order did not originate with Achashverosh (although, if and when he became aware of it, Achashverosh doesn't seem to protest).

This approach also sheds light on why the עַבְדֵי הַמֶּלֶךְ who are upset / perturbed by Mordekhai's refusal to bow report Mordekhai's behavior to Haman and not to Achashverosh. If Mordekhai was disobeying a formal royal edict, why not take their complaints directly to the king? It makes sense for these ministers to approach Haman if it was actually he who issued the decree in the first place. Practically speaking however, it made little difference who actually issued the order; it was something that everybody had to do. But considering that it seems to have originated with Haman, Mordekhai's refusal to comply was taken as a deeper and more personal demonstration of disrespect for his nemesis.

# Chapter Fifteen

Why does Mordekhai refuse to comply? At the end of the day, Haman's demand was surely petty, self-serving, and narcissistic, but was it so odious that it warranted Mordekhai to risk his life in disobeying it?

Taking a step back from the details of the story, it turns out that it's specifically Mordekhai's refusal to bow before Haman that leads Haman to look for a way to destroy the Jewish people and convince Achashverosh to issue a decree authorizing him to do so. Mordekhai's refusal wasn't just a personal decision. It had grave national and historical consequences. What gave him the right to put the entire Jewish people in mortal danger?

Admittedly, it's a somewhat unfair accusation. It's only in hindsight that the connection between Mordekhai's refusal to bow and Haman's decree against the Jewish people becomes clear. It's quite possible that Mordekhai could never have imagined that his actions would lead to Haman plotting to annihilate the entire Jewish people. Even knowing a little about Haman's personality, taking Mordekhai's insult as representative of the entire Jewish people still seems quite extreme, even for Haman. And even if Mordekhai could have somehow predicted Haman's extreme reaction, he could likely never have imagined that Achashverosh would go along with it. While that might exonerate Mordekhai's culpability regarding the Jewish people and assuming that Mordekhai felt that he was only making a personal defiant decision, he was certainly aware that in doing so, he was putting his own life at risk.

Reading between the lines, it doesn't seem that these servants were actually interested in deciphering what was actually going on in Mordekhai's head, but rather just trying to stir the proverbial pot. From the Megilah highlighting their consistent questioning despite never getting a satisfying response and the fact that these servants then report Mordekhai's activities directly to Haman, it seems as if they are intentionally trying to cause trouble. Even then, they approach Haman לִרְאוֹת הֲיַעַמְדוּ דִּבְרֵי מָרְדֳּכַי to see what he thinks of Mordekhai's refusal – as if there was actually a chance that Haman might find it within himself to recognize the pettiness of his demand. It's clearly not a genuine question, as the Megilah makes it quite clear that up until this point that Haman hadn't really noticed Mordekhai's lack of compliance. Only after these servants report Mordekhai's action to him does Haman begin to take notice; only now וַיַּרְא הָמָן כִּי אֵין מָרְדֳּכַי כֹּרֵעַ וּמִשְׁתַּחֲוֶה לוֹ (Haman noticed that Mordekhai does not kneel or bow to him).

Further, in their 'report' to Haman, the Megilah explains that these servants are looking to find out הֲיַעַמְדוּ דִּבְרֵי מָרְדֳּכַי כִּי הִגִּיד לָהֶם אֲשֶׁר הוּא יְהוּדִי (Will Mordekhai's refusal stand, as he told them that he is Jewish). It's unclear how or what the phrase כִּי הִגִּיד לָהֶם אֲשֶׁר הוּא יְהוּדִי is modifying or what relevance it has to the issue. Nonetheless, it is the only phrase that could be read as offering some reasoning behind Mordekhai's actions, leading some to interpret that Mordekhai refused to bow out of Jewish religious considerations. According to this reading, the servants in turn went to Haman to see if he this was a good enough excuse to exempt Mordekhai from the decree.

This is difficult on multiple levels. If it's true that Mordekhai's refusal was religiously based, why does the Megilah not mention that Mordekhai gave this answer when asked? More importantly, what religious issue would there be in bowing down to Haman? While Judaism generally reserves bowing for Hashem and specifically in the *Beit ha-Mikdash*, in Biblical times it was also a common manner of formally greeting people. Avraham bows to Efron, Yaakov bows to Esav, Moshe bows to Yitro, among so many more examples throughout Tanakh. It seems fairly benign with nary a word of censor or criticism by *Chazal*. And even if Mordekhai did not respect Haman, and even if Mordekhai thought that Haman was a narcissist who didn't deserve any honor whatsoever – that's a personal issue between the two of them which has nothing to do with Judaism. Why then should it matter כִּי הִגִּיד לָהֶם אֲשֶׁר הוּא יְהוּדִי?

* * *

It seems that *Chazal* were confounded by this same difficulty. From a strictly halakhic perspective, there doesn't seem to be any good reason to avoid bowing to Haman, particularly recognizing that Mordekhai was well aware that his failure to comply was effectively risking his life.

Perhaps in trying to make sense of this serious challenge, *Chazal* posit that Haman had fashioned some type of *Avodah Zarah* icon to his clothing, either an actual idol or an image of one crocheted into his coat or other garment. Meaning that in theory, regardless of what he thought of him, Mordekhai had no problem bowing to Haman out of respect. It's only because of the concomitant idolatrous practice involved that Mordekhai could simply not comply. So severe is the prohibition against idolatry, that one must be willing to give up one's life – and certainly risk one's life – to avoid any violation whatsoever.

But while this neatly explains Mordekhai's actions and resolves the inherent difficulty, it doesn't seem to fit all that well into the Megilah's narrative. Nowhere in the Megilah is Haman described as religious at all, let alone so fastidious in his religious practice that he would fashion an idolatrous icon to his clothing. Moreover, this answer is so straightforward that it begs the question why didn't Mordekhai actually offer that answer himself when repeatedly questioned (or if he did, why doesn't the Megilah mention it)?

But perhaps most importantly, this reason relates to a core fundamental Jewish belief – standing up against idolatry even in the face of death. Accordingly, if true, Mordekhai's was an act of deep faith, exhibiting true courage, and reflecting a sincere inner heroism. And although it is certainly a normative requirement, it's hard to know how many people would be able to persevere under such difficult circumstances, which makes Mordekhai's resolve that much more admirable and praiseworthy. Why then would the Megilah hide this fact and not proudly promote Mordekhai's reasoning as inspiration for future generations?

Even more challenging is the fact that bowing down to an *Avodah Zarah*-clad Haman isn't necessarily something for which Halakhah demands giving up one's life. Under the circumstances, Mordekhai would have been bowing to Haman solely out of fear of what Haman might do if he refused; Mordekhai would have been most certainly not intending to deify or otherwise ritually acknowledge the *Avodah Zarah* emblazoned on Haman's cloak. This is certainly not the 'classic' case of *Avodah Zarah* for which it's elementary that the Torah demands sacrificing one's life. In fact, the Talmud records a debate as to the propriety of such actions, not taking either side for granted. In the later halakhic literature, there is much debate among the commentators and Poskim how this all practically plays out.

* * *

But even assuming that there indeed was a question of the halakhic propriety of bowing to Haman, it's interesting to explore why the Megilah specifically highlights Mordekhai's refusal to comply. Surely there were other God-fearing Jews in Shushan who adhered to Halakhah who would have acted similarly. The Megilah paints a picture of Shushan teeming with Jews who presumably interacted with Haman on some level and yet the Megilah is silent on what they did in the face of Haman's demand.

It's certainly possible that the Megilah singles out Mordekhai's behavior because he stood out among his compatriots in refusing Haman's demand. Perhaps other Jews possibly complied with Haman's edict while Mordekhai stood his ground and refused. In fact, there is a sentiment in *Chazal* echoing such an idea that picks up on Mordekhai's description as an אִישׁ יְהוּדִי – a single individual, unique among his community, since he stood up for the essence of Judaism. However, this idea seems to run counter to other threads in *Chazal*'s approach that seem to indicate that there were other righteous Jews in Shushan at the time who presumably would also not have violated Halakhah to capitulate to Haman's decrees. If so, it seems safe to presume like the majority of Poskim that, under the circumstances, bowing to Haman would have been permissible. Why then the staunch refusal?

In reading in between the lines, R. Alkabetz suggests that, even if not technically violating a halakhic precept, bowing down to a narcissistic political leader should indeed offend the religious sensibilities of a devout Jew. The imagery of bowing down to anybody or anything other than Hashem is so repugnant, such that even if for some technical reason it would not constitute an actual violation of *Avodah Zarah,* it's something that would nonetheless offend the religiously sensitive.

Truth be told, the Jews had another available option; they could have simply avoided the situation. Those who could not or would not bow to Haman could make every effort to avoid confronting him and thereby not risk their lives nor complicate their religious convictions. In fact, from the Megilah's lack of any mention of the Jews of Shushan's behavior, Rav

Alkabetz argues that this is precisely what they did. The Jews of Shushan deliberately avoided Haman and if they saw him coming, would quickly get out of his line of sight so as not to have to be put in a compromising situation.

Mordekhai however, adopts a different tactic.

* * *

It's not just that Mordekhai refuses to bow to Haman but that he makes a point of it.

Unlike his urban compatriots, he makes no effort whatsoever to avoid confronting Haman. In fact, the Megilah describes Mordekhai's refusal as וּמָרְדֳּכַי לֹא יִכְרַע וְלֹא יִשְׁתַּחֲוֶה (Mordekhai will not kneel nor bow) – strangely phrased in the future tense. It's almost as if the Megilah is saying that Mordekhai intended his refusal to be a deliberate and defiant statement, opting to make a show of it. In fact, later in the story, Mordekhai is described as וְלֹא קָם וְלֹא זָע מִמֶּנּוּ – he didn't stand up or make any movement whatsoever. When Mordekhai saw Haman coming, he made sure to be absolutely still, so that nothing he did could even inadvertently be misconstrued as honoring or respecting Haman. The tone of the description gives the feeling that Mordekhai wanted Haman to see him just standing there and refusing to bow.

It's clear that there is something unique about Mordekhai and his refusal to comply; a refusal that particularly evokes Haman's ire at the entire Jewish people. What emerges is that Mordekhai is not just a simple foe but a contemporary representative of an ancient rivalry.

After being told of Mordekhai's refusal and finally taking note of it himself, Haman decides that he must annihilate all the Jews and not just Mordekhai, כִּי הִגִּידוּ לוֹ אֶת עַם מָרְדֳּכָי (Because they revealed to him [the identity of] Mordekhai's nation). Haman was able to make such a huge leap from killing one person to destroying his entire people once he realized that it was the Jewish people that were in question.

# Chapter Sixteen

Realizing that Mordekhai was Jewish was enough to convince Haman that the most appropriate reaction to Mordekhai's refusal to bow down to him was to kill off the entire Jewish people.

It's clear that it wasn't Mordekhai's actual identity that was in question. Throughout the Megilah, Mordekhai is described as הַיְּהוּדִי, a proud Jew who was easily identified as such. The servants who came to Haman didn't offer him any information about Mordekhai that Haman didn't already know. Haman was well aware of who and what Mordekhai was. But when the servants described Mordekhai as Jewish (and according to some commentators, explained to Haman that Mordekhai was refusing to bow on religious grounds), Haman quickly realized that this was as good an excuse as any to put his inner antisemitism into action. The servants didn't provide Haman with a reason to wipe out the entire Jewish people, just a convenient excuse to do so.

Haman didn't simply view all Jews as defiant because of Mordekhai's actions or start viewing the entire Jewish people negatively in light of his impressions of Mordekhai. Haman went much further.

Without missing a beat, Haman decides that the most appropriate reaction to the actions of one Jew is to annihilate the entire Jewish people. Not just Mordekhai, but the entire Jewish people. Haman had never met the overwhelming majority of the Jews of Achashverosh's 127 provinces nor had much to do with them at all, but nonetheless, it makes sense to him that they all must die.

It's clear that there is no logical connection between Mordekhai personally offending Haman and killing all the Jews of the Persian Empire as retribution. What is perhaps most disturbing is that this is Haman's first instinct. The Megilah is highlighting that Haman's wrath draws on something latent within himself, an inner hatred that was stirring within his heart well before this episode with Mordekhai. Mordekhai's refusal was simply Haman's excuse for acting on this basest of all emotions.

Indeed, when the Megilah offers no explanation for Haman's actions, it's because there is nothing that can explain his behavior. If it did, it would almost excuse Haman's actions or at least somewhat justify his emotions and feelings.

* * *

Interestingly, while not explicit in the text, there are additional clues to recognizing that this battle was more about larger issues of antisemitism and less about a personal vendetta between two of Achashverosh's ministers.

In classic biblical fashion, characters are often introduced together with their lineage. Mordekhai is the son of Ya'ir, the son of Shim'i, the son of Kish, from the *shevet* of Binyamin. Very little is known of Mordekhai's direct ancestors. As noted previously, the name Mordekhai only appears one other time in Tanakh, in the book of *Ezra* as one of the leaders of the effort to resettle the Land of Israel and rebuild the *Beit ha-Mikdash*. Given *Chazal's* general preference for 'conservation of characters,' they identify the Mordekhai of *Ezra* with the Mordekhai of the Megilah. Little to nothing is known of Ya'ir or Shim'i, particularly given that these are more common names. Kish, however, is mentioned elsewhere as a member of *Shevet Binyamin*; he was the father of Shaul *ha-Melekh*. Admittedly, some commentators assume that Mordekhai's lineage is not meant to be taken as literally as written. Meaning, while Ya'ir was his father and Shim'i, his grandfather, Kish was not his great-grandfather, but rather referred the distant ancestor, Kish father of Shaul. Regardless of the number of generations between the two (and perhaps it's even more compelling if Kish was a more previous ancestor), the Megilah is connecting Mordekhai to Shaul *ha-Melekh*'s lineage.

Haman's lineage is somewhat less descriptive, which is understandable, considering the general lack of familiarity most readers of the Megilah would have of the genealogical history of other nations. He is described as the son of Hamdata the *Agagi*. It's somewhat ambiguous whether *Agagi* directly describes Haman or his father, but the general impression is that this family was known as *Agagi*.

As an adjective, the term itself is not terribly descriptive. But if, similar to Mordekhai's lineage, it refers to a particular clan or ancestral heritage, there is only one such person in Tanakh that matches – Agag, King of Amalek during the lifetime of Shaul.

Admittedly, there is some debate as to Haman's precise lineage. The *Talmud Yerushalmi* (*Yevamot* 2:6) suggests that Haman was not actually from Amalek at all, but rather adopted their ideology, while *Masekhet Soferim* (13:6) indeed traces Haman's lineage back to Amalek (son of Elifaz, son of Eisav), but not actually to King Agag. Regardless of which version is historically more accurate, the Megilah is clearly identifying Haman with the historical Amalek and asking the reader to hearken back to the emotions, feelings, and thoughts that the mere mention of Amalek brings to the fore.

* * *

IN TRACING MORDEKHAI and Haman's lineages in precisely this manner, the Megilah is alluding to the battle between Shaul *ha-Melekh* and Agag. Shaul was the first Jewish king and one of his first missions was to destroy Amalek. Historically, Amalek was the nation that first attacked *Bnei Yisrael* as they left Egypt and the Torah demands that once having established a functional government in the Land of Israel that Amalek be wiped out.

Famously, when Shaul waged war against Amalek and won, he failed to wipe them out completely, an oversight for which Shmuel *ha-Navi* holds him accountable and takes him to task for it. It is for this reason, Shmuel tells him, that Shaul's kingship will not continue as Hashem will seek a more appropriate leader (who later turns out to be David *ha-Melekh*). Specifically, Shaul spares the Ameleki women and children, as well as Agag, the Amaleki king.

After confronting Shaul for his transgression, Shmuel himself kills Agag. But it wasn't soon enough. *Chazal* (*Megilah* 13a) relate that it was specifically on that night after being captured by Shaul but before being killed by Shmuel that he sired a child from which Haman descended. Indeed, others must have survived as well, since throughout *Sefer Shmuel*, the Amalekites are found still sparring with the Jews in various stories of many of them escaping capture and continuing to torment *Bnei Yisrael*. While Shaul was the first Jewish king to formally confront Amalek, he did not complete the task.

As the Megilah sets up the confrontation, Mordekhai and Haman are continuing this epic and historical battle. Even more specifically, it's a virtual reenactment of that famous battle between Shaul and Agag. Mordekhai, Shaul's direct descendant, must now face Haman, Agag's direct descendant, in what Haman hopes will be a battle to the finish. In the end, it turns out quite the opposite. Mordekhai is finally able to complete that which his ancestor Shaul could not – completely defeating Amalek (אֲשֶׁר יִשְׁלְטוּ הַיְּהוּדִים הֵמָּה בְּשֹׂנְאֵיהֶם – The Jews ruled over their enemies).

* * *

Amalek's original attack on *Bnei Yisrael*, fresh after crossing the Red Sea and their Exodus from Egypt, is completely unprovoked. There is scant reason why Amalek chooses to attack and, as such, Amalek is often depicted as the prototypical antisemitic people. Their hatred is deep seated and they need no reason to act upon these emotions of hate. More than just a battle between nations, the Torah sets up and portrays the battle with Amalek as one of good against of evil. If the fact that the Megilah does not offer a reason for Haman's decision to annihilate the Jews does not evoke the reader to conclude that antisemitism doesn't need a reason but only an excuse, then surely echoes of the original antisemitic battle between Amalek and *Bnei Yisrael* should stir those same feelings.

Historically, while Amalek is the first nation to attack the Jewish people for antisemitic motives, it's not the first instance in the Torah of antisemitic hatred and violence. From the Torah's perspective, the antisemitic enterprise actually begins with Eisav, the grandfather of Amalek (Elifaz son of Eisav's child was named and became the progenitor of Amalek). In fact, *Chazal* (*Sifrei Be-Ha'alotekha* 11) state quite unambiguously that הלכה היא בידוע שעשו שונא ליעקב (It is a settled matter of Tradition that Esav hates Yaakov), seemingly dating the root of all antisemitism to the conflict and confrontation between Yaakov and Eisav. It wasn't just a one-time sibling rivalry but the archetype of all such conflicts to come with strong echoes in the Megilah as well.

The word choice surrounding Haman's decision is unique and appears only one other time throughout the entire Tanakh – וַיִּבֶז בְּעֵינָיו לִשְׁלֹחַ יָד בְּמָרְדֳּכַי לְבַדּוֹ (it was too simple / degrading in his eyes to strike out only against Mordekhai). The word וַיִּבֶז is both unique and familiar, as the Torah describes Eisav's willingness to sell his birthright to Yaakov as וַיִּבֶז עֵשָׂו אֶת הַבְּכֹרָה (And Esav denigrated the birthright). Eisav 'denigrated' the birthright, found no value in it, and was more than willing to part with it in exchange for a bowl of stew. But it was this very sale of the birthright that Eisav later comes to not only regret, but for which he holds Yaakov accountable.

Before approaching his death and wanting to bless his children, Yitzchak calls his firstborn Eisav to receive the first and more prestigious set of blessings and the spiritual birthright that Yitzchak inherited from Avraham. Yitzchak is apparently unaware of the sale and transfer of the birthright from Eisav to Yaakov and, in his mind, is acting on that which is right and proper. Eisav doesn't correct his father or offer any hesitation at all before quickly preparing to receive that which he did not deserve. Rivkah is also unaware of the transaction and therefore devises a plan for Yaakov to deceive Yitzchak and receive the *berakhot* that he otherwise deserves. (Without any knowledge of the sale, Rivkah seemingly believes that it's more appropriate for Yaakov to receive the *berakhot*, even though, to her knowledge, Eisav might be their rightful heir.)

Yaakov goes along with the plan without mentioning to either of his parents that from his perspective – and, by right, Eisav's as well – no deception should have been necessary since Yaakov and Eisav had already agreed years ago that Yaakov would be Yitzchak's spiritual heir.

Having returned and found out that Yaakov had tricked Yitzchak and received the *berakhot* to become Yitzchak's spiritual heir, Eisav's anger knows no bounds, going so far that he plots to kill Yaakov. In expressing his utter frustration, he describes Yaakov as וַיַּעְקְבֵנִי זֶה פַעֲמַיִם אֶת בְּכֹרָתִי לָקָח וְהִנֵּה עַתָּה לָקַח בִּרְכָתִי (He hampered me twice: he took my birthright and now has taken the blessings that are rightfully mine). Aside from playing on the name Yaakov, the complaint is rather strange.

Yaakov did not *take* the *bekhorah*; Eisav willingly sold it to him. And even while Eisav sold it to him in exchange for some food, the Torah is quite clear that Eisav didn't value it at all – וַיִּבֶז עֵשָׂו אֶת הַבְּכֹרָה. It would be hard to argue that Eisav is now complaining that the sale be declared invalid since it was made under duress. Yaakov wanted something that Eisav couldn't care less about. From Eisav's perspective [certainly at the time], it was a completely win-win situation. To complain about it later seems disingenuous. To then claim that it's a double wrong – first, 'taking' the *bekhorah* and later 'stealing' the *berakhot* – is deliberately manipulative.

Eisav's consequent utter hatred for Yaakov (וַיִּשְׂטֹם עֵשָׂו אֶת יַעֲקֹב), which almost drove him to lethal violence, was completely baseless. Yaakov did not wrong him in any way. The sale was not only valid and legal, but Eisav was quite enthusiastic about trading something that to him had no value (וַיִּבֶז עֵשָׂו אֶת הַבְּכֹרָה) for a nice hot bowl of soup that he 'actually' enjoyed. The sale and subsequent trickery about the *berakhot* was just Eisav's excuse. It's for this reason that *Chazal* identify Eisav as the prototypical antisemite, grandfather of Amalek, and progenitor of worldwide hatred of the Jewish people.

The Megilah wants to insure that the reader pick up on this crucial detail. Haman's hatred wasn't rational, but instead reflected his inner antisemitism for which Mordekhai's refusal to bow to him was merely an excuse to act on his emotions. It's for this reason that no reason is given for Haman's actions. But that point is subtle and some readers may not pick up that a lack of information can also be a means of conveying a lesson.

The Megilah therefore traces Mordekhai and Haman's lineages back to generations many years prior, that bring to memory the battle between King Shaul son of Kish and Agag, King of Amalek. And just to insure that the point comes across as forcefully as possible, Haman's decision is introduced by language highly reminiscent (and in fact, used in the Tanakh only in these two instances) of the circumstances surrounding Eisav – the first and prototypical antisemite in *Chazal's* worldview – and his developing hatred for his brother Yaakov. All pointing to the fact that antisemitism doesn't need a reason, only an excuse.

# Chapter Seventeen

Having concluded that annihilating the Jewish people is the right move but recognizing that he needs Achashverosh's approval, Haman begins to put a plan together.

While many veteran readers of the Megilah take his next actions for granted, what Haman does next is indeed somewhat strange. Before approaching Achashverosh with his request, Haman sets up a lottery to determine the best and most appropriate day to execute his plan. The notion of resorting to a lottery is itself odd, but doing so even before discussing the matter with Achashverosh just highlights how out of place it really is. Even while it make sense that Haman wants to present Achashverosh with a complete and detailed plan, just pending his royal imprimatur, considering that he couldn't be sure that Achashverosh would even agree it comes across as somewhat presumptuous to already have preselected a date for the devastation.

The Megilah doesn't explain why Haman uses a lottery and from the general flow of the story, it takes it almost as second nature that casting lots is the most obvious and appropriate method to determine when to annihilate the Jewish people. From the Talmud's general historical accounting (detailed a little later), Haman cast this lottery on the 14th of Nissan. This is significant, as it turns out that the date that is ultimately randomly selected is a full 11 months later. In fact, according to some, it was the absolutely last possible day on which the lottery could have fallen.

While not overly detailed, the Megilah describes Haman as casting lots מִיּוֹם לְיוֹם וּמֵחֹדֶשׁ לְחֹדֶשׁ (from day to day and month to month) – from day to day and month to month. *Yosef Lekach* explains that Haman employed a method that he would select a date and would then cast lots to determine if that date was suitable. When he finished with the days of the month (1 to 30), he then moved on to the months themselves. As Haman was eager as ever to bring his plan to fruition, he made sure that the very next day (the 15th of Nissan) was certainly a viable option. He therefore cycled through the month starting with the 15th (the next day), until finally circling back around to the 14th. For the months, he started with that very month – Nissan – and cycled through the year until finally reaching Adar. Effectively, Haman wanted to insure that when he approached Achashverosh with the plan, it was going to theoretically be possible to start executing it the very next day. And without any fanfare or reaction from Haman whatsoever, the lottery just so happens to fall out on the 13th of Adar – the last possible date that Haman's system allowed for.

The Megilah presents the lottery's outcome without comment, not even acknowledging it as a fortuitous coincidence for the Jewish people. In fact, even while other commentators offer different interpretations as to the precise method Haman used to cast these lots and, according to their reckoning, the 13th of Adar wasn't the absolute latest date for it to fall out, the 'destined' date was still a good long while away. But as is the Megilah's style, it presents facts plainly and simply, all as mere coincidences.

It's of significant note that while the lottery itself occupies only a few short sentences in the Megilah and doesn't seem to play a particularly significant role in the plot, it's this very lottery that gives the holiday of Purim its name. But even in its current context, the whole notion of lots seems somewhat odd and out of place. Why would Haman even bother? There isn't any other indication in the Megilah that he was overly superstitious or religious. And even if casting lots indeed made sense to Haman for some cultural or religious level, why does the Megilah specifically choose to highlight this detail? It's clear that in retrospect, given the name of Purim for the holiday, this detail becomes an important element in the plot. But that just makes understanding the importance and symbolism of the lottery all that more important.

* * *

Interestingly, the lottery which initially appears as a seemingly insignificant detail, leads to the very name of the holiday, indicating, that perhaps understanding its deeper meaning holds a key to understanding the deeper message of the Megilah.

As discussed throughout, one of the Megilah's main messages is recognizing the *yad Hashem* in the world and learning how to respond and react to it. Accordingly, the lottery cast by Haman plays an important role in conveying this notion, as part of the continuing Mordekhai-Haman rivalry as reminiscent and representative of the eternal Jewish-Amalek battle.

Aside from founding and harboring the oldest and most insidious form of antisemitism, *Chazal* understood that Amalek ideology represents a life worldview completely at odds with Judaism. In commanding *Bnei Yisrael* to eternally remember the battle with Amalek, the Torah (*Devarim* 25:18) describes Amalek as אֲשֶׁר קָרְךָ בַּדֶּרֶךְ – how he [Amalek] met / attacked / surprised you on your journey. The ambiguity in the various translations stems from the unusual word choice of קָרְךָ, which more colloquially might be rendered as "he happened upon you." Rashi (and many others following his approach) emphasize that קָרְךָ stems from מקרה, meaning a coincidence or fortuitous happenstance. But while perhaps most grammatically precise, it's hard to know what it means in context.

A battle between two nations doesn't just happen coincidentally and in its original telling of the story, the Torah is quite clear that וַיָּבֹא עֲמָלֵק וַיִּלָּחֶם עִם יִשְׂרָאֵל בִּרְפִידִם – Amalek specifically approached *Bnei Yisrael* to wage war against them. And even in the later retelling, the Torah emphasizes וַיְזַנֵּב בְּךָ כָּל הַנֶּחֱשָׁלִים אַחֲרֶיךָ – attacked all the stragglers in the rear – clearly indicated a planned and thought-out military approach. There was nothing coincidental about Amalek's attack and was clearly devised and planned in advance. This forced non-literal reading of אֲשֶׁר קָרְךָ led many commentators to interpret אֲשֶׁר קָרְךָ as describing Amalek's intentions and outlook as opposed to the nature of the military battle.

This idea builds upon a notion prevalent in Jewish thought that the Jewish-Amalek battle was more than just a military struggle but [also] a conflict of ideas and outlook. Particularly in the context of the Megilah, this struggle is about recognizing Hashem's role in the world. The Jewish view, highlighted by Mordekhai and Esther (and later even Zeresh), recognizes Hashem as not only orchestrating world events from High Above, but also actively intervening if and when necessary.

On the opposite extreme, Amalek represents a worldview that world events occur at random and cannot be infused with any particular spiritual significance. It's for that reason that Amalek attacks *Bnei Yisrael* only a short few days after their Exodus from Egypt. The Jews had just finally left Egypt after an overtly miraculous 11 months of Divine plagues and proudly proclaimed their allegiance to Hashem as they triumphantly marched out of the land of their oppressors at His command. The Jews leaving Egypt were acutely aware of the spiritual significance of their journey; that it was not merely freedom from slavery and suffering but would instead transform into a freedom to serve Hashem and dedicate their lives to Him. It's this demonstration of *Bnei Yisrael* as the עם הנבחר and playing an important role in the spiritual unfolding of history that peaked Amalek's ire.

To Amalek, these notions were simply false and they couldn't stand for a brand new group of people declaring to the world an opposite worldview. Amalek was so heavily invested in their *weltanschauung* being the dominant outlook in the region [if not the world] that they felt duty bound to attack and hopefully destroy any nation or culture that advocated otherwise.

Haman, as Mordekhai's foil, represents the Amalekite approach. To Haman, nothing in history holds any spiritual meaning or purpose as – to his mind – everything that occurs is random and coincidental. It therefore makes perfect sense to Haman to cast lots to determine when to schedule the annihilation of the Jewish people.

In contrast, the Tanakh often describes a lottery as method of arriving or determining divine or spiritual sanction or meaning to an otherwise mundane and circumstantial selection. Haman however, doesn't appear to have any religious proclivities. Instead, consistent with his overall portrayal as a simple minded individual, he finds no hidden or special meaning in lotteries and lots. Considering his plot to destroy the Jewish people is of significant importance to him, Haman relies on what he knows and trusts – the 'power' of random coincidence – to help determine when the plan should take place.

This is likely the reason that Haman doesn't react when the lottery comes out to the very last possible date. For the average reader, this would seemingly indicate some supernatural or divine involvement in the matter. In fact, Ibn Ezra and *Yosef Lekach* interpret the delay as a Divine opportunity for the Jews to repent and thereby hopefully bring about a spiritual annulment of the royal decree.

It's not just that Haman's plan isn't immediately executable, it's almost a whole year away. He could have, if he wanted to, just decided that the decree would take place the very next day, week, or month. But he has no reaction whatsoever, since to Haman, a lottery is just about mere coincidence and chance; there isn't any meaning or Providence behind it. Since it was at least theoretically possible for the lottery to land on the absolutely last possible opportunity, Haman makes nothing of it.

* * *

The contrast couldn't be starker. Careful readers will note the fortuitous coincidence as no doubt the Jews of Shushan did once word of the specific events made their rounds and clearly see the *yad Hashem* even in the technical details in which their very annihilation is planned.

This continuation of the Jewish-Amalek rivalry, although subtle, is almost certainly intentional, further driving home the message of the Jewish value and axiom of seeking out, finding, and responding to the *yad Hashem* in the world.

From the Megilah's perspective, Haman's casting lots, as symbolic of his general Amalekite worldview, is neatly contextualized right after describing and hinting to the Mordekhai-Haman arch-rivalry, which hearkens back to the Shaul-Agag rivalry, which was a later manifestation of the Jewish-Amalek rivalry. Casting lots serves to cast Haman in his role as a foil to the message that the Megilah highlights throughout – recognition of the *yad Hashem* in the world and learning to react and respond to it.

# Chapter Eighteen

At first glance, Haman's request of Achashverosh sounds absurd. Haman tells Achashverosh that there is some nation, scattered among the Empire's provinces, who is strange and different. They have their own sets of values, morals, and rituals; like none other throughout all 127 lands. But they aren't satisfied in being somewhat more eclectic than most, since most tragically, וְאֶת דָּתֵי הַמֶּלֶךְ אֵינָם עֹשִׂים – they refuse to follow the king's rules. They don't fit in with everybody else and they flaunt their own culture and mores at the expense of the king's. These people are undesirable וְלַמֶּלֶךְ אֵין שֹׁוֶה לְהַנִּיחָם – it's not reasonable for the king to allow them to continue like this.

At no point does Haman actually identify who these terrible people might be. But perhaps even more interestingly, Achashverosh doesn't seem very interested in finding out. He asks no questions and isn't even the least bit curious to find out what it is that Haman has planned. Haman says אִם עַל הַמֶּלֶךְ טוֹב יִכָּתֵב לְאַבְּדָם – if it pleases the king, he should proclaim לְאַבְּדָם, to destroy 'them.' In context, the reference to 'them' is somewhat vague and seemingly deliberately so. Interestingly, in the rest of the Megilah, when Haman subsequently issues a kingly proclamation to put his plan into place, he is far more specific in what he wants to accomplish – לְהַשְׁמִיד לַהֲרֹג וּלְאַבֵּד – to annihilate, kill, and destroy. It's only when he is speaking to the king, trying to 'sell' his plan to Achashverosh, that Haman is vague with his words. But it's more than just the reference that is vague.

Haman offers Achashverosh 10,000 *kikar* of silver and still leaves his intentions equally ambiguous. Is it meant as a 'thank you gift' to Achashverosh for going along with Haman's plan? Or perhaps a means of compensating Achashverosh for the lost taxes that he will suffer with fewer tax-paying subjects?

R. Yehudah ibn Shoshan argues that Haman was intentionally vague, waiting to see Achashverosh's reaction and act accordingly. Haman understood that his request seemed a bit 'over the top,' to say the least. While he wanted to kill the Jews, he wasn't sure that Achashverosh would go along with the plan. But even if Achashverosh wouldn't go along, Haman was nervous that if Achashverosh thought that his request was so excessive, Achashverosh might think that Haman was going too far. He might have thought that Haman let his promoted status 'get to his head' and think that he now has the right and authority to do away with an entire people.

While Haman was certainly using his status to call in a favor, he didn't want it to cost him his position either. He certainly hated Mordekhai and the Jews, but he loved his position in the palace even more. Haman therefore needed to set up a situation in which he could pitch Achashverosh the idea of killing the Jews and at the same time, plausibly deny that that's what he actually meant.

Haman therefore deliberately worded his official request as לְאַבְּדָם – which he wanted Achashverosh to interpret as "destroy them" – meaning the Jewish people, but in context, could also be understood as "destroy them" – meaning the Jews' foreign culture and rituals. Depending on how Achashverosh would respond, Haman would know how to proceed. If Achashverosh seemed too perturbed by the extreme nature of the request, Haman could always fall back on the second interpretation, claiming that's what he really wanted all along.

* * *

Without asking even a single question or actually inquiring which nation Haman wants to obliterate, Achashverosh completely goes along with Haman's plan. He gives Haman his official royal ring for Haman to use to issue whatever proclamation Haman feels is most appropriate, וְהָעָם לַעֲשׂוֹת בּוֹ כַּטּוֹב בְּעֵינֶיךָ – to do with them whatever he sees fit. But that's not enough. In a magnanimous gesture, Achashverosh tells Haman to keep his money, Achashverosh doesn't need it. It was a nice gesture on Haman's part, but Achashverosh is happy to acquiesce even without the 'bribe.' But why?

The Megilah gives little reason or context for Achashverosh going along with this plan. In fact, Haman's plot doesn't really interest Achashverosh.

It's almost as if he couldn't care less what happens with these unnamed people. From Achashverosh's perspective, who really cares if דָתֵיהֶם שֹׁנוֹת מִכָּל עָם (their manners and ways are different than other nations)? He rules over 127 different provinces. Of course they don't all march lockstep with the same values, rituals, and customs. That's not enough of a reason to destroy a whole people. Also, while Haman presents the fact that דָתֵיהֶם שֹׁנוֹת מִכָּל עָם as leading directly to וְאֶת דָּתֵי הַמֶּלֶךְ אֵינָם עֹשִׂים, he doesn't give any proof or argument for his claim. Why should the two issues be connected at all? If Haman is trying to argue that this nation marches to the beat of its own drummer and ignores the king, why even bother mentioning what their private practices are? The two points aren't terribly relevant to each other, so why connect the two? And despite all this, Achashverosh gives Haman everything he asked for and more, with nary a question or comment.

It's hard to know what exactly was going through Achashverosh's mind at the time, but given the background to the beginning of the story, perhaps Achashverosh was playing shrewd politics once again. From just listening to Haman's argument, Achashverosh may have picked up on the fact that Haman has some personal connection to the issue. Achashverosh also must have realized that Haman was putting himself somewhat out on the line with this request. He knew that Haman would have been nervous to ask for something this big (which was why perhaps Haman was intentionally vague with the details of the request). It was a big favor that could have easily backfired and lost Haman his elevated royal position. So when Haman describes this unnamed nation in such negative terms, in a rather unpersuasive manner, and whose accusations don't seem to fit in with each other or paint a coherent narrative, Achashverosh realized that something was amiss. Why would Haman go out on such a limb with such a weak argument?

Achashverosh may have realized that aside from the challenges and burdens that Haman claims this unnamed nation poses to the Persian Empire, Haman also seems to have some skin in the game. For one reason or another, Haman seems to have a personal interest in getting rid of these people. Which is actually enough of a reason for Achashverosh to give Haman what he wants.

* * *

Achashverosh realizes that he needs Haman on his side. Assuming that Haman and Memukhan are one and the same, Haman has been a loyal and trusted advisor to Achashverosh for some time. Haman not only helped Achashverosh resolve the "Vashti issue" but did so in such a way that helped solidify Achashverosh's authority and quash the nascent and potentially growing Reactionary movement. Haman was proving himself as a Loyalist and somebody whom Achashverosh could count on. Furthermore, Achashverosh just narrowly escaped an assassination attempt and was looking for additional ways to secure his reign and position. This is very likely the reason that גִּדַּל הַמֶּלֶךְ אֲחַשְׁוֵרוֹשׁ אֶת הָמָן (King Achashverosh raised up Haman) in the first place.

After hearing Haman's rather weak arguments and realizing that Haman likely has a personal interest in the demise of this nation, Achashverosh capitalized on the political opportunity in front of him. This request was clearly something that Haman was both passionate about and personally invested in. It's also an easy thing for Achashverosh to 'give' to Haman. What better way to keep Haman as a faithful Loyalist than to buy his appreciation. From Achashverosh's perspective, it's politically expedient for Haman to feel that he got something from the king and be in his debt. Haman has done a lot for him and this is Achashverosh's opportunity to show his appreciation for those efforts at little political cost.

* * *

Reading the Megilah as is, it seems that Achashverosh is not in the least interested in destroying this unnamed nation and merely goes along with it so as to appease Haman. Achashverosh poses no questions about this elaborate plan. He doesn't ask anything about the accusation itself, not even for clarification on Haman's overly vague description of people from different cultures being different. Achashverosh doesn't even take the money that Haman offered him, indicating that Achashverosh is happy to do this favor specifically for Haman, to maintain and support their relationship. Moreover, as soon as Haman gets Achashverosh's approval and finishes sending out the proclamations, he and Achashverosh sit down to drink. For Achashverosh, the entire episode is just another means to reward a dear Loyalist for his service and maintain their relationship, which he immediately celebrates by inviting Haman for a drink. It's the final detail of the story, because after all, from Achashverosh's perspective, that is what the whole exercise was about.

What emerges from this story though, is the Achashverosh is completely unaware of any plan to kill the Jews. He never asks and Haman never offers that information. At the end of the story, when Esther finally reveals to him that there is a plot to kill her people, Achashverosh has no idea what she is talking about. Even before she mentions Haman's involvement or declares herself to be a Jewess, why didn't Achashverosh have any recollection of this whole episode with Haman, where Haman obtained Achashverosh's permission to do just that and destroy a whole nation just a few short days earlier?

Alternatively, Achashverosh does remember the episode but couldn't imagine that Haman would be such a fool to plot to actually kill the queen. While this episode will be analyzed in some detail later, Achashverosh likely stopped for a moment and realized that he has no idea who in fact his queen's kinsmen are and which nation did he exactly give Haman permission to annihilate. The whole thing seems to take Achashverosh by surprise, likely because he never took too much of an interest in the details in the first place. It's probably because the details weren't relevant to him at the time. Achashverosh was agreeing to Haman as a person, a minister in his court, and a Loyalist, not necessarily to his murderous plan.

Assuming this account to be accurate, it makes sense that Achashverosh would want to promote Memukhan. After his involvement with the Vashti affair, he demonstrated his faithfulness to Achashverosh and to Achashverosh's vision. As a clearly staunch Loyalist, Achashverosh shows his gratitude with Haman's promotion. The description of his promotion is also a fitting introduction to understanding Haman's request to annihilate the Jews, which from Achashverosh's perspective seemed to have been more about Haman than the Jews themselves.

# Chapter Nineteen

Haman wastes no time in putting his plan into place. According to numerous commentators, Haman recognizes that having hid the true details of his plan from Achashverosh may lead Achashverosh to reconsidering and even taking back his agreement should he later learn them. To insure against that possibility, Haman commissions letters to be sent to each of the 127 provinces that very day, knowing and relying on the Persian law that prevents and prohibits rescinding already-enacted royal decrees.

But while the Megilah clearly presents the speed with which Haman puts his plan into action, it is somewhat more ambiguous with exactly how he makes it known. The Megilah describes how Haman commissions scribes to transcribe a message to the vast kingdom, but subsequently notes that these letters were sent to אֲחַשְׁדַּרְפְּנֵי הַמֶּלֶךְ וְאֶל הַפַּחוֹת אֲשֶׁר עַל מְדִינָה וּמְדִינָה וְאֶל שָׂרֵי עַם וָעָם – the various levels of administrative government within each province. These letters were then handed to runners and messengers to distribute them throughout the kingdom. Given the vast nature of the empire and its sheer size, this was no small feat and Haman needed to rely on an already existing governmental system of proclamations and messaging. It makes sense that Haman would send these letters specifically to the governing authorities. After all, they would be the ones who would ultimately be responsible for executing the plan. While this is seemingly the simple approach to the story, there are a number of challenges to contend with, some literary and others, more fundamental.

After recording that the books / letters were sent to the administrative officials of each province, the Megilah continues, פַּתְשֶׁגֶן הַכְּתָב לְהִנָּתֵן דָּת בְּכָל מְדִינָה וּמְדִינָה גָּלוּי לְכָל הָעַמִּים לִהְיוֹת עֲתִדִים לַיּוֹם הַזֶּה (The text of the document was that a law should be declared in every province; to be publicly displayed for all the people, so that they might be ready for that day) without elaborating whether or not this פַּתְשֶׁגֶן הַכְּתָב is another way of referring to those very books / letters, or to something different. The Megilah describes this פַּתְשֶׁגֶן הַכְּתָב as specifically being גָּלוּי לְכָל הָעַמִּים – open and accessible to everyone. On the face of it, this also makes sense. Annihilating an entire people is not something that government administrators can pull off on their own; they need the buy-in of the populace as well. It makes sense that there might also be a public proclamation to get the people – those who will have to actually put the plan into practice – ready for what is to come. But if these proclamations were public and open, why does the Megilah very shortly note that Mordekhai somehow found out about Haman's plot? If these פַּתְשֶׁגֶן הַכְּתָב were publicized widely, shouldn't everybody have known about what was going on? Why does Mordekhai then have to send proof to Esther to convince her that this was actually taking place? These details also seem to point to an indication that at least some aspect of Haman's plan was still somewhat secret and that Mordekhai had somehow found out information that was not publicly available.

Additionally, the content of the פַּתְשֶׁגֶן הַכְּתָב (assuming it was a separate document) is far less detailed than the books / letters that Haman sent to the administrators. While the original letters specify לְהַשְׁמִיד לַהֲרֹג וּלְאַבֵּד אֶת כָּל הַיְּהוּדִים מִנַּעַר וְעַד זָקֵן טַף וְנָשִׁים (to annihilate, kill, and destroy all the Jews, from children to the elderly, infants, and women), this latter פַּתְשֶׁגֶן הַכְּתָב is completely devoid of any detail whatsoever. It merely notes that the people should be עֲתִדִים לַיּוֹם הַזֶּה – ready to act / anticipate the coming 13th of Adar. Lastly, after the letters were sent, the Megilah describes וְהָעִיר שׁוּשָׁן נָבוֹכָה – the city was in a state of confusion; not sadness or melancholy, but confusion. If the content of the public פַּתְשֶׁגֶן הַכְּתָב merely commanded people to anticipate or get ready for the upcoming 13th of Adar without providing any detail as to what will take place, it makes sense that people might be somewhat antsy, anxious, and somewhat confused.

Leaving aside the textual challenges, from a more strategic perspective, Haman was left with somewhat of a dilemma. He needed to convince the general populace of 127 different provinces to rise up on a specific date and kill their neighbors. Given Haman's vicious internalized antisemitic perspective on the world, he likely didn't think that this task was all too difficult. The challenge was that in the long interim between authoring the letters and their eventual execution, the Jews would have ample time to come up with a plan of their own. They might find some way to band together for a defense strategy, or flee e*n masse* before the plan's date of execution, or devise some political solution to avoid or cancel the entire plan altogether. While it's unlikely that Haman took this into consideration, if the plan was made public it would create really awkward and difficult social interactions between the Jews and their neighbors for the next 11 months. How are people supposed to do business with each other if each party knows ahead of time that come the 13th of Adar, one will be royally commanded to kill the other?

It's for many of these reasons that many commentators assume that Haman sent two different sets of letters – a private communication to the government administrators and a broadly publicized one for the general public. This neatly explains the seeming repetition of sending the letters and explains that differences existed between them.

Malbim argues that the government officials received sealed letters that they weren't supposed to open until the 13th of Adar while the public letters just told the general population to be ready for the 13th of Adar when the content of the official's letters would be revealed. Gra takes a slightly different approach, agreeing that the public was only told to prepare for the 13th of Adar but that the government administrators were given full disclosure about what was to happen. Both agree that it was important to Haman to hide the plan's gory details with the general populace, particularly lest word spread to the Jews who might find some way to save themselves.

But even while commentators debate the details of how these one or two similar or different sets of letters were sent, publicized, and distributed, practically speaking, Haman failed in his objective. Word quickly got out about the details of the plan and got out quickly. Already on that very day, the details somehow were leaked to Mordekhai, who after a brief period of sadness and mourning, sprang into action. And it wasn't just Mordekhai with his lofty palace credentials that somehow helped him get a hold of the hidden details, but rather

> וּבְכָל מְדִינָה וּמְדִינָה מְקוֹם אֲשֶׁר דְּבַר הַמֶּלֶךְ וְדָתוֹ מַגִּיעַ אֵבֶל גָּדוֹל לַיְּהוּדִים וְצוֹם וּבְכִי וּמִסְפֵּד שַׂק וָאֵפֶר יֻצַּע לָרַבִּים.
>
> And in each state and place that the decree of the king arrived, there was great mourning for the Jews; with fasting, crying, and eulogies; sackcloth and ashes were widespread.

The Jews of the various provinces also quickly found out. Apparently, despite Haman's best efforts, plans to annihilate whole swaths of the Kingdom are not easily kept hidden for long.

# Chapter Twenty

When Mordekhai initially approaches Esther with the information about Haman's decree, he suggests (or more properly, demands) that she approach Achashverosh to beg him to reverse it. Esther hesitates and points out that Mordekhai's plan isn't viable. After all, Achashverosh does not take to uninvited visitors very well. She even seems somewhat surprised that Mordekhai, clearly a prominent Shushan personality, is apparently unaware of this particular peculiarity.

> כָּל עַבְדֵי הַמֶּלֶךְ וְעַם מְדִינוֹת הַמֶּלֶךְ יוֹדְעִים אֲשֶׁר כָּל אִישׁ וְאִשָּׁה אֲשֶׁר יָבוֹא אֶל הַמֶּלֶךְ אֶל הֶחָצֵר הַפְּנִימִית אֲשֶׁר לֹא יִקָּרֵא אַחַת דָּתוֹ לְהָמִית
>
> All the servants of the king and nations of his kingdom know that any man or woman who enters the inner chamber without being summoned is certainly put to death

This was common knowledge, not just in the palace but throughout the kingdom.

Why was Mordekhai suggesting something that is so blatantly obvious that it won't work? Even if, by some miracle, she could even get through the front door without being put to death – which she thinks is unlikely – she would have to first explain to Achashverosh why she even cares about the Jewish people and Haman's decree. After all, Achashverosh doesn't know that Esther is Jewish. While it's true that he hasn't asked, which indicates to her that it wasn't terribly important to him, nonetheless, the Megilah repeatedly highlights the fact that Esther deliberately kept this from him. It would be a touchy subject for her to broach under 'normal' circumstances, let alone when asking for a huge favor.

And even that side discussion in itself is risky. Once she reveals her true identity, how will Achashverosh react? Will it matter at all to him? Will he, already weary of political insurrection from within his own court, identify Esther with the Jews of Yerushalayim, whom he believes to be rebellious and violent? In fact, why wouldn't he make that immediate association? Isn't that the precise reason that Esther hid that information from him in the first place? Not only would Achashverosh have to process what it means for him to be married to a Jewess, he would also need to quickly calculate what it means that she intentionally hid this from him until now. All of this adds up to a vanishingly small chance that approaching Achashverosh and begging him for mercy, as Mordekhai suggests, would be successful. She can't go along with it.

Frustrated with Esther's hesitation, Mordekhai must now rouse her to action, convince her that "she can do it!," and get her to save the Jewish people. She needs an inspiring pep talk, something that will motivate her to take the risk, realizing that it's the only way to save the Jewish people.

Shockingly, Mordekhai's 'rousing speech,' is anything but uplifting.

But hidden within it is the secret to the story of the Megilah.

* * *

MORDEKHAI OPENS WITH a somber note, אַל תְּדַמִּי בְנַפְשֵׁךְ לְהִמָּלֵט בֵּית הַמֶּלֶךְ מִכָּל הַיְּהוּדִים – don't pretend that you will be safe just because you live in the palace. Not that this was necessarily on Esther's mind, but realistically speaking, why not? Esther hasn't told Achashverosh that she is Jewish and apparently, it was something that she was able to effectively hide from him; clearly, it wasn't otherwise obvious. Haman would similarly not have known and couldn't be aware that his plan included killing the newly appointed queen. And even if Haman was aware that Esther was Jewish (even though it's hard to know how he would be), he wouldn't have been foolish enough to include her in the decree; he would have found some way to exclude her or make some exception for the queen.

Assuming that Haman and Memukhan are one and the same person, he was the minister to previously recommended banishing Vashti. It wouldn't look good for him if he now wanted to kill off the newly minted queen as well. But even without that loaded history, Achashverosh would likely not take too kindly to acquiescing to allowing his wife to be killed just to fulfill some random decree of Haman. Of course Haman never intended for Esther to be killed. What then was Mordekhai driving at?

Not leaving his assumption that open ended, Mordekhai continues that

> כִּי אִם הַחֲרֵשׁ תַּחֲרִישִׁי בָּעֵת הַזֹּאת רֶוַח וְהַצָּלָה יַעֲמוֹד לַיְּהוּדִים מִמָּקוֹם אַחֵר וְאַתְּ וּבֵית אָבִיךְ תֹּאבֵדוּ וּמִי יוֹדֵעַ אִם לְעֵת כָּזֹאת הִגַּעַתְּ לַמַּלְכוּת.
>
> On the contrary, if you keep silent in this moment, relief and redemption will come to the Jews from another source, while you and your father's house will perish. And who knows, perhaps it's for this moment that you have attained your royal position.

On a superficial level, it's hard to know how these two sentences flow together. He starts by chastising Esther that she shouldn't think that she will be safe in the palace and continues that if she doesn't take any initiative, then the Jews will be certainly saved by some other means. Mordekhai is fully confident in Hashem's salvation; it could be through Esther, but הרבה שלוחים למקום (Hashem has many messengers) and He isn't limited by the current political actors in the Shushan palace. But if that were to happen, then "Esther and her family will be lost" and "perhaps, this is the reason you reached the throne." Mordekhai is expressing two different points, both of which can stand on their own regardless of whether or not Esther feels safe in the palace.

Firstly, and perhaps most importantly, Mordekhai is demonstrating his complete faith in Hashem, who will not abandon His people. The Jewish story will most certainly not end in Shushan and by some means or another, the Jews will survive. This is the ultimate statement of faith. No matter how dire the situation, no matter that he cannot necessarily foresee a possible way to reverse Haman's decree, Mordekhai is absolutely confident in Hashem's salvation. Mordekhai recognizes that this alternative plan may not include his or Esther's own survival, but in the larger scheme of things that isn't of historical significance.

What matters is that the Jewish story doesn't end and this is one of the clearest expressions in Tanakh of the eternity of the Jewish people, of כלל ישראל, even if not of every member of the then-current Jewish people. When it comes to matters of historical significance, it's the nation as a whole that is the focus, not the individual players. Just because the chess pieces seem lined up in a particular way doesn't necessarily mean that we can predict how He will move them. But let there be no mistake, Mordekhai assures Esther, Hashem's people will survive; they will win, it's only a matter of how and when. This is one of the most moving moments of the entire Megilah, an expression of pure faith in the eternal covenant between Hashem and His people.

But while inspirational, it's not a terribly effective argument. If Mordekhai is trying to convince Esther to confront Achashverosh and beg for his mercy, how does telling her that whether or not she steps up to the plate will not matter in the long run possibly help his cause?

Many of the commentators pick up on this difficulty and offer various interpretations. Rashi understands Mordekhai as reasoning with Esther. While it's true that she currently feels safe in the palace, who knows what Achashverosh will think of her next year, when Haman's decree finally comes to fruition? With Achashverosh, nobody can really predict how or in what directions the political winds will sway so many months from now. She shouldn't rely on her status as Achashverosh's queen as a means of saving herself and possibly even her family; that can change at any moment. Rashi is trying to connect the two ideas by reading Achashverosh's fickle nature into the subtext. But while plausible, it doesn't seem to read well, since if Mordekhai is indeed confident that רֶוַח וְהַצָּלָה יַעֲמוֹד לַיְּהוּדִים מִמָּקוֹם אַחֵר, then even if Esther was no longer a favored persona in Achashverosh's palace, why should she, more than any other Jew, be at an increased risk?

In *Tokpo shel Nes*, R. Rahamim Hai Havitah ha-Kohen adds a little bit to Rashi's understanding that seemingly tries to address this problem. He explains that Mordekhai is really trying to get Esther to act right now – meaning in the month of Nissan, a full 11 months before Haman's decree is set to happen. Esther responds that she hasn't been or been called to Achashverosh for the past month, but it's highly likely that he will call for her before next Adar (when Haman's decree is set for). It's not worth risking her life to enter Achashverosh's chambers without being called if there's a really good chance that she will have the opportunity to speak with him anyway without endangering herself. He understands that Esther is willing to participate in the plan. She isn't saying no, just simply suggesting a means of mitigating the potential risk.

Mordekhai however, is concerned that waiting will only increase the problem. Haman may want to assure that his plan becomes a reality by consistently approaching Achashverosh throughout the upcoming year, to bolster support for his plan. He fears that Haman will concoct more accusations against the Jews, building on Achashverosh's fears and possible resentment of them (if Haman chooses to reveal the identity of the nation in question). All of this will make it far more difficult for Esther to intervene when she is eventually called to him.

If Esther delays too much, Mordekhai is concerned that, at best, she might get an exemption for herself and her family. But once Achashverosh would be so emotionally (and financially) invested in Haman's plan, he won't be so willing to rescind it in its entirety. Because of Mordekhai's steadfast belief that the Jews will ultimately survive, he's concerned that if Esther does approach Achashverosh, but does so too late to avert the decree and Hashem finds some other way to save the Jews, Haman may still remain in his position of power and harbor deep resentment and animosity toward Esther for her efforts to thwart his plans.

While this approach paints Esther in a more favorable light – in that she doesn't hesitate about acting on behalf of her people more generally, only about the actual timing – and it nicely interrelates to Esther's previous claim that she hasn't been called to Achashverosh in the last month, it's also difficult to read so much into these few lines of text to substantiate that this is really what Mordekhai had in mind.

But if this is indeed one of "the" moments of the Megilah as the ultimate declaration of faith in Hashem and His relationship with the Jewish people, perhaps that in itself is the clue to understanding Mordekhai's argument.

Mordekhai needs to get Esther to act and act quickly. His message to her was quite clear and having grown up in his home, Esther was likely quite receptive to it, having heard it – or more likely seen Mordekhai live it – for quite some time.

# Chapter Twenty-One

Mordekhai saves the most important and fundamental message for the very end; it's the last thing Esther hears from him: וּמִי יוֹדֵעַ אִם לְעֵת כָּזֹאת הִגַּעַתְּ לַמַּלְכוּת – And who knows, perhaps it's for this moment that you have attained your royal position. Nothing happens randomly; there are no coincidences in life. While we often do not and cannot understand why world events happen in the way in which they do, they are most certainly not random or left up to chance. Hashem is behind everything but only sometimes makes Himself and His manipulating the story and history plainly obvious.

This is the main lesson of the entire Megilah – something that the reader is encouraged to take cognizance of but more importantly, to see how the characters in the Megilah itself internalize this idea and in doing so, adapt their lives to it. Mordekhai is telling Esther that it is certainly no mere coincidence that she was specifically chosen as Achashverosh's queen. While there was an elaborate selection process focused entirely on superficial qualities and seemed to be a completely random and uninspired choice – and perhaps this is why the Megilah highlights the process in excruciating detail – it was all masterfully orchestrated by Hashem.

Initially, Mordekhai was most likely perplexed by Esther's selection. Of all the girls in the kingdom, why specifically select Esther, the nice Jewish girl who had to be cajoled / forced to 'apply' for the position? Even realizing that nothing happens randomly, until this point in time Mordekhai didn't understand why Esther was chosen, and even now, he can only speculate.

But what he is telling Esther is that if you look carefully enough, sometimes you can get a glimpse of Hashem's plan for the world. While it's often hidden, there are some details of His plan that manage to peek through the lattice. Mordekhai senses that this is exactly what is happening right now. As the queen, Esther is in a unique position to save the Jewish people. There is nobody with more access or ability to influence his decision. And even while Achashverosh hasn't called for her in the last month, she is better situated than anybody else to intervene.

It's true, Mordekhai freely admits, that whether she acts or not, Hashem will find some way to save the Jewish people. Haman's decree will certainly not outmaneuver or overpower Hashem's historically earlier promise to *Bnei Yisrael* to never abandon them. And it's also true, that if Esther doesn't use her unique position to intervene, there will be something that will change what currently seems to be the unbending predictable outcome. But if Esther just sits back for a moment and takes in the whole picture, she will realize that she can be part of His plan. She didn't become the queen for no reason; this was all part of His plan.

Mordekhai is teaching her that even though it's true that if she doesn't step forward Hashem will implement a plan B, if Esther can come to recognize that she is already part of Hashem's plan, she can make a difference. If she realizes that perhaps לְעֵת כָּזֹאת הִגַּעַתְּ לַמַּלְכוּת – this may be the very reason that Hashem orchestrated her selection so she can take that next step and participate in His plan.

Mordekhai knows full well that this isn't the safe choice. Esther would likely be put at no risk if she does nothing and simply stays quietly within the palace; it's more than likely that Haman's decree won't affect her. But what will be of her legacy? Of her place in the historical Jewish story?

Esther must choose whether she wants to play a pivotal role in the trans-historical Jewish people and take an active role in implementing Hashem's plan or merely sit on the side as a bystander. In fact, Mordekhai doesn't actually say that if she stays in the palace she won't escape Haman's decree. Instead, he tells her that אִם הַחֲרֵשׁ תַּחֲרִישִׁי בָּעֵת הַזֹּאת and sit on the sidelines, then וְאַתְּ וּבֵית אָבִיךְ תֹּאבֵדוּ. Mordekhai highlights Esther's role as part of the Jewish people; otherwise, why even reference בֵּית אָבִיךְ? What he is saying is that if she sits this one out, if she does not take the opportunity to step up and actively play a part in Hashem's plan, then, despite her prominent role in the Persian royal story, she and her legacy will be completely forgotten from the historical Jewish narrative. While she may physically survive, her potential contribution to the Jewish people, to the Jewish legacy, will be lost to eternity.

* * *

MORDEKHAI'S GOAL IS to motivate Esther to grab the reigns of history and look beneath the surface to see what is 'really' happening. His goal is for her to recognize that she is where she is for a particular reason.

This is her moment.

If she believes that Hashem is the Master of the world and the Author of history, then she will recognize that He has set things up in such a particular manner just so that she will use her position to save the Jewish people. Mordekhai needs to show her that for all that Judaism teaches about humility, stepping up in this situation isn't an act of hubris, but of profound faith. Faith that Hashem runs the world. Faith in Hashem's promise to His people that He will never abandon them. And faith in Hashem who has already set into motion a plan that will save His people, of which she is a vital player. Mordekhai is teaching Esther that it's not enough just to stand by and look for ways in which Hashem makes Himself visible, but that when you see it, it demands a response.

It worked. Esther got the message loud and clear. She recognizes that her position in the royal palace was part of her larger role in the historical Jewish story and she rises to the occasion.

# Chapter Twenty-Two

Before taking any action, Esther exhorts Mordekhai,

> לֵךְ כְּנוֹס אֶת כָּל הַיְּהוּדִים הַנִּמְצְאִים בְּשׁוּשָׁן וְצוּמוּ עָלַי וְאַל תֹּאכְלוּ וְאַל תִּשְׁתּוּ שְׁלֹשֶׁת יָמִים לַיְלָה וָיוֹם.
>
> Go gather all of the Jews in Shushan and fast for me, and do not eat and do not drink for three days, nights and days.

This is one of the most overtly religious activities described in the entire story, and even then, it's not clearly spelled out. There is no framework given for this particular fast, nor does it seem to be accompanied by anything else. This wasn't necessarily anything new either, as the Megilah just previously records,

> וּבְכָל מְדִינָה וּמְדִינָה מְקוֹם אֲשֶׁר דְּבַר הַמֶּלֶךְ וְדָתוֹ מַגִּיעַ אֵבֶל גָּדוֹל לַיְּהוּדִים וְצוֹם וּבְכִי וּמִסְפֵּד שַׂק וָאֵפֶר יֻצַּע לָרַבִּים.
>
> And in each state and place that the decree of the king arrived, there was great mourning for the Jews; with fasting, crying, and eulogies; sackcloth and ashes were widespread.

Fasting was part of the generalized, somewhat haphazard mourning that was already taking place throughout the Jewish communities of the Persian Empire. While fasting most certainly has religious overtones and is a tool used in a communal response to calamity and tragedy, the previous description seems somewhat spontaneous and unorganized. It's listed together with other mourning practices and while for many Jews it may have been an act of faith or part of their *teshuvah,* the Megilah leaves its description as somewhat secular.

This might give credence to Ibn Ezra's quotation of Rav Sa'adyah

Gaon that the Megilah was written at Achashverosh's behest for a Persian audience who might not have appreciated a direct reference to forms of *Avodat Hashem*. Alternatively, even according to *Chazal*'s tradition that the Megilah was written by Mordekhai with רוח הקודש, perhaps Mordekhai was aware that the story would become widespread within Persian society and therefore thought it was wiser to only obliquely reference actual instances of *tefilah*, a clue that all Jewish readers would be sensitive to, but their Persian compatriots would not necessarily find offensive.

Regardless, the Targum and *Midrashim* elaborate in exquisite detail about the mass *teshuvah* campaign Mordekhai embarked on, gathering the entirety of the Shushan Jewish community in solidarity for fasting, *teshuvah*, and *tefilah* for the success of Esther's mission. This wasn't fasting as sign of mourning, but part and parcel of a mass movement of communal repentance.

As Rambam (*Hilkhot Ta'aniyot* 1:4) describes, the Torah demands that when the Jewish community is faced with adversity, that we reach inward and upward: in a demonstration of repentance and contrition as well as deepening our connection and devotion to Hashem. He describes the the ancient rabbinic practice of complimenting that *teshuvah* effort with communal fasting.

There is some debate among the commentators whether the fast was actually 72 hours long, whether it included some necessary breaks, or whether the continuous nature of the fast was optional for the more pious among the Jews while others took some time off, but the issue is largely irrelevant for the purpose of understanding the rest of the story.

* * *

WHILE ONLY REFERENCED, Esther's charge to Mordekhai of לֵךְ כְּנוֹס is an uncommon and interesting way to ask him to gather the people as opposed to the more commonly found קבץ or אסוף. Perhaps the intention is to draw the reader's attention that he was to gather the people together for a collective unified purpose (Rav Alkabetz). Even while previously, some had already been mourning and even fasting independently, this was Mordekhai's [successful] attempt to help them all focus their efforts and energies together on a specific targeted communal outcome.

The goal wasn't only that each person participate, but that they do so in a communal sense. כְּנוֹס is the same verb that describes a בית כנסת the location specifically set aside for communal prayer. The Talmud repeatedly extols the virtues of communal prayer and *teshuvah* that far supersedes the efforts of the same individuals when left to their own devices, describing it (*Berakhot* 8a) as the quintessential עת רצון and that Hashem will never find fault or repugnancy with specifically communal *tefilah*.

Esther requests that וְצוּמוּ עָלַי – fast for me. But how can one person's not eating or drinking affect somebody else? Clearly, she didn't mean for it to be taken literally.

What she was asking for was communal *tefilah*. She requests that Mordekhai לֵךְ כְּנוֹס אֶת כָּל הַיְּהוּדִים הַנִּמְצְאִים בְּשׁוּשָׁן – gather all the Jews in Shushan together. There is nothing particular about fasting that requires a communal gathering or effort. But there is tremendous value in a תענית צבור of communal efforts, particularly of תפילה בצבור. While not eating and drinking is a central component of a תענית צבור, its essence is so much more than that. It's a day of communal חשבון הנפש, congregational repentance, and a societal reassessment and resetting of wayward value systems. In fact, the *Targum* interpolates וְצַלּוֹ קֳדָם מָרֵי עָלְמָא into Esther's very request. The *Targum Sheni* offers much Midrashic detail on the specifics of how the prayer service unfolded.

Just as there is some debate as to the extent of the fast, so too the commentators debate the precise dates on which these fasts took place. The only date provided in the Megilah itself is when Haman sent his decree throughout the lands – precisely 11 months before they were to be executed, on the 13th of Nisan. The next date in the Megilah itself is not until the 23rd of Sivan when Mordekhai sends word that Achashverosh has finally granted the Jews permission to defend themselves (and essentially revoke Haman's decree [to be discussed in detail later]). The details of the intervening events are left somewhat ambiguous.

* * *

Chazal clearly have a tradition that at least part of the fast took place during the holiday of Pesach and several *Midrashim* describe discussions that happened at the time as to the propriety of fasting on a *Yom Tov*. The indication seems to be that Mordekhai approached Esther on the very day that Haman's decree was issued. He wanted her to intervene as quickly as possible, which he felt would give her the greatest chance to succeed in her mission. The debate among the commentators is whether the three day fast began on that same day – the 13th of Nisan and lasted through the 15th – or whether it only began on the next day – the 14th of Nisan, lasting through the 16th. The Megilah itself is not only silent on the matter but doesn't even seem to give any clues as to the timing of any of these events.

In order to piece together the timeline, the commentators try to juggle various *Midrashim* – each one addressing a different point in the story and which may be at odds with each other (representing different perspectives among *Chazal* as to various aspects of the story). In trying to find themes and commonalities among the various *Midrashim*, there seems to be a general consensus that the episode with Haman parading Mordekhai on a royal horse throughout the streets of Shushan took place on the 16th of Nisan.

The Gemara and various *Midrashim* note that when Haman approached Mordekhai to inform and invite him on this rather strange spectacle, Mordekhai was in the midst of teaching his students about the קרבן העומר – as particularly relevant for that day – which was brought on the 16th of Nisan. And even while the timeline is subject to debate, the majority consensus opinion seems to be that the fasting started only on the 14th – the day after Haman issued his decree – and lasted through the 16th.

This also makes intuitive sense. The Megilah is clear that the discussion between Mordekhai and Esther took some time with multiple messengers carrying messages between the pair a number of times. Mordekhai only began his quest to convince Esther to confront Achashverosh after Haman had already issued his decree, which would have also taken some time. Such that even while Esther devised her plan on that very same day – the 13th of Nisan – starting to fast on that very day would mean starting late in the afternoon. The Jews of Shushan would only get word of the fast somewhat later, likely toward the evening. If the very idea was לֵךְ כְּנוֹס אֶת כָּל הַיְּהוּדִים and bring everybody together, it wouldn't make sense for each person to start fasting as soon as they heard about the idea.

It would make a lot more sense that Esther determined that a three day fast was appropriate and planned for it to begin the next day so that everybody could begin together. [Admittedly, this reading requires interpreting the phrase ויהי ביום השלישי – when Esther entered Achashverosh's chambers – to refer to three days since the letters were sent, meaning the 15th of Nisan and not referring to the three days of fasting (which would have ended only on the 16th of Nisan). But given the preponderance of evidence, many of the commentators prefer this conclusion.]

Reconstructing the timeline, if the story of Haman parading Mordekhai throughout Shushan took place on the 16th, it would mean that Esther's first party was the day prior, on the 15th of Nisan. Practically speaking, if her fast started on the 14th, it would mean that Esther was fasting during the very party that she was hosting, which seems somewhat odd. In fact however, Rav Alkabetz suggests that that is precisely what happened – Esther did not eat or drink during the first party. But far from being odd, he supports this contention from the text itself.

As Achashverosh and Haman prepare for the first feast, the Megilah describes them as וַיָּבֹא הַמֶּלֶךְ וְהָמָן אֶל הַמִּשְׁתֶּה אֲשֶׁר עָשְׂתָה אֶסְתֵּר (And the king and Haman came to the feast that Esther prepared); while for the second feast, it describes the pair as coming לִשְׁתּוֹת עִם אֶסְתֵּר הַמַּלְכָּה (to drink with Queen Esther). They joined Esther's first party, with no mention of her participation; it's only during the second party that the Megilah highlights לִשְׁתּוֹת עִם אֶסְתֵּר הַמַּלְכָּה, indicating that she drank with them. Given the proximity of the two stories, the change in language is clearly deliberate and, Rav Alkabetz argues, supports the notion that Esther was fasting on the 15th of Nisan during the first party.

But even according to Rav Alkabetz, the three day fast extended through the 16th of Nisan, when the second party took place. Why was Esther no longer fasting then? Maharal argues that in fact, this was all part of Esther's original plan. In halakhic terminology, a fast extends for as long as one accepts it on himself or herself. He argues that when Esther declared the three day fast, she accepted upon herself something slightly shorter so that she would be able to drink with Achashverosh and Haman at that fateful second party. He finds a hint to this idea in the text as well. When Esther presents her idea to Mordekhai that she is willing to approach Achashverosh only after the Jews fast on her behalf for three days, she says וּבְכֵן אָבוֹא אֶל הַמֶּלֶךְ (And as such I will come to the king), with וּבְכֵן having the numerical equivalent of 72, precisely the number of hours in the three day fast. But just prior to that, when she describes her own participation in the fast, she says גַּם אֲנִי וְנַעֲרֹתַי אָצוּם כֵּן (I and my maidservants will fast as well), with the verb describing fasting strangely in the singular as she seems to be describing not only her actions but those of her servants. Maharal explains that the numerical equivalent of כֵּן is 70, indicating that per her plan, she alone won't be fasting the entire 72 hours as she will be hosting a party for Achashverosh and Haman toward the end of the third day and it would be inappropriate for her not to participate in the feast. Because of this, she undertook a slightly shorter fast – 70 instead of 72 hours – than the rest of her Shushan comrades, so that she would be able to host and participate in that second party toward the end of the afternoon of the 16th of Nisan.

Aside from offering a precise accounting of the details, Maharal finds tremendous significance in the confluence of the Purim story with the קרבן העומר. The קרבן העומר offered on the second day of Pesach, the 16th of Nisan, was an offering of barley from the crop that specifically grew that year. In fact, it is considered the "first" of that new crop inasmuch as grain from the previous year (that grew since last Pesach) is not allowed to be eaten until the קרבן העומר is brought in the *Beit ha-Mikdash*.

Maharal explains that the קרבן העומר represents our acknowledgment and acceptance of Hashem as the ultimate Master of the natural world. As a demonstration of our gratitude, we offer a קרבן to him before we can partake of that very grain. Barley was chosen, Maharal explains, as throughout Tanakh it symbolizes the earth, nature, and physicality in general. It's that very acknowledgment that is at the heart of the Purim story as well.

The 'miracles' of the Megilah are not overt, like the splitting of the Red Sea or the Ten Plagues, but are all manifestations of Hashem's desire and ability to orchestrate the natural world to meet His goals. The entire Purim story teaches that Hashem is behind all that which may appear to be 'natural' and normal; He just sometimes cloaks Himself in the mantle of nature when acting in this world.

* * *

The Midrash (*Va-Yikra Rabbah* 28:6) elaborates somewhat on the interaction between Haman and Mordekhai when Haman comes to invite Mordekhai to be paraded throughout the streets of Shushan as the king's favored minister. Clearly dejected and certainly disheartened at having to publicly show favor and grace to his mortal enemy, Haman first greets Mordekhai's students, who, as mentioned, are studying the laws of the קרבן

העומר. After learning that it was an offering that was historically brought on that very day, Haman asked what precious material it consisted of, to which the students answered that it was merely barely. Given the connection between their lesson and that particular day, Haman assumed that there was some connection between some lesson of the קרבן העומר and his sudden reversal of fortune. He figured that the merit of this special mitzvah must be so great that it seemed to 'protect' Mordekhai on this very day.

He therefore wondered how many tons of barley were offered on that day – assuming that it was the great sacrifice on behalf of the people, willing to give up large sums to their God that helped secure their safety on that day. The students responded that only a simple עִשָּׂרוֹן (a volume measurement between approximately 2-4 liters) was necessary. Slightly taken aback, Haman responded that "Your small עִשָּׂרוֹן managed to outweigh my 10,000 *kikar* of silver" that he offered Achashverosh to allow him to annihilate the Jews.

More than just the 'equivalency' of these two amounts, Maharal notes that it's the lesson contained within the קרבן העומר – that Hashem is the true and sole Author of history – that protected the Jewish people and ultimately foiled Haman's plot.

From a Jewish perspective, this is the crux around which the entire story's fulcrum turns – when the Jewish people turn to Hashem for help, He does not desert His people. It's perhaps therefore fitting that this is one of the classical instances in which many of the commentaries find an additional level of interpretation, one that isn't necessary to read the story as is, or even to understand the decisions behind the characters' various actions, but one that works on a deeper level. As a book written with רוח הקודש, many commentators find hidden meanings within the text that often enrich the story and add to its relatability.

On that deeper level, many wonder why was it that Hashem allowed Haman to almost succeed in eradicating the Jewish people. While questioning Divine judgment is not something to be taken lightly, it's common within Rabbinic literature to search for a reason or cause that may have led to the [almost] calamity.

# Chapter Twenty-Three

Some find a clue to the Jews' almost downfall within Haman's accusation against them. When Haman presents Achashverosh with the opportunity to kill the Jewish people (albeit without identifying them actually as the Jews), he describes them as עַם אֶחָד מְפֻזָּר וּמְפֹרָד בֵּין הָעַמִּים – a scattered and separate people – seemingly meaning that they don't integrate within society and are found throughout the kingdom.

The 'deeper' understanding is that Haman is insinuating that even among themselves they are מְפֻזָּר וּמְפֹרָד – disorganized and more importantly, not unified. The accusation of a lack of unity among the Jewish people, the lack of אחדות, is particularly biting, especially when it comes from an arch enemy of the Jews. It means that not only did Haman hate the Jewish people and harbor a deep seated and almost intrinsic antisemitism, but that he observed, watched, and studied the Jews of his time to find their fundamental flaw. And according to this reading, he found it.

When the Jewish people are מְפֻזָּר וּמְפֹרָד and have no אחדות among themselves, they don't stand a chance against oppressors and those who wish them harm. It's important to remember that while this was a relatively recently exiled community – having been forced out of Israel after the destruction of the *Beit ha-Mikdash* less than 70 years earlier – many of the younger men and women in Shushan grew up never knowing a Jewish homeland or Jewish sovereignty. Exile didn't only mean finding a new home in a new country but a daily recognition that your homeland and your people were destroyed. Even up to five years before Achashverosh, the Jews still lived under the Babylonian regime, the same nation that destroyed the *Mikdash* and threw them out of their land. Given an existence that most modern readers thankfully cannot relate to on even an elementary level, it's inappropriate for a modern reader to judge the Jews of that time for their social situation. Nonetheless, clearly Hashem found fault with it and allowed Haman to take advantage of the Jews' disadvantaged state.

But realize this is also the secret to the redemption. The story specifically starts to turn when the Jews change their behavior. לֵךְ כְּנוֹס אֶת כָּל הַיְּהוּדִים – bring them all together in a show of solidarity. Mordekhai is showing them that they are all part of a team and need to count on each other. It's when they are no longer מְפֻזָּר וּמְפֹרָד that on a spiritual / mystical level Haman's decree starts to slowly crumble.

In fact, it's why, Rav Alkabetz explains, that in remembrance of the Purim story that Mordekhai later instituted the mitzvah of מִשְׁלֹחַ מָנוֹת אִישׁ לְרֵעֵהוּ – sharing of gifts. The miracle of Purim turned on the Jewish people coming together and overcoming inner strife and it's therefore appropriate to commemorate that miracle with similar acts of camaraderie and friendship. The Halakhot of Purim are meant to create and deepen an awareness of how we were redeemed, with a key component of that being the very notion of לֵךְ כְּנוֹס אֶת כָּל הַיְּהוּדִים.

* * *

THIS SAME IDEA may also explain an interesting passage in the Gemara (*Megilah* 13b) that connects the story of Purim to the building of the *Mishkan*:

> אמר ריש לקיש: גלוי וידוע לפני מי שאמר והיה העולם, שעתיד המן לשקול שקלים על ישראל, לפיכך הקדים שקליהם לשקליו והיינו דתנן באחד באדר משמיעים על השקלים.
>
> Reish Lakish said: It was revealed and known in advance to the One Who spoke and the world came into being, that in the future Haman was going to weigh out shekels against the Jewish people; therefore, He arranged that the Jewish people's shekels that were given to the Temple preceded Haman's shekels. As we learn in the Mishnah (*Shekalim* 1:1): On the first of Adar, we announce the collection of half shekels for the annual contribution to the *Beit ha-Mikdash*.

At the simplest level, this Gemara is explaining the otherwise unlikely connection between the collecting of the מחצית השקל and the holiday of Purim. In commemoration of this annual contribution, in post *Mikdash* times, we have the practice of reading פרשת שקלים – the description in the Torah of the very first collection of half shekels – on the Shabbat preceding Rosh Hodesh Adar (or on Rosh Hodesh Adar itself when it occurs on Shabbat). Ostensibly the two have nothing to do with each other.

The half shekels were used to purchase communal sacrifices, which the Talmud derives must be renewed yearly. With the ritual year beginning with Nisan, it made sense to start the public collection a month earlier so as to give time for people to contribute and for the money to make its way to Yerushalayim. Ostensibly, this has nothing to do with the holiday and commemoration of Purim, which was set by Mordekhai and Esther on the dates of the Persian Jews' redemption, the 14th and 15th of Adar.

Aside from finding meaning in the mere coincidental occurrence within two weeks of each other, a close look at Reish Lakish's statement raises further difficulty. What exactly is Reish Lakish driving at by noting לפיכך הקדים שקליהם לשקליו – this is the reason that Hashem arranged for *Bnei Yisrael*'s shekels to precede Haman's? *Bnei Yisrael*'s shekels preceded Haman's not by a mere two weeks, but by almost 1,000 years!

The first collection of half shekels was coordinated by Moshe Rabbenu in the Desert in the very first year that the Jews left Egypt. The story of Purim happened just short of 70 years after the destruction of the first *Beit ha-Mikdash*, a great many years later. But that seems to be Reish Lakish's focus – not just the ritual cycle of the Jewish calendar, but the entire structure of Jewish history was orchestrated such that the origination of the Jewish contribution of the half shekels would precede Haman's plot.

Driving the point even further, *Tosafot* demonstrates that עֲשֶׂרֶת אֲלָפִים כִּכַּר כֶּסֶף (ten thousand *kikar* of silver) that Haman offers to Achashverosh was actually precisely equivalent to the total amount of *shekalim* that were collected during *Bnei Yisrael*'s sojourn in the Desert (other commentators have alternate methods of arriving at essentially the same point – demonstrating an equivalence between the two amounts). Clearly, Reish Lakish is not referring to mere historical precedence, but to a deeper connection between the two ideas.

* * *

There is a well-known idea that the Torah commands that each person contribute only a half shekel as teaching that each person, on his or her own, is incomplete without the benefit of others. That in order to be counted as a whole, in order to make a difference on the national level, people need to join together; by him or herself, each person is only a half. This lesson is particularly apt in light of the Gemara's explanation that at the very first collection of half shekels in the Desert, each person had to contribute to three separate collections (for a total of a shekel-and-a-half each): for the census, the communal sacrifices, and to be used as part of the building of the *Mishkan*.

The notion of requiring others to be 'complete' clearly underscores the necessity for a half shekel when it comes to the census. The same is also true of communal sacrifices – for them to truly take on a communal character, no single person can lay claim to them. While the communal aspect of the sacrifices wouldn't change if each person gave a full shekel instead, the continued focus that each member of *Bnei Yisrael* needs each other is an important lesson when it comes to communal sacrifices as well.

And perhaps while less obvious, the lesson is even more appropriate when it comes to the third collection. These half shekels were melted to form the אדנים – the foundation connectors of the *Mishkan*. The *Mishkan* was comprised of many tall beams of gold covered wood, and these silver אדנים from the melted half shekels – two for each pillar – served as the supports and foundation. The lesson here is both figurative and physical. Not only do the half shekels come to build a 'whole nation' out of disparate parts by focusing each person's need on the other in order to 'count,' it also formed the very foundation of the *Mishkan*. The *Mishkan* and later the *Beit ha-Mikdash* served to mark a physical location and vehicle for approaching Hashem. If so, the very idea of the Jewish people forming and maintaining a relationship with Hashem was founded – both figuratively and literally – upon all of *Bnei Yisrael* coming together as a whole.

Putting all of these ideas together, this then might be the full import of Reish Lakish's statement. Haman was able to succeed in issuing a decree of annihilation against the Jewish people, because we were מְפֻזָּר וּמְפֹרָד, with the redemption coming when we came together as כְּנוֹס אֶת כָּל הַיְּהוּדִים. Reish Lakish is arguing that the seeds of this idea were planted many generations ago, when Hashem commanded the mitzvah of מחצית השקל whose message was that only through coming together as a whole, recognizing each person's need for another, that we can 'count' as a people and form a relationship with Hashem.

לפיכך הקדים שקליהם לשקליו to teach us that the way to counteract the שקלים of Haman – of his accusation of מְפֻזָּר וּמְפֹרָד – is through our own שקלים – the mitzvah of מחצית השקל, which highlights our unique national abilities when we recognize the power of community and unity.

In fact, the Mishnah that describes the public announcement of the commencement of the shekalim collection season specifically chooses the verb משמיעים and not something more common, such as מודיעים or מפרסמים. It's possible that the term משמיעים connotes more than just hiring a town crier to publicly proclaim the onset of the fundraising season, but rather להשמיע indicates something more subtle – announcing but also getting the message across. The goal wasn't only to collect a half shekel from each Jew but also – in that very process – to teach and hopefully internalize the message of the half shekel, the very interdependence of the Jewish people.

Hearkening back to the story of Purim as a 'continuation' or culmination of the initial and subsequent battles between the Jewish people and Amalek, it's interesting that when King Shaul prepares to battle Amalek and gathers the people, the *Navi* (1 *Shmuel* 15:4) describes וַיְשַׁמַּע שָׁאוּל אֶת הָעָם (Shmuel announced [made heard] to the nation) – using that same verb וישמע instead of the more colloquial ויאסוף or ויקבוץ. The *Navi* might be driving at the very same point. Amalek initially attacked the rear of *Bnei Yisrael*'s camp, hoping to separate them from the rest of the group and thereby succeed. Much like their later descendant Haman, Amalek's power lay in recognizing that when the Jews are מְפֻזָּר וּמְפֹרָד – be it in Shushan or in the Sinai Desert – they are more susceptible to attack and conquer. To combat this notion from the outset and to mentally prepare the Jews for the monumental battle, King Shaul specifically וַיְשַׁמַּע שָׁאוּל אֶת הָעָם – doesn't just collect soldiers, but gathers them for a collective purpose. It's when *Bnei Yisrael* are united that Hashem more favorably sheds His countenance upon us and grants us success.

# Chapter Twenty-Four

It's interesting that the Megilah doesn't report what Esther actually planned. And there was most certainly an intricate plan. After all, Mordekhai had just pushed Esther to speak with Achashverosh to revoke Haman's decree but that isn't what she does. Esther starts party planning and inviting Achashverosh and Haman to a series of two feasts.

And even when Achashverosh turns to Esther at the first feast to see what's really going on and what he can do for her, she coyly suggests that if the king would be so kind as to grace her with his presence at the second meal, she will be able to finally talk to him. For the reader approaching the story for the first time, it seems pretty clear that Esther has a plan and that Mordekhai seems to approve of it and go along with it, although the Megilah leaves the reader somewhat in the dark as to its specifics. It's only through watching the events unfold that the reader can try to reconstruct Esther's plan.

While an intriguing literary technique both to avoid repetition and create intrigue, reconstructing the plan based on the eventual events assumes that everything that occurs is because it's all going according to plan. It's hard to know, in making such a reconstruction, if there were any changes or challenges that required reconfiguring or reassessing what might be the next best move. It's quite possible that Esther's plan may have changed midway (perhaps even more than once), but as long as the characters continue to roll with the story, the reader would never know.

Even though the story is readable as is and assuming that everything works out exactly as Esther had hoped it would when she originally devised her plan, such a reading leaves many challenging aspects and episodes that render such a reading somewhat tenuous. But what's at stake isn't simply a search for an authentic biblical historicity, but as will be argued, a more nuanced and closer reading demonstrates that Esther not only changed her plan midway, but that she did so because she internalized the essential message of the Megilah.

It's Mordekhai's insistence and Esther's eventual recognition that it's always Hashem who runs history and that when you are able to get a glimpse of how it might be playing out that you have a chance to rise to the occasion and be a part of the Divine plan for the Jewish story. And it's that very point that Esther takes to heart midway through her plan that forces her to reassess, recognize the *yad Hashem* that is at play, and again rise to the occasion to save the Jewish people.

# Chapter Twenty-Five

Esther gathers her strength and, in a feat of courage, comes up with a plan to confront Achashverosh and save the Jewish people. She realizes it is risky and recognizes that she may lose her life. Mordekhai reassures her that the risk is necessary and worthwhile – as the fate of the entire Jewish people is on the line – and as noted earlier, וּמִי יוֹדֵעַ אִם לְעֵת כָּזֹאת הִגַּעַתְּ לַמַּלְכוּת – perhaps, just maybe, the rather unlikely selection of Esther as Queen of Persia was Divinely orchestrated so that she could intervene at this precipitous moment in history.

It all begins by inviting Achashverosh and Haman to a party. She offers no rhyme or reason for the invitation or the celebration, but there are several subtle clues indicating that she is planning an intimate affair.

In describing how she is about to execute her plan, she tells Mordekhai that she hasn't been called to be with the king for over a month. Presumably, Achashverosh is also aware that he hasn't been with his wife in some while. And even though he does maintain some type of a harem (בֵּית הַנָּשִׁים), he apparently finds some value and possibly fealty in marriage, since he didn't really need to get married after Vashti, but still found some value in doing so. Esther uses this tension to her advantage.

She prepares for entering Achashverosh's private chambers by וַתִּלְבַּשׁ אֶסְתֵּר מַלְכוּת, which *Chazal* interpret as being enveloped in רוח הקודש, but whose simple meaning seems to be that she dressed in fancy and regal attire. Esther wants to appear attractive and seductive to her husband.

When she finally approaches Achashverosh, the Megilah describes her entrance in excruciating detail.

וַתַּעֲמֹד בַּחֲצַר בֵּית הַמֶּלֶךְ הַפְּנִימִית נֹכַח בֵּית הַמֶּלֶךְ

> Esther stood in the courtyard of the inner chamber of the king, opposite the king.

Esther precisely positions herself just outside of Achashverosh's chambers, such that

> וְהַמֶּלֶךְ יוֹשֵׁב עַל כִּסֵּא מַלְכוּתוֹ בְּבֵית הַמַּלְכוּת נֹכַח פֶּתַח הַבָּיִת
>
> And the king was sitting on his royal throne in the royal chamber opposite the entrance.

From Achashverosh's throne, he'd be able to catch a glimpse of her through his open door. He finally does see Esther and

> וַיְהִי כִרְאוֹת הַמֶּלֶךְ אֶת אֶסְתֵּר הַמַּלְכָּה עֹמֶדֶת בֶּחָצֵר נָשְׂאָה חֵן בְּעֵינָיו
>
> When the king saw Queen Esther standing in the courtyard, she found favor in his eyes.

He is excited to see her.

There is repeated mention and focus on Esther's stance and her precise positioning. Since this is all part of her plan, it makes sense. She wants to be seen and she needs Achashverosh to invite her into his chambers. In the context of וַאֲנִי לֹא נִקְרֵאתִי לָבוֹא אֶל הַמֶּלֶךְ זֶה שְׁלוֹשִׁים יוֹם (and I haven't been summoned to the king for the past thirty days), she dresses up and stands in a seemingly seductive manner, all enticing Achashverosh to invite her in.

Clearly excited to see her, Achashverosh is willing to do for her whatever she asks. At that point, Esther realizes that the first stage of the plan was successful. She was in and aroused Achashverosh's interest. She couches her entrance and request in a somewhat intimate connotation, not having been with Achashverosh in over a month and now inviting him (and Haman) to a private party.

Esther clearly piqued his interest and Achashverosh is more than happy and eager to attend. Achashverosh insists on moving things along quickly, eagerly anticipating what Esther has in store. But more than just rushing to the party, Achashverosh is quite clear that he wants to hurry specifically לַעֲשׂוֹת אֶת דְּבַר אֶסְתֵּר (to fulfill Esther's command). He is excited about Esther's idea and wants to do whatever she'd like. At the party too, he is quite magnanimous in being overly gracious, offering Esther עַד חֲצִי הַמַּלְכוּת (even as much as half the kingdom). Clearly over the top, the Megilah is highlighting Esther's success in seducing Achashverosh and keeping him interested.

But then there's the elephant in the room. If Esther intends on hosting an intimate party for her husband, who she hasn't seen in over a month, why bring Haman along? Esther not only gives no indication why Haman should be there, but she seems to almost want Achashverosh to wonder about it for a bit.

When she invites him to the party, she describes it as הַמִּשְׁתֶּה אֲשֶׁר עָשִׂיתִי לוֹ (the feast that I prepared for him) – leaving the object of the sentence – לוֹ – somewhat ambiguous. In context, יָבוֹא הַמֶּלֶךְ וְהָמָן הַיּוֹם אֶל הַמִּשְׁתֶּה אֲשֶׁר עָשִׂיתִי לוֹ (the king and Haman should come [singular] to the feast that I prepared for him) seems like it should refer to Achashverosh – meaning that she is inviting Haman to tag along to a private, intimate party for the royal couple.

And while that may seem somewhat strange, the alternative is equally perplexing. Could לוֹ refer to Haman and she means to invite Achashverosh to a party that she has prepared for Haman? But what would she be celebrating with Haman? Ostensibly, Esther and Haman have nothing to do with each other and the Megilah doesn't even record that they've ever even spoken to each other. What could she possibly want with him? And even if she did have something to discuss with Haman, why arrange an intimate party in her husband's presence? If there was some political or governmental matter to discuss, couldn't she just have summoned him to her chambers? Why a party? And why intimate? Could there be something else going on between the two of them?

* * *

Although perhaps somewhat strange at first glance, perhaps this is precisely what Esther wanted Achashverosh to think. Esther didn't misspeak when she referred to the party that she "made for him." She was quite deliberate with her word choice, leaving her intentions clouded and planting the idea that perhaps, just maybe, she and Haman might be having a hidden relationship behind Achashverosh's back. If so, it explains a lot about Esther's plan, her intentions, and her actions.

If she was to try to save the Jewish people, the simplest way to do so would be to get rid of Haman. She assumed that once he would be out of the way, his decree would be nullified and the Jews would be saved. But as a senior member of the palace, Haman wasn't somebody she could arrange to have killed without anybody noticing. And because of Haman's close relationship with Achashverosh, it was highly unlikely that she could convince Achashverosh to get rid of him. After all, Achashverosh just promoted him and has grown to trust him as a faithful Loyalist. What she needed was a way to drive a wedge between Haman and Achashverosh; a reason for Achashverosh himself to want Haman out of the picture. Esther's plan is to do just that: by convincing Achashverosh that she and Haman are having an affair.

As the ultimate form of disrespect, Achashverosh would have no choice but to kill Haman. This would be true even if Achashverosh didn't care much for marital fidelity, but all the more true coming from Achashverosh who publicly shamed and punished Vashti for disrespecting him. Adding insult to injury, if indeed Haman and Memukhan are one and the same, it would be more than just slightly ironic that the person who suggested banishing Vashti for disrespecting the king would himself engage in such behavior.

But beyond simple disrespect, whether just as a husband or even as the king, the thought of Haman and Esther together would highlight an additional fear for Achashverosh. The Megilah already described how anybody who merely entered the king's chambers without a formal invitation would be put to death. Assuming Haman and Esther were indeed having an affair, Achashverosh could know with certainty that Haman realized that he'd be putting his life at risk. Why would he be willing to do that? It seems to go beyond merely getting a thrill out of 'living on the edge' but perhaps is part of a larger scheme.

Achashverosh promoted Haman as a trusted advisor and somebody who he could count on, who commanded authority with the ministers and people around him. But maybe all of this honor and authority had gotten to his head. Perhaps Haman was planning on taking advantage of the precarious political situation in Shushan and himself mount a coup. He already had much popular support and was quickly becoming a force to reckon with in the Persian Empire. And what better way to assert his authority by demonstrating his power even over Achashverosh, by 'stealing' his wife.

From Achashverosh's perspective, if indeed Haman and Memukhan are one and the same, it would continue the pattern established earlier in the Megilah by Memukhan himself of using marriage as a political tool. (But even if Memukhan and Haman are distinct individuals, using marriage politically is something that Achashverosh had clearly utilized earlier in the story, of which Haman is no doubt aware.) Clearly, aside from opportunity (Haman was a frequent guest of the palace and Esther attests that she hadn't been with Achashverosh in over a month), Haman also had a potential motive to even risk his life in pursuing Esther.

* * *

Esther no doubt realized that it takes two to tango and if Achashverosh would kill Haman for having an affair with the queen, he'd do the same with her. She would be risking her life to save the Jewish people. While not a simple decision, she took Mordekhai's encouragement to heart – וּמִי יוֹדֵעַ אִם לְעֵת כָּזֹאת הִגַּעַתְּ לַמַּלְכוּת – perhaps Hashem arranged things in just such a way that a Jewish queen of Persia would be in the position to sacrifice her own life to save her people. Esther likely realized the extreme unlikelihood that she, of all the women selected, would end up as queen. And given that she now was chosen and that the chance to save the Jewish people presented itself precisely because of her position – it's not a coincidence but a Divinely orchestrated opportunity.

She recognized the sacrifice she needed to make and came to terms with it, וְכַאֲשֶׁר אָבַדְתִּי אָבָדְתִּי (and if I shall perish, then so be it) – recognizing that if her plan went **well** that she would end up dead. It was likely not an easy decision to make and speaks to Esther's fortitude of spirit and steadfast *emunah* in willing to sacrifice herself for the good of the Jewish people. It also explains what she asks of Mordekhai to do to prepare for her plan – she asks Mordekhai to declare a three day fast.

As noted previously, the fast was obviously not about losing weight or cutting down on carbs, but rather was clearly intended as a communal *teshuvah*. All of this is necessary because Esther isn't just going to play politics, she is going to sacrifice her life on behalf of the Jewish people; מסירות נפש in the literal sense of the term. Willing to give up her life to save her nation is more than just politically sound, it's a deeply religious act. For Esther, it's a supreme act of faith, recognizing that she has the opportunity to be part of the historical Jewish narrative. She views this as a mitzvah opportunity – according to most *Poskim*, not one that she would be required to undertake, but one that is certainly permissible – and is seeking Divine assistance in insuring its success.

Praying on behalf of another is a tried and true Jewish practice, dating all the way back to the times of Avraham. It's a form of *tefilah* that has particular significance and is an active demonstration of care and concern for another. But beyond the 'standard' benefits and advantages of praying on behalf of others, the Jews of Shushan weren't just praying for Esther but also for themselves. It was their lives on the line that Esther was trying to save and protect. Their very survival depended on her success and it's therefore particularly fitting to include and involve them in this *tefilah*.

# Chapter Twenty-Six

Trying to sow suspicion as to her relationship with Haman, Esther needs to allow the tension to build. She begins by inviting Achashverosh to a party with overtly sensual connotations and asks to have Haman present as well. She even deliberately misleads Achashverosh by indicating that she is making the party "for him," leaving the person in question – Achashverosh or Haman – somewhat ambiguous. She wants to leave him guessing. As Rabbi David Fohrman (*The Queen You Thought You Knew*, 43) points out, the "not knowing" precisely what is going on is part of the tension Esther is trying to build.

The Megilah doesn't describe the party in much detail other than Achashverosh asking Esther what he can do for her. For the past month or so, Achashverosh couldn't be bothered enough to call for Esther and now, for the second time in only a few hours, is seemingly willing to go to the ends of the earth for her – עַד חֲצִי הַמַּלְכוּת. Knowing one of the secrets to Achashverosh's heart, Esther's seductive plan is clearly working.

And while Achashverosh uses virtually the same language in asking Esther what he can do for her, Esther responds just as similarly. He offers up to half his kingdom and she invites him to another party. She needs the possibility of her alleged affair with Haman to fester in Achashverosh's mind for a while longer. She wants him to mull it over, consider all the reasons that it probably doesn't make much sense and then realize how and why Haman would gain from such a dalliance.

In fact, instead of just inviting the two of them to the party like she did the first time, Esther plays up her request. She repeats and focuses on how she'd like Achashverosh to do something special, just for her. Esther makes it less about the actual request and more about their relationship.

> אִם מָצָאתִי חֵן בְּעֵינֵי הַמֶּלֶךְ וְאִם עַל הַמֶּלֶךְ טוֹב לָתֵת אֶת שְׁאֵלָתִי וְלַעֲשׂוֹת אֶת בַּקָּשָׁתִי
>
> If I find favor in the eyes of the king and if it is good for the king to agree to my request and accede to my desire...

Her immediate response to Achashverosh's request, שְׁאֵלָתִי וּבַקָּשָׁתִי (my request and my desire), introduces her actual request by making it personal. What she really wants, what she *really, really, really* wants, is Achashverosh's approval. Many Megilah readers have the practice of embellishing the טעמי המקרא (musical cantillation notes) of these last two words, adding a musical quality to the tension in the dialogue.

Esther's plan is not so much about the specific parties or what festivities will ensue but rather what Achashverosh will be thinking both during and in between them. She wants him confused, unsure of where and with whom she stands. She therefore needs to pull his emotions in opposite directions. She makes her request all about their relationship – if he really loves her, then he'll do what she asks, while also making sure that Achashverosh is quite clear that she wants Haman there as well. Adding to the ambiguity of her intentions, she is planning the second party for both of them – הַמִּשְׁתֶּה אֲשֶׁר אֶעֱשֶׂה לָהֶם (the feast that I shall make for them) – which seems to indicate that when she originally said אֶל הַמִּשְׁתֶּה אֲשֶׁר עָשִׂיתִי לוֹ as an invitation to the first party, it was intentional. If Achashverosh thought that the first party was geared toward only one of them, Esther is quite clear that she clearly intends the second party for both. In fact, as Rabbi David Fohrman points out, perhaps she is trying to make him wonder if he really heard her correctly earlier in the day when she said אֲשֶׁר עָשִׂיתִי לוֹ. Did she really plan the party for only one of them? Was that a slip of the tongue? A Freudian slip perhaps? Or did he simply not hear her properly the first time?

* * *

It's intriguing to consider what Achashverosh was actually thinking at the time. As a nervous and apprehensive monarch who is working to solidify his authority and who has already fended off at least one assassination attempt, he had conflicting emotions and theories pulling him in different directions.

Achashverosh no doubt realized that he hadn't called for Esther in some while. Did Haman pick up on that?

Achashverosh had been promoting Haman among the other ministers. But Haman was supportive of Achashverosh's regime! It was certainly because of his loyalty to Achashverosh. Or perhaps was Haman climbing the political ladder to be able to eventually throw Achashverosh off his perch on its highest rung?

When Esther invited him to this party, she was clearly trying to seduce him. Clearly, it was because she missed him and desired his company. Or was the whole thing just a ruse? Why else would she invite Haman? What was he doing there anyway?

And worst of all, if Haman and Esther were indeed conspiring against him, Achashverosh wasn't going to allow them to get away with it! But were any of these concerns real or were they simply the anxious ruminations of a nervous king, somewhat unsure of how well his kingship was appreciated and received by his ministers and subjects?

The Megilah gives us only brief biological details about Esther and we don't know much about her as a person, but if her plan was to convince Achashverosh that she was having an affair with Haman, she was very good at what she was doing. After all, Achashverosh couldn't just lash out at the two of them with only vague thoughts and concerns. Even if he was quick to get rid of his former queen, Achashverosh only put it into practice on the advice of his advisors. So too, getting rid of Haman without more evidence, without being more sure about what was happening, was a liability. If his suspicions were wrong, Achashverosh would lose one of his most trusted and loyal advisors. And even if his suspicions were justified and Haman was indeed trying to take over his throne, Achashverosh would need to make sure that getting rid of Haman wouldn't merely bolster the opposition. He couldn't afford to have Haman viewed as a martyr for 'the cause' which might embolden others to take over from where he left off. The tension in Achashverosh's mind was very real.

Which is precisely where Esther wanted him.

This was all part of her plan, to plant the seeds of possible infidelity and sedition and let them fester and grow until Achashverosh would have no choice but to act. She didn't expect him to reach any conclusions yet and wanted him to keep mulling over all of those very thoughts, which is why she invited them both to a second party the next day. Esther wanted

Achashverosh to spend the rest of the day and that night wondering about Haman's intentions, questioning Haman's character, and wondering whether the same minister who advised Achashverosh to get rid of Vashti is now trying to 'steal' Achashverosh's current queen.

Esther wants Achashverosh thinking and worried about what might come next. She promises him that if he and Haman join her party tomorrow, she will answer the king's request – וּמָחָר אֶעֱשֶׂה כִּדְבַר הַמֶּלֶךְ (and tomorrow I shall do as the king spoke). What could she possibly want that she can't tell him today? Is she just playing 'hard to get' to peak his excitement? Why then is it necessary to have Haman present? Why must it wait until tomorrow? And with all those questions still on his mind, Esther and Haman leave the palace.

* * *

The question is, how does Esther anticipate the rest of her plan playing out? If everything goes as she predicted, Esther hopes that Achashverosh shows up to the party the next day flustered, anxious, and on edge. Haman will also show up – oblivious to Esther's plan – seemingly in a far better mood, thinking that the reason for his invitation is simply bolstering his confidence that he is finding favor in the eyes of the royal couple. He knows nothing about Esther trying to plant the notion of a possible illicit relationship with him and would understandably resist any such suggestion, if he only picked up on it being insinuated.

For her part, Esther couldn't simply tell Achashverosh about her [non-existent] affair with Haman. He would deny it outright and be rightfully offended at the mere suggestion. It would put Achashverosh in the awkward position of having to choose between his queen and his senior advisor about something fundamental to his continued rule. As far as a plan goes, Esther could not be confident in what Achashverosh would choose. If so, it seems unlikely to be part of her plan. (Additionally, it is somewhat hard to imagine how she could simply bring up the idea of an affair with her husband in the course of any normal discussion.)

Esther would have to figure out some way to convince Achashverosh that she was romantically involved with Haman without allowing Haman the opportunity to reject the idea. It's hard to know what her play would be.

She could have chosen to accuse Haman of taking her against her will as a demonstration of his power within the palace. But if so, why not just tell Achashverosh outright. Why bother with the parties and seduction? It also wouldn't make sense in light of Esther's repeated seductive invitations to a sensually themed party.

This leaves Esther to come up with some plan that would be so convincing that Achashverosh would have to believe it, even above and beyond any of Haman's protests to the contrary. Readers of the Megilah are left guessing what precisely she had in mind because before she was able to execute that last crucial piece of her plan, everything in Shushan changed.

# Chapter Twenty-Seven

As an aside, it's clear from the end of the story that merely getting Haman out of the way didn't automatically lead to Achashverosh rescinding Haman's decree. While it will be explored in more detail later on, it's clear that Mordekhai and Esther thought that Haman and his evil decree would die together. They anticipated that once Haman was killed there would be some automatic means by which his decree would be revoked or rescinded. This is exactly why Esther was willing to sacrifice her life to be killed with him.

If she were successful in convincing Achashverosh that she was having an affair with Haman, Achashverosh would kill both Haman and Esther. If she thought that even after Haman's death she would still have to appeal to Achashverosh to rescind the decree, then it would have had to have been part of her plan. But if her plan, successfully executed, would have resulted in her death, how exactly would that have come about? Even though Mordekhai would remain, he would be in no particular position to appeal to the king. He wouldn't want to identify as Esther's family, since – if her plan had succeeded as she envisioned – she would have just been put to death for infidelity. The only clout Mordekhai would have wouldn't be any different from what he had before. If Mordekhai didn't think he could directly appeal to Achashverosh while Haman was alive, why should he think that he could successfully do so after Haman and Esther would have been killed?

One possible suggestion might be that Esther's plan was that once Haman was out of the picture Mordekhai would step in and take his place. With that newly elevated status, Mordekhai would be in a position to try to influence Achashverosh to rescind Haman's decree. But even while potentially plausible, there are two reasons that it doesn't seem very likely.

Having just been betrayed by his trusted minister Haman, Achashverosh would no doubt be somewhat hesitant in appointing somebody to take his place. Even if he would position Mordekhai to fill Haman's shoes, Achashverosh would likely keep him on a short leash and not be so willing to go along with everything he asked. It's such a shot in the dark that it doesn't seem reasonable for Esther to sacrifice her life just to be able to possibly give Mordekhai the opening to maybe be in the position to persuade an otherwise reticent king to go along with another advisor's scheme involving whole cultures within his kingdom.

But even if this pessimistic perspective on the chances of Mordekhai's success in rescinding the decree are misplaced, it's still unlikely that this was actually part of the original plan.

At the end of the day, while Esther lives, Achashverosh does indeed kill Haman. And even when the opportunity presents itself for Mordekhai to slip into that very role and try to wield enough royal influence to rescind the decree, it's not what he does. Instead, it's Esther who beseeches Achashverosh – the only time she cries throughout the Megilah – begging him to spare the Jewish people. It's an emotional scene, with Esther desperately pulling at Achashverosh's heartstrings and appealing to his sense of compassion and love for her. The Megilah's description of her desperation – וַתִּפֹּל לִפְנֵי רַגְלָיו וַתֵּבְךְּ וַתִּתְחַנֶּן לוֹ (She fell before his feet and cried and begged him) – is real, raw, and impassioned. What the Megilah seems to be trying to make clear is that it's clearly not part of the original plan, but their only move left at this point.

What emerges from between the lines is a keener understanding of Esther's original plan. She was going to try to convince Achashverosh that she and Haman were having an affair, which would lead to Achashverosh killing both of them – but more importantly Haman – and *ipso facto* cause Haman's decree to automatically dissolve or be rescinded. As anybody whose read the Megilah knows, that's not how the plan pans out. Something changes along the way.

# Chapter Twenty-Eight

Achashverosh cannot sleep. After the events of the previous day, he has a lot to worry about and is quite nervous. While the Megilah offers no specific reason for his insomnia, it contextualizes it as the night between the two parties, which is all the Megilah thinks is necessary for the reader to understand what is going on. After offering the reader an initial impression of Achashverosh as generally anxious about solidifying his leadership and cautious about establishing his authority, the concern about a possible political-romantic liaison between Haman and Esther just play off his already precarious mental state.

Up until now, Achashverosh not only considered Haman to be a loyalist but among the most promising of his cadre. But after reflecting on Haman's character and actions for the better part of the day, Achashverosh is no longer sure that loyalty is indeed where Haman's heart lies. Achashverosh starts collecting memories that might more accurately paint Haman as ambitious, rather than as necessary loyal.

Haman is the one who originally suggested 'getting rid' of Vashti. But that was just to help support Achashverosh's reign, wasn't it? He starts to wonder whether it was actually an act of loyalty, defending the honor of Achashverosh's throne, or, thinking about it further, perhaps Haman was instead positioning himself as the mover and shaker of the nascent Persian monarchy, cementing his ascendancy in the palace for an eventual coup.

And it only got worse.

Haman had just come to Achashverosh with a request to completely 'get rid' of some unnamed nation that Haman described as dangerous. Haman convinced Achashverosh that it was for the 'betterment of the kingdom,' but was it really? Was Haman defending the power and extent of Achashverosh's authority and demonstrating his loyalty to the crown? Or was he more interested in crafting the character of the Empire to his own liking? What was Haman really thinking?

Achashverosh married the daughter of the former Babylonian king as a political move. Was Haman thinking along similar lines in seducing Esther away from him? Achashverosh simply could no longer be sure of who Haman really was and perhaps this uncertainty was most troubling of all.

It's understandable that that night נָדְדָה שְׁנַת הַמֶּלֶךְ (The king's sleep was troubled) – his mind wasn't at peace.

* * *

And in what seems like an ancient Persian equivalent to counting sheep, Achashverosh asks to have some bedtime stories read to him. It seems that he needs to find some way to relax and forget about all that troubles him. But if that's his goal, his book selection seems odd. The סֵפֶר הַזִּכְרֹנוֹת דִּבְרֵי הַיָּמִים (Book of Remembrances and History) records events and happenings in the palace, Shushan, and the Persian Empire at large. These aren't necessarily the most riveting, engaging, or even relaxing stories. It would be something akin to reading C-SPAN transcripts from the past year's committee meetings. While an accurate description of past events, why specifically choose to fall asleep to the recollection of political events and not a collection of stories or soothing poetry?

While it's certainly 'coincidental' that his servants 'just happen' to read about how Mordekhai intervened to foil an assassination plot against Achashverosh, it's clear that these are the types of stories that he asked to be read. The 'coincidence' is only in the selection of this particular story, not in the genre.

Achashverosh wasn't interested in an ancient Persian equivalent of counting sheep to help calm his mind. Rather, he specifically wanted to hear stories of people's loyalties to the Empire. Given the possibility of Haman's potential revolutionary activities, Achashverosh wants to take stock of members of his government and try to assess their loyalties. He realizes that he may have severely misjudged Haman and needs to make sure that he has an accurate perspective on his other ministers and high ranking officials.

Achashverosh isn't actually trying to fall asleep at all. He realizes that he has more important things to worry about for the day ahead. He chooses the סֵפֶר הַזִּכְרֹנוֹת דִּבְרֵי הַיָּמִים because he is looking for clues of how to deal with the developing political turmoil. This is why Achashverosh isn't surprised to hear about Mordekhai; these are the precise stories that he is looking to inquire further about.

While the Megilah presents the selection of this particular story as merely coincidental, it is at the same time trying to push the reader to recognize that randomness and coincidence have no place in a deeper understanding of this entire story. This, as noted earlier, is the central theme of the Megilah.

Ibn Ezra (4:14) quotes Rav Sa'adyah Gaon to the effect that Mordekhai wrote the Megilah at Achashverosh's behest (which is why Mordekhai deliberately omits Hashem's name from its text, lest it not be properly respected by the unfaithful), indicating that it was intended for the Persian masses. But even while the Gemara debates the topic, it ultimately concludes that the Megilah was written with a certain level of רוח הקודש and, by incorporating it into the Biblical canon, recognize that it's primarily intended for the faithful or those seeking out faith. The reader comes to the Megilah aware that it contains a spiritual and religious lesson and so when Mordekhai earlier chastises Esther to confront Achashverosh by recognizing that her station in this world is Divinely ordained – the message that nothing happens randomly is clearly hammered home.

By this point in the Megilah, the reader is acutely aware of the central message. While the Megilah presents ample reason and explanation for selecting specifically this story to be read to Achashverosh, it's clear to the reader that something else is going on 'behind the scenes.' It's true that there is plenty of political turmoil amiss and it makes perfect sense for Achashverosh to be seeking out allies. But from all potential allies to 'randomly' choose, Achashverosh specifically hears about Mordekhai. In fact, *Chazal* highlight this point as well.

While the simple meaning of בַּלַּיְלָה הַהוּא נָדְדָה שְׁנַת הַמֶּלֶךְ refers to Achashverosh being unable to sleep, *Chazal* add an additional level of interpretation and explain that it's a veiled reference to the King of Kings, Who on that night started putting things into play to thwart Haman's plot. By interjecting Hashem into the story line, *Chazal* are hinting at the same message – regardless of what may appear to be normal and natural, Hashem is ultimately behind everything.

Perhaps this 'perfect coincidence' is the Megilah's way of signaling to the reader that things are about to change for the Jews. When the Talmud debates the precise requirements of reading the Megilah on Purim, R. Shimon bar Yochai notes that it's appropriate and sufficient to read only from this very section, of בַּלַּיְלָה הַהוּא נָדְדָה שְׁנַת הַמֶּלֶךְ. The Gemara elaborates that the reading is supposed to encapsulate the תקפו של נס – the extent and drama of the story's miracle, which it suggest begins on this night. It's at this point that the reader is aware that something supernatural is taking place, that while the characters in the Megilah are playing out their own respective parts, the Puppet Master from Above is coordinating the events.

* * *

It's a 'perfect coincidence' because reading about Mordekhai is so completely natural, normal, and easily explained, but at the same time it's clear to the reader that it's part of the Divine plan for the salvation of the Jewish people. For the religiously sensitive reader – and assuming that it's them to whom the Megilah is geared – *Chazal*'s extrapolation of הַמֶּלֶךְ to also include the King of Kings in this context is both clever and obvious. The Megilah wants the reader to both appreciate how coincidental the reading selection is, such that none of the servants or Achashverosh himself are surprised by it, and at the same time so clearly directed by the One Above. It's likely for this reason that many Ashkenazim have the tradition to chant the word המלך in the traditional *Yamim Nora'im* melody, driving the point home that it's the King of Kings who is ultimately responsible for what is taking place.

Mordekhai's message that Hashem ultimately controls the world and that when able to see His hand peeking through, Esther must rise to the occasion and respond – isn't meant for Esther alone but for all the Megilah's readers for all time. It's a lesson that the Megilah hopes the reader walks away with just as the characters in the Megilah itself did.

And so after having internalized Mordekhai's message, the reader is primed to recognize Achashverosh's servants selection of the story of Mordekhai foiling the assassination plot as clearly not random or coincidental. Because this is when the message becomes most obvious; it's the point *Chazal* identify as when the story starts turning miraculous.

* * *

Mordekhai was very visibly identified as Jewish, and by right should have harbored no love toward the Persian Empire generally and Achashverosh in particular. Mordekhai could have easily kept the information about the assassination plot to himself and it's quite likely that nobody would have ever found out that he knew about it. Even if it became known that Mordekhai knew about the plot, nobody knew that he had an 'in' with the queen and wouldn't have blamed him for not intervening. And even if somebody thought that, armed with this knowledge Mordekhai could have and should have acted, given Achashverosh's general relationship with the Jews anybody would have most certainly understood his hesitancy in getting involved. That he nonetheless intervened to save Achashverosh's life signified to the king that, despite any misgivings, Mordekhai has a profound loyalty to the kingdom. Mordekhai is definitely somebody that Achashverosh would want to keep around.

Particularly with what the next day might bring, Achashverosh needs to know who he will be able to count on for their integrity and fealty to the kingdom. Thinking about all the reasons Mordekhai would have had for wanting Achashverosh dead, but still doing the right thing, Achashverosh knew that even if he wasn't the Empire's strongest supporter, Mordekhai, in particular contrast to whom Haman might turn out to be, was a man of integrity who can get things done.

But when he doesn't hear a follow up to the story of Mordekhai's involvement, Achashverosh gets a little nervous – מַה נַּעֲשָׂה יְקָר וּגְדוּלָּה לְמָרְדֳּכַי עַל זֶה (What grand and great thing was done to Mordekhai for this?). He assumes that Mordekhai was repaid in some way and not just by a token 'thank you card.' Achashverosh wonders only what type of יְקָר וּגְדוּלָּה Mordekhai received, not whether or not he received it.

יְקָר וּגְדוּלָּה is a recurring descriptive phrase in the Megilah, which gives some clue as to Achashverosh's meaning. He clearly didn't mean that Mordekhai should have gotten some token honor, but something far more substantial. The Megilah used similar phrasing to describe Achashverosh's motivation in hosting a party for the ministers of his Empire, to show off יְקָר תִּפְאֶרֶת גְּדוּלָּתוֹ (the glory and grandeur of his greatness). The lavish party displayed his vast riches, from rugs to mugs, couches to cutlery, almost to the point of absurdity. Such was the thanks he assumed Mordekhai received.

Achashverosh is almost shocked when he hears that nothing was done – לֹא נַעֲשָׂה עִמּוֹ דָּבָר (nothing was done for him). Nothing at all, not even a token thank you. Aside from general common decency, Achashverosh quickly realizes the potential political cost for this oversight. Mordekhai went above and beyond what Achashverosh would or should have expected, not only saving his life but demonstrating his loyalty to the kingdom in the process. It was a golden opportunity to reward Mordekhai and demonstrate how much he values Mordekhai's commitment to the Empire.

Showing his gratitude – and certainly if he did so in a lavish manner – would demonstrate how important loyalty is to Achashverosh and would have only served to enhance their relationship. If he had only reciprocated at the time Achashverosh could have easily ingratiated himself to Mordekhai, somebody for whom it would be natural for Achashverosh to call upon when necessary.

While hindsight is always 20/20, this was an easy problem not only to avoid but would have been an investment that Achashverosh wishes he could cash in on right now. And while he is still contemplating what could have been, and how it would have been nice to know that Mordekhai could be counted as a certain loyalist, he suddenly gets very nervous.

Without pausing even for a minute and with anxiety in his trembling voice, he blurts out מִי בֶחָצֵר (Who is in the courtyard)? In the midst of deliberating about whom among his staff and ministers he can trust, wondering about the possibility of a castle insider trying to foment a rebellion and possibly having an affair with his wife, he thinks he hears an intruder walking around outside!

# Chapter Twenty-Nine

The Megilah doesn't mention or describe anybody or anything causing a particular noise. The story flows directly from Achashverosh asking what reward was given to Mordekhai to his servants responding that nothing was done and without missing a beat or reacting in any way, Achashverosh demands to know who is outside.

The Megilah eventually informs the reader that Haman has decided to visit Achashverosh at this late hour of the night, but it's somewhat telling that this bit of narrative only appears after describing Achashverosh's question. It seems that the Megilah is trying to highlight the quick pace of the conversation and Achashverosh's general nervousness, not even pausing to catch the reader up on what is transpiring.

Achashverosh clearly has a lot on his mind and, while surprised, isn't completely shocked to learn that it's Haman who is prancing around the palace at night. Concerned that his worst fears are materializing in front of his very eyes, Achashverosh grants Haman an entrance to his chambers.

It's important to remember that Haman has no idea what is going on in Achashverosh's mind. He has no idea that Achashverosh thinks that Haman is involved with Esther, nor does he have the slightest inkling that he is being played. The Megilah is quite clear that Haman was ecstatic after the first party, walking out of it שָׂמֵחַ וְטוֹב לֵב (happy and good hearted). Haman felt that he was finally being recognized for the faithful and loyal minister that he was.

From his perspective, both the king and queen are treating him in a manner that he feels fitting to his devotion to the kingdom. Haman is proud of how far he's come and upon arriving home, shares his pride with his family and friends. Gloating, he tells them all about

> כָּל אֲשֶׁר גִּדְּלוֹ הַמֶּלֶךְ וְאֵת אֲשֶׁר נִשְּׂאוֹ עַל הַשָּׂרִים וְעַבְדֵי הַמֶּלֶךְ.
>
> All that the king has elevated him and raised him up above the other ministers and royal servants.

likely something that they've heard from him innumerable times previously. He's particularly gratified that the king and queen are now taking a personal interest in him.

> אַף לֹא הֵבִיאָה אֶסְתֵּר הַמַּלְכָּה עִם הַמֶּלֶךְ אֶל הַמִּשְׁתֶּה אֲשֶׁר עָשָׂתָה כִּי אִם אוֹתִי וְגַם לְמָחָר אֲנִי קָרוּא לָהּ עִם הַמֶּלֶךְ׃
>
> Queen Esther did not invite anybody else to the party she had with the king other than me and even tomorrow I am invited by her with the king.

In context, the Megilah is setting up Haman's pride and prestige in contrast to the seeming despise that Mordekhai accords him. It's almost ironic, that despite all of these accomplishments, how far he's come, and how special he's being treated, that he simply can't handle the fact that Mordekhai won't bow to him. The Megilah is clearly painting Haman as a pathetic, egocentric fool, who, the reader will come to anticipate, will eventually fall from grace and receive that which he deserves.

So when Haman enters Achashverosh's chambers that night, it's to ask a personal favor from the king. He not only has no reason to think that Achashverosh is suspicious of his motives, but Haman likely feels that it's a fortuitous moment. When better to ask for a favor then when the king and queen are thinking so highly of him anyway? To Haman it's a no-brainer. To readers of the Megilah, it's dramatic irony – at Haman's expense.

* * *

Completely unaware of what Achashverosh is thinking, Haman is almost giddy to get his request out, so confident that Achashverosh will grant him whatever he requests. In further irony – again at Haman's expense – Haman has no idea that Achashverosh has just read about Mordekhai saving Achashverosh's life and how Achashverosh owes Mordekhai a debt of gratitude. Haman has no idea that Achashverosh is looking for allies and just found a strong candidate in Mordekhai, who Achashverosh hopes to be somebody he could trust if and when the situation arose. None of that possibly crossed Haman's mind as he prepares himself to ask Achashverosh permission to hang Mordekhai.

Those who have already read the story know that Haman will never get the opportunity to make this request, but when reading the Megilah for the first time, the suspense if very real. Who will speak first? If Haman jumps right into it before Achashverosh can ask him anything, Haman will almost certainly be sealing his fate. Even while Achashverosh does not have any concrete evidence against Haman, he has many concerns and reasons for suspicion.

If Achashverosh hears that Haman wants to kill Mordekhai – the very person whom Achashverosh just read about and now considers an honest broker who he could possibly count on should a rebellion erupt – that might have been the straw that broke the camel's back. If Haman was really trying to take over, it makes sense that he'd want to get rid of as many of the king's confidants and loyalists as possible before making his move. Nervous as he already is, Achashverosh might not be able to take it anymore and would immediately decree Haman's death. If so, what will happen with the Jews? It's precisely these emotions and thoughts that the Megilah tries to evoke with its dramatic rendition of Haman's entrance – וַיָּבוֹא הָמָן (Haman entered).

Building the tension of the moment, the *trop* (musical cantillation notes) surrounding Haman's entrance are extended and dramatic (*zarka-segol*), prompting the reader / listener to pay attention and foreshadowing a point of interest.

In reality, Achashverosh never allows Haman the opportunity to make his request. Instead, Achashverosh immediately starts questioning Haman. He doesn't even bother asking what Haman is doing there. Quite frankly, he's fairly certain that Haman is prancing around the palace looking for Esther, an accusation that Haman would no doubt adamantly deny and offer some other excuse for being there, which Achashverosh would not actually believe. In truth, Haman was certainly not coming to the castle to be with Esther, since in reality, they have no actual relationship.

In further dramatic irony, if asked, Haman's 'excuse' for being there in the middle of the night would have actually been the truth, a truth though that Achashverosh wouldn't believe, which is likely why he doesn't even bother asking.

* * *

ACHASHVEROSH HAS THE opportunity to try to see what's on Haman's mind. He can't ask Haman straight out what's going on, because, regardless of the truth, Haman will adamantly deny it and Achashverosh wouldn't likely believe him in any event. But more importantly, Achashverosh isn't 100% sure that something is actually going on between Haman and Esther or that Haman is actually vying for the throne. These are just his suspicions – seemingly well-founded suspicions – but at this point, nothing more.

Achashverosh doesn't want to cavalierly throw out such an accusation until he has proof and so, even if he could find some way to believe Haman, Achashverosh wouldn't want to ask Haman straight out in any event. Achashverosh needed to come up with a scheme by which he might be able to assess Haman's motives without letting on that he is harboring suspicions against him. Achashverosh needed to find some line of questioning that would appear completely natural and appropriate, but at the same time, particularly crafted to determine what Haman harbored in his heart.

Recalling that throughout the Megilah, Achashverosh is continually portrayed as a thoughtful, calculating ruler while Haman is described as an egomaniacal fool, the conversation between them takes on a deeper meaning.

* * *

WHEN ACHASHVEROSH ASKS Haman, מַה לַעֲשׂוֹת בָּאִישׁ אֲשֶׁר הַמֶּלֶךְ חָפֵץ בִּיקָרוֹ (What should be done to a man whom the king wants to honor?), Achashverosh is very much aware that Haman will interpret the question about himself. It won't be explicitly stated, but assuming that Achashverosh's assessment is correct, it will reveal what Haman thinks that he himself deserves. Haman however, consistent with his portrayal throughout the Megilah, is not quite as astute and doesn't realize that Achashverosh is testing him. In Haman's mind, Achashverosh's question makes a lot of sense and is clearly about him.

Haman has been consistently promoted and now invited to a private party with the royal couple. They are clearly interested in making him feel special and valued. Achashverosh's question is just the next step: how could Achashverosh take the appreciation he shows Haman to the next level? What could Achashverosh do for Haman that would show everybody how much the king values and appreciates his loyalty?

From the standpoint of the servants in the king's private chambers at the time, the line of questioning also seemed quite appropriate, albeit from a completely different perspective. They had just finished reading about Mordekhai to whom no gratitude was shown after saving the king's life. It makes sense then that Achashverosh would be interested in figuring out something to do for Mordekhai and that Achashverosh would look for advice from one of his trusted advisors.

In this rather clever manner, the Megilah manages to build intrigue by setting up a situation in which each of the various characters has a different perspective as to Achashverosh's motives in questioning Haman. Haman assumes that Achashverosh it talking about him, looking for ways to show Haman how much he means to the kingdom. The servants in the room assume the questioning is leading to doing something for Mordekhai, whom they just read about, while Achashverosh is using all of this merely as a ploy to try to size up and learn more about what Haman is thinking.

# Chapter Thirty

Achashverosh opens with a question that he is confident will get Haman's attention, since Haman, self-interested as ever, assumes everything is always about him. What Achashverosh is looking for is Haman's attitude as well as his response. Achashverosh is trying to catch Haman somewhat off guard and see if that might give him some clue as to his inner thoughts. Knowing that Haman will interpret the question about himself, Achashverosh wants to know what Haman thinks Achashverosh could and / or should do for him to best express how much Haman means to the Persian government and people.

On the simplest level, it speaks directly to Haman's ego, playing off Haman's misguided perception of the day's earlier events that he is continuing to rise in the ranks of importance in the eyes of the royal couple. But from Achashverosh's perspective, it's vital to understand how Haman views himself vis-à-vis the monarchy and his role in the kingdom.

Haman's response is far worse than Achashverosh could have ever imagined. Haman basically says that Achashverosh should treat "this person" (who Haman assumes is referring to himself) like the king himself. יָבִיאוּ לְבוּשׁ מַלְכוּת אֲשֶׁר לָבַשׁ בּוֹ הַמֶּלֶךְ וְסוּס אֲשֶׁר רָכַב עָלָיו הַמֶּלֶךְ וַאֲשֶׁר נִתַּן כֶּתֶר מַלְכוּת בְּרֹאשׁוֹ – dress him like the king, have him ride on the king's royal chariot, and place the royal crown on his head. But for Haman, external appearances aren't sufficient. What's the point of getting all dressed up if only a handful of people in the palace might notice? Haman suggests a more robust public relations campaign for this "individual."

> וְנָתוֹן הַלְּבוּשׁ וְהַסּוּס עַל יַד אִישׁ מִשָּׂרֵי הַמֶּלֶךְ הַפַּרְתְּמִים וְהִלְבִּישׁוּ אֶת הָאִישׁ אֲשֶׁר הַמֶּלֶךְ חָפֵץ בִּיקָרוֹ וְהִרְכִּיבֻהוּ עַל הַסּוּס בִּרְחוֹב הָעִיר וְקָרְאוּ לְפָנָיו כָּכָה יֵעָשֶׂה לָאִישׁ אֲשֶׁר הַמֶּלֶךְ חָפֵץ בִּיקָרוֹ.

> And give the dress and the king to one of the king's official ministers and they shall dress the person whom the king wants to honor and parade him on the horse throughout the city and proclaim before him, "This is what shall be done to a man whom the king wants to honor!"

A successful public relations campaign needs to insure that it's abundantly clear what is going on. This kingly attired individual needs to be paraded around town in a manner that makes it clear that he's not just playing dress up with the king's clothing. He most certainly 'deserves' a regal escort and wagon driver, who is clearly identifiable as the king's personal guards. Haman wants it to be clear to all the spectators – and he most certainly envisions that there will be many of them – that it is Achashverosh himself who is bestowing this tremendous honor. If it was just any old servant leading the horse, an onlooker may not immediately conclude that the rider is receiving specifically royal treatment. He needed somebody clearly identifiable as one of Achashverosh's שָׂרֵי הַמֶּלֶךְ הַפַּרְתְּמִים.

To insure the success of this public relations campaign, Haman insists on adding a vocal element to this spectacle: the wagon driver should also be publicly announcing that this parade is in honor of "one to whom the king wants to show favor!" Even if the hubbub of a royal carriage making its way through the streets and alleys of Shushan wouldn't garner enough of an audience, the incessant screaming out of כָּכָה יֵעָשֶׂה לָאִישׁ will surely rouse the interest of many interested onlookers. Haman is trying to orchestrate a public spectacle and the larger the public and the larger the spectacle, the better. The underlying theme of the entire charade is promoting his image (after all, he assumes that it's him who will be sitting on that horse) and continuing to boost his ego.

Achashverosh couldn't care less about any of these details. All he hears is that Haman is orchestrating a coronation ceremony for himself. Who else but the king himself appears in royal robes, in a royal chariot, led by a royal wagon driver, and worst of all, wearing the royal crown! Already concerned that Haman is vying for the throne, this is precisely what Achashverosh hears in Haman's description. Unbeknownst to him, Haman is playing directly into Achashverosh's worst fears and concerns. While completely unaware and entirely unintentionally, Haman is confirming all of Achashverosh's suspicions.

All Achashverosh knows right now is that Haman must be stopped.

* * *

BUT EVEN WITH this last stunt and with all his suspicions, Achashverosh has no concrete proof of Haman's intentions or alleged affair with Esther. Nonetheless, Haman's last soliloquy cannot go unanswered; he is clearly going too far. Regardless of his intentions, what does Haman want with a pseudo-coronation ceremony anyway? At this point, Haman's motivations matter very little. Certainly if Haman is vying for the crown, but even if he is not, Haman must be quickly put in his place.

Achashverosh therefore commands that Haman do everything he just described, but to somebody else. Let Haman, the highest minister in the land, dress somebody else, put the crown on somebody else, and parade somebody else throughout Shushan. Achashverosh insists that every detail be followed, so long as it's Haman doing all of this to somebody else. Right now, Achashverosh's particular interest isn't necessarily in giving honor to any specific person but more focused on making sure Haman realizes who is really in charge.

Achashverosh realizes that Haman is thinking about himself (which is why he started this line of questioning in the first place) and even without the concerns of the past day, Haman's suggestion definitely makes Achashverosh quite uncomfortable. While perhaps innocently well intentioned, it's a dangerous precedent to set to let anybody act as the king, even for just a little while, lest he start thinking too much along those lines. The concern and hesitation is a thousand fold more magnified when there is reason to believe that the minister in question already started thinking along those lines, possibly has a plan for bringing it about, and may have already started putting it into play!

Achashverosh's response to Haman is quick and decisive. מַהֵר קַח אֶת הַלְּבוּשׁ וְאֶת הַסּוּס כַּאֲשֶׁר דִּבַּרְתָּ – "do exactly what you just said," just to somebody else. Let it be Haman who does all of this to somebody else, so as to make sure that Haman remembers that he isn't actually in charge. By dressing, crowning, and parading somebody else throughout Shushan, Haman will learn his place. He is a subject of the king and will do whatever the king says whenever he says to do it. Let Haman realize that the king is the only one promoting and demoting officials within his palace and it is within that framework alone that Haman can operate. It's almost irrelevant to Achashverosh who it is that Haman will be dressing and parading throughout Shushan; only that it's Haman that will be in the subservient role.

Practically speaking though, Achashverosh needs to select somebody for this role and has little time to think who might be most appropriate. He quickly remembers that he was just reading about Mordekhai when Haman suddenly appeared outside. How perfect? Achashverosh needed to do something to show gratitude to Mordekhai and the exact situation just presented itself. It will do quite nicely, killing two birds with one stone – repaying Mordekhai and teaching Haman a lesson.

It's somewhat unclear if Mordekhai would have otherwise received such an over the top show of royal gratitude and appreciation. While Achashverosh certainly needed to thank him and more importantly guarantee his continued loyalty to the crown, dressing him up like the king and parading him through the streets of Shushan seems excessive. But the precise details of Mordekhai's reward are not Achashverosh's priority right now. Achashverosh is more interested in making sure Haman remembers his proper place in the royal food chain and the best way to do that is to take every detail that Haman thought that he deserved and have Haman do them to somebody else. Mordekhai as Mordekhai has very little to do with what Achashverosh is trying to accomplish. That he just happens to be that 'somebody else' is simply fortuitous. It's just another of the Megilah's 'convenient coincidences.'

The extreme irony of the situation is not lost on the reader. Haman initially came to Achashverosh to ask for permission to hang Mordekhai. He walks out of Achashverosh's chambers parading Mordekhai throughout the streets of Shushan. Suffice it to say, after his discussion with Achashverosh, Haman is smart enough to not ask about hanging the very man to whom Achashverosh wants to accord so much honor.

From Haman's own perspective, this whole episode is just very confusing. It becomes clear to him that Achashverosh seemingly has it in for him, but he has no idea why that should be. Haman clearly doesn't have a clue that the king suspects him of having an affair with Esther. If that thought even entered Haman's mind, he wouldn't be so foolish as to snoop around the palace in the middle of the night, even if it wasn't for any illicit purpose. Haman is also completely unaware that Achashverosh suspects that he might be fomenting a rebellion and trying to take over. If he were aware, he would recognize that, if so, it's not the right time for him to ask for kingly favors. This is particularly true with his specific request, since he is asking Achashverosh for permission to kill one of the other ministers. If he realized he was under suspicion for seditious behavior, he wouldn't want to add any more fuel to the fire by asking about getting rid of one of his colleagues.

* * *

And so Haman finds himself doing that which he just hours ago thought impossible. Instead of presiding over the unceremonious hanging of Mordekhai, Haman is instead proclaiming Mordekhai's greatness throughout the streets of Shushan as he escorts him in a most regal manner.

וְהָמָן נִדְחַף אֶל בֵּיתוֹ אָבֵל וַחֲפוּי רֹאשׁ (Haman was pushed into his home, his head covered in mourning). This is the second time that Haman is described as entering his home all upset. The difference is that this time it makes sense that he should be so distraught. In describing these two instances of coming home similarly, the Megilah is trying to build a comparison between them. Ironically, the circumstances behind his sadness are diametrically opposed to each other.

The first time, on the previous day, he cannot contain his misery and gloom that Mordekhai won't bow down to him. Haman is so upset, that he cannot even come up with the simple plan to get rid of Mordekhai that his wife and advisors have to suggest to him. This second time, he enters his home 'rightfully' upset. He doesn't necessarily understand why, but the very person who he wanted hanged was instead just paraded around Shushan as the king's most favorite minister. Mordekhai, the minister who refused the royal edict to bow to Haman, who even made a point of not bowing down to Haman, that same Mordekhai whose refusal to bow led Haman to concoct an entire scheme to destroy the entire Jewish people, was being showered with praise – כָּכָה יֵעָשֶׂה לָאִישׁ אֲשֶׁר הַמֶּלֶךְ חָפֵץ בִּיקָרוֹ.

And if that wasn't enough. Achashverosh had Haman himself dress, crown, and lead Mordekhai through the streets of Shushan. Anybody watching this spectacle would quickly perceive the balance of power between Mordekhai – beautifully regaled in the king's finest robes and crown, riding upon a royal stallion – and Haman, the dutiful minister, completely subservient to any and all of the king's demands. One can only imagine Haman's face while parading Mordekhai throughout the city of Shushan and actually calling out כָּכָה יֵעָשֶׂה לָאִישׁ אֲשֶׁר הַמֶּלֶךְ חָפֵץ בִּיקָרוֹ. This is the same person that Haman simply could not stand at all, that he couldn't even wait the mere 11 months until all the Jews would be killed. Mordekhai was Haman's self-created arch-nemesis and just thinking about the spectacle of him having to parade Mordekhai around the city made Haman's blood boil.

And so when Haman enters his home אָבֵל וַחֲפוּי רֹאשׁ, it's completely understandable. Not only was Haman terribly embarrassed, but now his plan had no chance of coming to fruition.

After this parade, there was no way that Haman could convince Achashverosh to hang Mordekhai. But aside from figuring out what to do next, there must have been more going on inside Haman's head and heart. Until now, Haman thought that he was the most beloved of all the ministers, the most loyal to the crown, whom Achashverosh knew he could count on when times became difficult. And now, Achashverosh put him in this rather demeaning position.

* * *

DID ACHASHVEROSH KNOW about Haman's plan to hang Mordekhai and was trying to pre-emptively thwart it? It's possible, but highly unlikely. After all, Haman's wife and advisors came up with the plan just that previous night. They suggested that Haman tell Achashverosh about it first thing in the morning so that he could get rid of Mordekhai even before the second scheduled party. They saw how much Mordekhai bothered Haman and wanted Haman to be able to 'properly' enjoy that second feast, which he simply was unable to do so long as Mordekhai was not dealt with.

When they suggested waiting until morning to speak with Achashverosh, it wasn't a delaying tactic. Zeresh and the advisors are quite clear that Mordekhai needs to be dealt with as quickly as possible. It just seemed like common courtesy not to disturb the monarch in the middle of the night with a personal request. But Haman, in his egocentric zeal, needed to deal with it right then and there and so runs out of his house to see if he can have an immediate audience with Achashverosh.

In truth, Haman was likely pretty sure that he wouldn't be able to speak with the king that night. The Megilah is clear that it's only because Achashverosh couldn't sleep that he was even awake when Haman entered the palace. So what then was Haman's plan?

If Achashverosh had a more 'normal' night, then he would have been asleep when Haman arrived. It's hard to imagine that Haman would have woken him to ask him for this personal favor. It's hard to even imagine that the palace guards would even let Haman into the king's chambers once Achashverosh fell asleep. Even in the nights when Achashverosh cannot sleep, Haman does not actually gain entry to the king's chambers until Achashverosh gives explicit permission. What then was Haman thinking? Or did he simply let his excitement get the better of him?

Regardless of what would have played out on a 'normal' night, that wasn't what Haman encountered. We can only speculate as to what Haman's plan would have been, but it's not terribly relevant. What the Megilah seems to be highlighting is the ecstatic excitement that so consumed Haman with visions of killing Mordekhai that he acted irrationally. With that tremendous build up, Haman's fall comes down much harder. It's not just that Haman is treated as a regular servant, but that he must cater to and glorify his arch-nemesis Mordekhai. The Megilah wants the reader to appreciate the emotional roller coaster that Haman went through that night – from thoughts of grandeur and success to utter distress. And what might be most stressful of all is that he has no idea why it was happening.

# Chapter Thirty-One

When Haman arrives home אָבֵל וַחֲפוּי רֹאשׁ (his head covered in mourning) after parading and celebrating Mordekhai's accomplishments throughout the streets of Shushan, Zeresh recognizes that something is amiss. She knows all too well that her husband is often easily upset. Just the day prior, even as he was coming off a personal high from being invited to Esther's party, merely noticing that Mordekhai did not bow to him as he passed was enough to completely destroy Haman's mood. In fact, leaving Esther's party is the only time in the entire story that Haman is described as happy. And in a pathetic contrast, the Megilah highlights that וְכִרְאוֹת הָמָן אֶת מָרְדֳּכַי בְּשַׁעַר הַמֶּלֶךְ (And when Haman saw Mordekhai at the palace gates) – as Haman is still so elated from his special treatment by the royal couple, even during those moments of excitement, the mere sight of Mordekhai is enough to disrupt his whole demeanor. But Zeresh realizes now that something is different. Haman's אָבֵל וַחֲפוּי רֹאשׁ-ness is not just a more exaggerated expression of his generally easily-upset attitude, but reflects something deeper.

She recognizes that there is certainly something going on in Shushan, that there is some larger plan in place, and that Haman is most certainly not in control of it.

From Zeresh's perspective, Haman's meeting with Achashverosh the previous night – the night the Megilah describes as נָדְדָה שְׁנַת הַמֶּלֶךְ and who *Chazal* interpret is a reference to King of Kings and the Gemara tells us is the beginning of the תקפו של נס story – was a key turning point. Haman came to Achashverosh that night because he wanted to take advantage of the unique opportunity presented to him. From Haman's perspective, Achashverosh and Esther think of him as the most loyal of their ministers – he was the only one invited to their party – and feel a need to express their recognition, appreciation, and gratitude toward him. If there was ever a time when Haman would be able to cash in on a favor, it would be now. From Haman's perspective, it's a win-win all around. It's not a tremendously big request – just killing off a single person – and it wouldn't particularly affect Achashverosh all that much. Knowing that Achashverosh gave Haman permission to exterminate a whole group of people just on his say-so, even without identifying the group in question, Haman was pretty confident that Achashverosh would agree.

It would be a serious understatement to say that that intended encounter did not go exactly as Haman had planned. Of all the possibilities he could have imagined as outcomes of that request, what actually happened certainly never even entered Haman's mind. But instead of just dashing Haman's plans, the Megilah actually boosts Haman's hopes and dreams before having them crash down.

When he starts talking to Achashverosh, Haman actually thinks that Achashverosh is still trying to show his gratitude and appreciation to him – וַיֹּאמֶר הָמָן בְּלִבּוֹ לְמִי יַחְפֹּץ הַמֶּלֶךְ לַעֲשׂוֹת יְקָר יוֹתֵר מִמֶּנִּי (Haman said [thought] to himself: Who could the king possibly want to honor more than me)? Self-absorbed as ever, Haman could not fathom that Achashverosh might actually even consider showing appreciation to anybody else. More than just planning on getting rid of his arch-nemesis, Haman is now thinking that he is going to be able to do it in style, with the pomp and circumstance deserved by such a loyal minister as he. All of this just makes the dramatic turn of events so much starker.

Zeresh realizes this. She sees history unfolding before her eyes in which everything her husband hoped for, every plan he had and thoughts about how to execute them, were completely turned on their heads. It's not that Haman wasn't able to achieve his goals, but that the way in which everything turned out was "too coincidental" to actually be a coincidence. The outcome was the complete opposite of what Haman set out to accomplish. Not only was Mordekhai not hanging from a tree by day's end, but Haman was personally proclaiming Mordekhai's greatness throughout Shushan. It seems likely that prior to this moment, Haman was not even aware that Mordekhai held a special place in Achashverosh's eyes, which is why he had the temerity to ask Achashverosh permission to kill Mordekhai. But now the tables were completely turned. Achashverosh was very publicly displaying and demonstrating his admiration and appreciation for the previously unheard of (from Haman's perspective) Mordekhai at the very public expense of Haman, who up until now had considered himself the most favored minister, loyal and faithful as always.

What becomes clear to Zeresh is that there is a larger plan in place in which Haman is but a pawn. She realizes that something larger and more powerful must be controlling these events to account for the utter and complete reversal of fortunes and plans dramatically unfolding right before her very eyes.

Zeresh didn't see any specific sign or symbol that indicated that a plan was clearly in place. The plan that she became aware of was one operating 'behind the scenes,' not obvious and not easily seen or appreciated. While not directly referencing Hashem or any other divine power, Zeresh understands that a power she cannot see, one more powerful than she or Haman, is controlling world events.

This is what she means when she tells Haman

> אִם מִזֶּרַע הַיְּהוּדִים מָרְדֳּכַי אֲשֶׁר הַחִלּוֹתָ לִנְפֹּל לְפָנָיו לֹא תוּכַל לוֹ כִּי נָפוֹל תִּפּוֹל לְפָנָיו.
>
> If Mordekhai, before whom you have begun to fall, is of Jewish heritage, you will not overcome him; you will fall before him to your ruin.

Zeresh isn't suddenly blessed with the gift of prophecy and the Megilah gives no hint that she is or ever has attempted to divine future events. What she is saying is that if you look a little bit deeper, if you don't just stop at that which appears superficial, but look to see what's 'behind' that which is going on, you start to see a pattern emerge. The plan she sees taking hold is the complete and utter reversal of everything Haman set out to accomplish.

When Zeresh sees how Haman's plan to ask permission to kill Mordekhai is completely flipped on its head, what she sees is a plan to thwart Haman's aspirations. She then puts two and two together. What just happened with Mordekhai might be the beginning of something larger. If there is a design to thwart Haman's strategies, perhaps that extends not just to his personal strife with Mordekhai but to his other plans as well, namely his larger plot to destroy the Jews.

It's quite striking that Zeresh has no idea that Mordekhai might happen to be Jewish (she says אִם מִזֶּרַע הַיְּהוּדִים ), even though the Megilah continuously presents and describes him as מָרְדֳּכַי הַיְּהוּדִי , indicating that his Judaism was part and parcel of Mordekhai's identity. All Zeresh knows is that

Mordekhai is some low-level palace minister who disrespects her husband in such a heinous and public fashion that Haman wants to have him killed. From her perspective, although both involve killing, this has nothing to do with Haman's plot to destroy the Jewish people, albeit perhaps reflective of her husband's unhealthy way of dealing with difficult life challenges. She had no reason to think that these events were linked in any way. But if, just if, if happens to be that Mordekhai also just happens to be Jewish and there is more connecting these two events than she previously realized, there might be a deeper connection.

Zeresh sees what took place during the previous night and earlier that very day and takes notice of the complete and total reversal of roles and fortunes that ensued. She isn't completely sure what it all means or how this newly discovered plan will pan out, but recognizes that it's too coincidental to be an accident. Something larger is going on.

She realizes that if this larger background 'something' is about thwarting Haman's own plan and there is some connection between Haman's plan to kill Mordekhai and his plan to annihilate the Jewish people, then perhaps just like the former is being so completely twisted against him, so too his plan against the Jews. But if she is right, not only will Haman's bigger plans never be able to be executed, but through some means, Haman will also experience a significant role reversal and dramatic turn of fate.

* * *

Recognizing that something larger than Haman is in control of the situation, Zeresh reasons that if this Mordekhai fellow happens to have some connection to Haman's plot against the Jews, then Haman should be aware that the latter is also unlikely to succeed. She recognizes what we might describe as a Divine Hand guiding then-current events and tries to get Haman to become cognizant of it as well. As the entire Megilah makes no explicit mention of God, it doesn't put His name in Zeresh's realization either. But, for the reader – either counting himself among the faithful or one seeking faith – the insinuation is obvious. Even when there are no overtly obvious signs of Hashem's guiding history, politics, or personal and communal experiences, sometimes a closer look, a little deeper than just that which appears superficially obvious, gives a different, broader, and more accurate perspective.

Zeresh could have interpreted the events of that morning as a mere random coincidence. She could have thought that things happen and there isn't always a reason why. Zeresh had no idea that Mordekhai was even Jewish, let alone the impetus for Haman's entire plan. Other than perhaps reflecting her husband's disturbing trend of wanting people dead, the fact that one plan didn't pan out exactly as expected shouldn't have anything to do with the other's potential success. But Zeresh saw a deeper message in the events taking place around her. She wasn't satisfied viewing the unfolding history as a sequence of random events with no rhyme or reason. She chose to look a bit deeper and saw the Hand of Hashem (even if she didn't or couldn't identify it as such) guiding history. Zeresh therefore points out to Haman that he might want to start paying attention to these details as well. If Haman's two plans are connected (which the reader knows they are even if Zeresh does not) and there is a larger scheme in place by which Haman's downfall is already underway, then it was quite clear to Zeresh that neither would ever come to fruition.

* * *

Haman didn't have time to contemplate his wife's wisdom since עוֹדָם מְדַבְּרִים עִמּוֹ וְסָרִיסֵי הַמֶּלֶךְ הִגִּיעוּ (They were still speaking with him when the messengers of the king arrived). He doesn't have time to think, to contemplate, or to even revise his plan if he wanted to. Haman is rushed off (וַיַּבְהִלוּ – They rushed) to the palace. Whereas he was previously ecstatic about having been invited to the first party and originally elated that he would be able to attend once again, now the palace guards need to practically drag him out of his house off to the palace. He may not have believed Zeresh, or not wanted to believe her, but he doesn't even get a chance to respond before he is whisked off.

# Chapter Thirty-Two

Esther, for her part, sets the stage of the second party similar to the first. But while the external appearances may have been similar, each of the attendees is dramatically different than they were just the day before.

Achashverosh was clearly excited for the first party. After all, his wife who he hadn't seen in some while seemed excited to see him and planned a romantic feast. Clearly a reason for celebration. But now, Achashverosh is a lot wearier. He has concerns about Haman's intentions and possibly even Esther's as well. After wondering why Haman was even invited to the party and then discovering Haman snooping around the palace at night, Achashverosh is becoming more and more suspicious of Haman's motives. Was he only after the queen as a romantic prospect, which would be bad enough. Or was Haman planning something far more nefarious and seditious? And what was Esther's role? Was Haman coercing or forcing her into his plot? Was this what the meals and their selective attendance about – to try to get him to stop? Or was she also part of the plan that somehow had something to do with these parties? The only thing Achashverosh was certain about was that he wasn't certain about anything. He walked into that party not knowing what to expect.

Haman was also a changed man. Yesterday he joined the royal feast with a sense of triumph, assuming that the royal couple was acknowledging him for his trusted and loyal leadership in the Persian government. But after the previous night's events and having to parade his arch-nemesis throughout the streets of Shushan while publicly singing his praises, Haman was likely not anxious with anticipation for this party to begin. In fact, the Megilah points out that Haman had to be hurried off from his home to come to the party. He was reflecting on the previous day's events with his wife and advisors – who were quick to note that they likely indicated Haman's downfall – when the king's messengers quickly whisked him off to the palace. To describe Haman's state of mind as he joined that feast as simply harried is somewhat of an understatement.

*   *   *

But despite any similarities to yesterday's festivities, Esther too is a changed woman. She completely pivots from her original plan to adapt to the changing realities of the day.

When she and Mordekhai first devised a plan to save the Jews, she had hoped that the only way to persuade Achashverosh to kill Haman and revoke his edict was by convincing him that Esther and Haman were having an affair. While it would eventually get them both killed, the goal of saving the Jewish people would be met. Or at least so they thought. But after that roller coaster night, another option presented itself.

Watching Haman fall from the king's good graces in a mere few hours, she realized she had another opportunity. Esther likely did not know the precise details of what led Achashverosh to demand that Haman parade Mordekhai throughout the streets of Shushan. After all, this was all decided in a few minutes in the middle of the night in the king's inner chamber. She may not have even known that Haman was planning on asking permission to execute Mordekhai that very next day. That was a private discussion that Haman had with Zeresh and his advisors. But what she did see was that the arch-nemesis of the Jews, somebody whom yesterday she thought was too powerful to be brought down, who was above any possible political maneuvering, was clearly demonstrating his subservience to Achashverosh.

But it's not just that she saw a fundamental change in Haman and Achashverosh's relationship. It's the precise way in which she saw it demonstrated that spurred her to action. After all, if for whatever reason Achashverosh wanted to accord some honor to Mordekhai, he could have found anybody else in the palace to parade Mordekhai through the city. It would have made far more sense to command a standard wagon drive, or perhaps even the king's wagon driver with the task. When Esther realized that Achashverosh specifically chose Haman for this job, she picked up on the fact (much like Zeresh did) that something else was afoot.

Just two days earlier, Esther was initially moved to action when Mordekhai taught her that it's her responsibility to not only seek out the *yad Hashem* in the world, but to respond to it when possible. That perhaps her appointment as the Persian queen was all Hashem orchestrating an elaborate prologue so that she may be primed and positioned to act when necessary. It's a message she sincerely took to heart and decided was worth risking her life to accomplish. And it's not just something that she thought about once, but a notion that was continually on her mind.

So when she saw this complete and utter reversal of fortunes, when she realized that Haman was no longer held in such high esteem in Achashverosh's eyes, she knew that this was no coincidence. It was all part of the *yad Hashem*. With her life on the line and the entire Jewish people davening for her success, she saw Haman parading Mordekhai around Shushan as a peek through the lattice, discerning the *yad Hashem* to which she had to respond.

It wasn't just about recognizing that Hashem was demonstrating to her that today it would be a lot easier to drive a wedge between Haman and Achashverosh, but that it was specifically Mordekhai who was being paraded around. Even if she knew nothing of Haman's plot to kill Mordekhai that very day, she was certainly aware of their rivalry. It wasn't a secret. Mordekhai was the unofficial leader of the Jews of Shushan and Haman was the second to the king. Mordekhai made a point of not bowing down to Haman even while other of his fellow Jews may not have had such courage. Mordekhai was also a teacher in the community and would want his students and constituents to know about what he believed to be proper behavior. It seems quite obvious that the Jews of Shushan, if not the entire city of Shushan, were keenly aware of the enmity between Haman and Mordekhai.

So when Esther realizes that Achashverosh no longer holds Haman in such high esteem and that this very demonstration was brought about by a complete reversal of fortunes between Mordekhai and Haman, it's clear to her that this is *yad Hashem*. Just a few days earlier Mordekhai approached Esther, originally in sackcloth, begging her to do whatever possible to stave off Haman's decree. The balance of power was clearly in Haman's favor. This, this morning, was a clear demonstration that the tables had turned.

It was most certainly not a coincidence that these two elements were intermeshed – the combination of the two just strengthened the notion in

Esther's mind that this was indeed *yad Hashem* and that she may have to alter her plans accordingly. For Esther, they both led to the same conclusion: Haman is experiencing a downfall and she would be wise to take note.

Esther realizes that she may no longer have to risk her life to accomplish the same goal. There are other ways of getting rid of Haman that do not necessitate her to die in the process. If not only Haman's relationship with Achashverosh had deteriorated, but that on some larger *yad Hashem* level Haman even manages to experience a downfall, it may be far easier to change tactics and present her accusation against Haman directly to her husband. She no longer needs to resort to the facade of an affair, which was complicated enough, when as of this morning, Achashverosh would be open and amenable to hearing a more direct accusation and acting upon it.

Changing tactics would certainly require tying up some loose ends. She would have to find ways that wouldn't leave Achashverosh confused by her previous actions. The first party and even the invitation to the second were all made as part of Esther's plan of convincing Achashverosh that she and Haman were having an affair. In altering her approach, she would now have to figure out how all these elements fit into this new plan so as not to confuse Achashverosh. At first she tried to create a sense of suspicion in his mind and now, she would be completely pivoting to a different direction. But very cleverly, instead of confusing him, as the Megilah will soon describe, Esther manages to use all of these elements to her advantage.

Esther's changing of tactic, while going unmentioned in the text, is fundamental to central theme of the Megilah. The lesson of the Megilah is in fact double tiered: both for the reader to understand and seek out *yad Hashem* in his or her own world but also to appreciate that this is exactly what is happening within the story of the Megilah itself. This is the second time that Esther recognizes Hashem's hand in current events and rises to the occasion to be part of the Divine outline for the Jewish historical story.

* * *

BUT AS FOR the party itself, it seems to have proceeded similar to the first. After some while, Achashverosh once again turns to Esther to see what she might want and what he could do for her. Esther, recognizing that Achashverosh wants to know what is going on, begins her accusation. She makes it quite clear from the start that she isn't asking for a simple favor, but for Achashverosh's most serious consideration

> תִּנָּתֶן לִי נַפְשִׁי בִּשְׁאֵלָתִי וְעַמִּי בְּבַקָּשָׁתִי.
>
> Let my life be granted me as my wish, and my people as my request.

Her life and that of her people are in danger. This was certainly not something that Achashverosh was expecting. She turns to him asking that he intervene and save them all.

There is something startling and unsettling about simply leaving the request as such and perhaps much that could be said for that tactic, but Esther chooses to continue.

> כִּי נִמְכַּרְנוּ אֲנִי וְעַמִּי לְהַשְׁמִיד לַהֲרוֹג וּלְאַבֵּד וְאִלּוּ לַעֲבָדִים וְלִשְׁפָחוֹת נִמְכַּרְנוּ הֶחֱרַשְׁתִּי כִּי אֵין הַצָּר שֹׁוֶה בְּנֵזֶק הַמֶּלֶךְ.
>
> For we have been sold, my people and I, to be destroyed, massacred, and exterminated. Had we only been sold as bondmen and bondwomen, I would have kept silent; for the adversary is not worthy of the king's trouble.

Even understanding that Esther might want to add a little context to the stark reality that she just presented Achashverosh, what relevance does this actually have to her request? Is she trying to convince Achashverosh that she would have sat silently if she and her people were merely sold *en masse* into slavery instead of being decreed to death? It's hard to believe and it's certainly not a terribly convincing argument.

It seems instead that Esther is intimately aware of how Haman convinced Achashverosh to agree to his plot. After all, Mordekhai, a palace insider, filled her in on all the details. The Megilah specifies that Mordekhai told Hatakh to tell Esther everything that occurred as well as to show her the edict that was put up in Shushan, subtly indicating that she should look for similarities and differences. As noted earlier, Haman only tells Achashverosh that he wants לְאַבֵּד this unnamed nation, but the proclamation that Haman issues clearly delineates לְהַשְׁמִיד לַהֲרוֹג וּלְאַבֵּד – clearly indicating that the earlier omission was purposeful.

She was effectively saying that if everything had actually gone according to what Achashverosh had assumed all along, she would not have brought the issue up at all. The problem was that Achashverosh was fooled by Haman into agreeing to something he didn't necessarily approve of. Whether or not

Achashverosh would have actually agreed to an explicit decree to annihilate the Jews (or some other unnamed nation) isn't particularly relevant at this point. Perspectives on this span the gamut and reflect the general debate as to whether Achashverosh harbored preconceived antisemitic motives. What matters is that Achashverosh wasn't told the truth.

Assuming that Achashverosh was starting to put things together and recalled the conversation with Haman from just a few days earlier, this is starting to make a lot of sense. There was a conversation about doing something to some nation, but there was no talk of death. Achashverosh was well aware that he was not only respected but also feared, that he and his decisions were final. Nobody would dare swindle him in such a way. Which is precisely what Esther is driving at.

If the person responsible for this decree were even remotely interested in the betterment of the Empire, this isn't what he would have done – כִּי אֵין הַצָּר שֹׁוֶה בְּנֵזֶק הַמֶּלֶךְ. This צָר who is out for her and her people's blood, doesn't have the king's best interests in mind; he is doing all of this for selfish egotistical reasons. If he really was aiming for the betterment of the kingdom, he should have been forthright with his request. But even then, how would that help the Empire? Losing a whole collection of presumably tax-paying citizens doesn't do much for the national betterment. Clearly, this צָר, was motivated by his concerns which led him to lie and trick Achashverosh.

Achashverosh is flustered, angry, and completely beside himself. He can't even gather his thoughts straight to ask Esther what is going on.

וַיֹּאמֶר הַמֶּלֶךְ אֲחַשְׁוֵרוֹשׁ וַיֹּאמֶר לְאֶסְתֵּר הַמַּלְכָּה

King Achashverosh said and he said to Queen Esther

the Megilah mentions that Achashverosh talks and then immediately reports that he addressed Esther. There is no dialogue reported after the first וַיֹּאמֶר. Did he actually say anything? If not, why mention it? It seems that in his anger and frustration, Achashverosh rose to yell and scream, but couldn't actually get the words out. He wanted to say something but was so simultaneously confused and angry that while he rose up to talk, he didn't have anything to say.

Slowly gathering his thoughts, he finally beams at Esther,

מִי הוּא זֶה וְאֵי זֶה הוּא אֲשֶׁר מְלָאוֹ לִבּוֹ לַעֲשׂוֹת כֵּן

Who is he and where is he who dared to do this?

Who could possibly have the temerity to do such a thing? The question is deliberately ambiguous – is he upset at somebody plotting against his queen or at being lied to? It didn't really matter, since both were egregious enough to incur the king's wrath.

Rising slowly from her seat, Esther points at the incredulous and completely befuddled Haman, sitting right across the table.

## Chapter Thirty-Three

Achashverosh is very confused. Who really is Haman and why does he want to kill Esther? Only a few moments ago, Achashverosh was concerned that Haman was having an affair with Esther and now she tells him that Haman is not only trying to kill her, but her entire people as well. Who even are her people? Where does she come from? But more importantly right now, what is going on with Haman? He gave Achashverosh advice a few years earlier to get rid of Vashti and now he's trying to kill Esther? Just last night, Haman was snooping around the palace, presumably to be romantically involved with Esther (or so Achashverosh thought) and now he wants her dead? But Achashverosh never did actually ask Haman what he was doing outside his chambers. Why was he even there?

There is clearly a lot going on, some of which Achashverosh thinks he understands and a lot more that he's clearly aware that he doesn't quite have a handle on yet. But in a government and kingdom where sedition and rebellion are constantly on the mind, nothing is too far fetched.

And then Achashverosh does something quite uncharacteristic. Instead of immediately reacting, instead of blurting out something, or making a rash decision, he gets up and leaves the party to catch a breath of fresh air. While clearly angry, he recognizes that he needs some time to figure out how best to respond.

* * *

Haman for his part is clearly scared and embarrassed, but also somewhat confused. What in the world is Esther talking about? When did he ever plan on killing her? Or her nation? Which nation does she even come from? Having kept her secret so well hidden, Haman, like Achashverosh, is completely unaware that Esther is Jewish.

It must have occurred to him at some point, while וְהָמָן נִבְעַת מִלִּפְנֵי הַמֶּלֶךְ וְהַמַּלְכָּה (And Haman cringed in terror before the king and the queen), to put two and two together and realize that Esther is in fact Jewish and she was referencing his decree to destroy the Jewish people in about eleven months' time. Having just come from one of the more difficult mornings of his life, it's understandable that Haman might be somewhat off his game, but still, he couldn't believe what was unfolding in front of his very eyes. What was once a sure-fire plan not only to get rid of Mordekhai but also of his miserable fellow Jews, was now being used to show that he was trying to kill the queen. His whole world was quickly unraveling.

But even that which seemed to be his personal disgust with Mordekhai was now being blown completely out of proportion. Zeresh's last words to him as he was quickly brought from his home to the party were ringing in his ears – אִם מִזֶּרַע הַיְּהוּדִים מָרְדֳּכַי אֲשֶׁר הַחִלּוֹתָ לִנְפֹּל לְפָנָיו לֹא תוּכַל לוֹ כִּי נָפוֹל תִּפּוֹל לְפָנָיו (If Mordekhai, before whom you have begun to fall, is of Jewish heritage, you will not overcome him; you will fall before him to your ruin). What she may not have realized, but what the Megilah was clearly foreshadowing, was that even when it came to his plans for the rest of the Jewish people, לֹא תוּכַל (you will not succeed). At the time, he likely didn't fully appreciate what Zeresh meant.

Clearly, Haman was not going to be able to hang Mordekhai as had previously planned, certainly not any time soon. Even if he had optimistically hoped that in eleven months time Achashverosh will forget about his special treatment of Mordekahi and allow him to be killed with the rest of the Jews, this was becoming less and less likely. In what appears to Haman to be an out of the blue occurrence, Mordekhai is now establishing himself as a loyal and faithful minister of the king. And even if Mordekhai otherwise kept to himself, who knows how powerful and influential he might become?

Not realizing that Achashverosh may have instructed Haman to parade Mordekhai around Shushan more with the intent to put Haman in his place than to celebrate Mordekhai, Haman was likely nervous about Mordekhai's increasing influence in royal affairs. At some point, Achashverosh might start thinking so highly of him that Mordekhai might be in a position to even cancel Haman's original decree.

But was that really what Zeresh meant? It would certainly be a situation of לֹא תוּכַל לוֹ – Haman will not succeed in taking down Mordekhai. And it even might foretell Haman's eventual fall from royal grace. Whereas he previously had the king's ear and was able to squeeze out an edict to destroy the Jewish people, with Mordekhai rising in the ranks he might be able to thwart Haman's plans. But even if this more pessimistic perspective described Haman's mood on his way to this second party, he could never have imagined that the previous night's events might portend his own death. Is this also what Zeresh meant? Her words were likely reverberating in his head all while Esther was talking, not being exactly sure what they might mean. As hard it is may have been for Haman to believe, he now saw himself falling rather quickly at the indirect hands of the Jews.

* * *

NOT ONLY WAS he unable to carry through with his plan to hang Mordekhai, but, "coincidentally," it just happened to turn out that the queen herself was Jewish. And instead of Esther approaching Haman and looking for a personal exemption from the decree, she flipped the situation on its head. She painted the decree as Haman trying to kill the entire Jewish people, including Queen Esther.

It's interesting to wonder what was Haman thinking when he was listening to Esther's accusation against him? She only revealed the identity of the villain at the very end of her remarks, leaving Haman wondering the whole time to whom she was referring. And even while Haman most certainly remembered his request from Achashverosh to kill out the Jews, he could never have imagined that this could have had anything to do with Esther.

If he did think back only a short while ago to Zeresh's warning before being dragged out of his house, he might have started to have an inkling of where Esther's accusation was going. While at first he likely couldn't have figured out how she was involved, he likely started wondering how terribly coincidental it would be for Esther to be Jewish. It would be the capstone to his already dramatic-irony fueled past 24 hours. The rug was being slowly pulled out from under him.

* * *

Listening to Esther's blistering accusation and realizing the fatal flaw of his plan, Haman נִבְעַת מִלִּפְנֵי הַמֶּלֶךְ וְהַמַּלְכָּה , trying to hide his face and at the same time realizing that there was nowhere to run. Noticing that Achashverosh steps outside for a breath of air to clear his head, Haman plays the only move he has left. He begs for his life from Esther.

Haman knows Achashverosh too well to think that he won't be severely punished, recognizing that כָלְתָה אֵלָיו הָרָעָה מֵאֵת הַמֶּלֶךְ (for he saw that the king had resolved to destroy him). From Haman's perspective, Achashverosh just heard that Haman wants to kill his queen and her entire people, for seemingly no reason whatsoever. Only a few hours earlier Achashverosh demeaned Haman by forcing him to parade Mordekhai through the streets of Shushan. And now this. While Haman was somewhat confused and unsure as to Achashverosh's motivation for doing so, how much more did Achashverosh need to hear before deciding that getting rid of Haman was the next best move?

The Megilah doesn't tell us what Haman actually said to Esther, only that he עָמַד לְבַקֵּשׁ עַל נַפְשׁוֹ מֵאֶסְתֵּר הַמַּלְכָּה (remained to plead with Queen Esther for his life). Was he looking for mercy? What could he have possibly offered or said to her that would grant him clemency? She just outed him to Achashverosh as an אִישׁ צַר וְאוֹיֵב (a man who is an adversary and enemy), who has it out for her and her people. Why would she act mercifully toward him? Haman really had no argument to make; he was at a total loss for words. What could he say to Esther? That he didn't realize that she was Jewish and therefore part of the plan? He could try to tell her that he never meant to kill her, only her people. But why would that convince her to act mercifully?

And in his pathetic attempt to beg for his life, he was nervous and shaking, not trying to think of what Achashverosh will have in store for him when the king reenters the party room. And just at that moment, as Achashverosh steps back into the room, Haman, nervous as ever, standing beside Esther, 'coincidentally' falls on top of her.

Watching this take place in front of his very eyes, Achashverosh simply loses it. We don't know if his walk outside helped clear his mind to figure out what to do with Haman and it's possible that Achashverosh was still working out the various permutations and possibilities as he walks back in. But seeing Haman on top of his wife is the straw that broke the camel's back – הֲגַם לִכְבּוֹשׁ אֶת הַמַּלְכָּה עִמִּי בַּבָּיִת ([Does he mean] to ravish the queen in my own palace?)! Is Haman now trying to sleep with her? Just a minute ago, Haman stood silently while Esther openly declared that Haman is trying to kill her. While perhaps still confused, to Achashverosh, it made little difference – he was done with Haman.

* * *

The Megilah's narrative word choice in describing his seemingly minor incident is quite deliberate. The entire episode is described in the past tense (וְהַמֶּלֶךְ קָם, וְהָמָן עָמַד, וְהַמֶּלֶךְ שָׁב), except for Haman losing his balance and falling on top of Esther – וְהָמָן נֹפֵל (And Haman was falling), in the present tense. Further emphasizing the word choice, the traditional rendering of reading the Megilah chants the word with a *ravi'a*, a falling note, complementing the simple meaning of the word with an audible cue. There is a clear and intentional attempt to grab the reader's attention to focus on what otherwise appears to be an accident, a clearly unintentional action.

But even while it eventually is the nail in Haman's coffin, it doesn't add all that much to the story. Even if Achashverosh hadn't caught Haman laying on top of Esther, Achashverosh would have likely killed him just for plotting to kill the queen. And it's even quite likely that if when he reentered the room Haman would have been standing next to Esther begging for his life, upon hearing that Haman was planning on hanging Mordekhai, Achashverosh would have almost certainly promptly put him to death anyway.

Considering that it's not terribly significant in terms of the plot, the Megilah could have simply noted it without much fanfare and moved on. In highlighting the word and the action with both a change in tense and audible cue, the Megilah is doing more than focusing on a particular misstep, but instead calling the reader to connect what is taking place at the party with Zeresh's foreboding warning to Haman just prior to his coming to the party.

She had just warned him, אִם מִזֶּרַע הַיְּהוּדִים מָרְדֳּכַי אֲשֶׁר הַחִלּוֹתָ לִנְפֹּל לְפָנָיו לֹא תוּכַל לוֹ כִּי נָפוֹל תִּפּוֹל לְפָנָיו. The very same verb, ליפול that Zeresh repeats three times is the very word that the Megilah draws the reader's attention to. Making this connection is so important that the Megilah switches tenses and has the Megilah reader chant the word in a more meaningful and attention grabbing manner, to make sure that the point clearly comes across, if not to Haman, then certainly to the readers of the Megilah.

The Megilah makes such a big deal about this connection because understanding it lies at the heart of the Megilah's message – Hashem has a plan for the world, we just aren't always privy to see it very clearly.

# Chapter Thirty-Four

From Achashverosh's perspective, everything about what just happened makes little sense. He came to the party thinking that Haman and Esther were having an affair and plotting to take over the throne. He then learned that not only are they not romantically involved, but that Haman actually wants to kill Esther. But why in the world would he want to do that other than to start his own revolution? And before he is able to process all of this, Achashverosh now sees Haman laying on top of Esther, apparently trying to rape her right in front of the king. Achashverosh doesn't know that Haman was begging for his life and 'happened' to trip. All he knows is what he sees and none of it makes sense to him. But at the end of the day, it becomes quite clear that Haman must go. הַדָּבָר יָצָא מִפִּי הַמֶּלֶךְ וּפְנֵי הָמָן חָפוּ (No sooner did these words leave the king's lips than Haman's face was covered). They both knew very well what the next immediate step was going to be.

But even before given the chance to scream out "off with his head!," Charvonah shows up – a previously unheard of court minister ready to share some information with the king. His entrance to the party is somewhat strange. Presumably, the party was a private affair – after all, Esther's original intent was to plant the seeds of a possible romantic liaison between herself and Haman and convince Achashverosh that it was real – and was not open to every palace passerby. How Charvonah entered the room without anybody noticing or even asking permission to enter is left ambiguous. Why, even after entering the room and taking in what otherwise appears to be an absurd scene (Haman laying on top of Esther and Achashverosh reprimanding him), he continues to deliver his message, is similarly left unaddressed. Nonetheless, Charvonah seems to be aware of Haman's precarious situation and although the Megilah offers no reason that Charvonah would want to specifically harm Haman, Charvonah makes sure to place the final nail in Haman's coffin.

Directly following up on Achashverosh's rhetorical הֲגַם לִכְבּוֹשׁ אֶת הַמַּלְכָּה עִמִּי בַּבָּיִת ([Does he mean] to ravish the queen in my own palace?), Charvonah adds in that if trying to attack or rape Esther in Achashverosh's own palace wasn't enough, גַּם הִנֵּה הָעֵץ אֲשֶׁר עָשָׂה הָמָן לְמָרְדֳּכַי אֲשֶׁר דִּבֶּר טוֹב עַל הַמֶּלֶךְ עֹמֵד בְּבֵית הָמָן גָּבֹהַּ חֲמִשִּׁים אַמָּה (Additionally, there is a tree standing at Haman's house, fifty amot high, which Haman made for Mordekhai—the man whose words saved the king). Not only is Haman plotting against the king's wife, he is also plotting against the king's loyal supporter! Romantic relationship or not, this was more than sufficient proof for Achashverosh that Haman's ego and ambitions had gotten the better of him and that if he wasn't stopped right now, Achashverosh may have a rebellion on his hands.

It's possible that Achashverosh may have been casually aware that Haman didn't particularly care for Mordekhai, but even then, the true extent of Haman's utter despise and hatred for Mordekhai likely came as somewhat a surprise. Haman never got a chance to present his case to Achashverosh against Mordekhai and wasn't able to request special permission to have Mordekhai hanged. And if the earlier contention that Achashverosh was blithely unaware of the identity of the nation that Haman requested to annihilate, he had no reason to think that Mordekhai was included among them, let alone had been the catalyst for the entire plan to begin with.

All of this was too much for Achashverosh to take in. He came to the party thinking that Esther was having an affair with Haman only to learn the Haman was actually trying to kill her, to walking in on Haman seemingly trying to rape her, to then learning that Haman has a plan to murder Mordekhai, the only loyal minister Achashverosh knows he can count on. While he might not be sure exactly of each character's individual motivations, machinations, or goals, Achashverosh is quite certain that Haman must go. Now.

Responding immediately and emotionally to Charvonah's information, Achashverosh commands תְּלֻהוּ עָלָיו (hang him [Haman] upon it) – a fitting dramatic irony to seal Haman's fate. But even while feeling accomplished in taking that final step in getting rid of Haman, Achashverosh now needs to figure out what in the world is going on in his palace.

* * *

Recognizing that the Megilah should be read and understood on several levels, keeping the underlying message of the Megilah in mind, it's possible to understand Charvonah's role somewhat differently. Although he is only introduced for the first time in this instance, the Megilah only records וַיֹּאמֶר – And he said. It does not mention that he entered the room or that he appeared. He is described as אֶחָד מִן הַסָּרִיסִים (one of the ministers) and when he starts speaking, he begins with גַּם הִנֵּה (Additionally, there is), which sounds like he is continuing some other thought.

It's possible that he was actually stationed inside the room, guarding the door from the inside. He doesn't appear out of nowhere but was in the room the whole time watching the tense-transforming-into-ridiculous scene unfolding before him. Charvonah hears Esther's accusation against Haman, watches Haman walk over to Esther to beg for his life, and stares in disbelief as a trembling Haman falls on top of Esther just as Achashverosh walks in from the patio.

It's unclear if Charvonah completely understands what is going on or realizes that Esther's accusation against Haman referred to his decree against the Jews. She never mentions it explicitly, nor does she ever indicate that she is Jewish. Esther only tells Achashverosh that Haman is out to kill her people. Charvonah hears this and then watches as Haman's last plead for mercy turns completely on its head when Achashverosh reenters the room to find him laying on top of Esther. The whole thing seems altogether 'too perfect.'

Charvonah quickly realizes that he is aware of another one of Haman's plots, also against somebody close to the king – Mordekhai. Charvonah recognizes that there is clearly something 'larger' going on, that Haman, who was previously held in such esteem by Achashverosh, who was able to finesse a decree from him to destroy a whole nation, is currently in freefall. He sees what we might describe as the *yad Hashem* operating in the palace of Shushan and responds.

As if completing a previous thought, Charvonah pipes up to inform Achashverosh, גַּם הִנֵּה הָעֵץ אֲשֶׁר עָשָׂה הָמָן לְמָרְדֳּכַי אֲשֶׁר דִּבֶּר טוֹב עַל הַמֶּלֶךְ (the man whose words saved the king). Not only was Haman plotting against the queen, he is also plotting against another royal supporter, אֲשֶׁר דִּבֶּר טוֹב עַל הַמֶּלֶךְ. Clearly, Haman is trying to bring down the king and it is during these few moments that it completely starts to unravel. When Charvonah sees that happening, he steps up and takes an active part of history. He too sees the *yad Hashem* (even if he may not have articulated it as such) and responds to the situation.

# Chapter Thirty-Five

At this point, even though everything seems to be working out for Esther, it doesn't seem to fit in with her original plan. At some point, she decided to change tactics.

Esther successfully raised Achashverosh's suspicions about Haman, such that when the time came Achashverosh decreed Haman's quick demise. While as veteran readers of the Megilah we have come to expect Achashverosh to react quickly and decisively, it's important to consider that this wasn't a guaranteed outcome; at least Esther didn't think so.

Instead of simply presenting her situation to Achashverosh in a more straightforward fashion and pleading with him to save her people from genocide, she orchestrates an entire plan to raise Achashverosh's suspicions about Haman. Clearly, Esther didn't think that a simpler approach would have succeeded. The Jews were just as much in peril the day prior to Esther approaching Achashverosh as they were on the day she finally got him to act; nothing changed except for Achashverosh's perception of Haman's character and motives.

And even after all of that – persuading Achashverosh that Haman was up to no good and begging him for her life and the life of her people – the outcome was still not certain. Esther recognized that Achashverosh was calculated and would likely make whatever decision would best suit him politically.

When Esther pleads for the life of her people at that second party, Achashverosh as no idea who her people actually are. But even if he did know, it's hard to know if that would have moved him very much to sympathy. Practically – and more importantly, politically – speaking, would it really have mattered to Achashverosh if the Jewish people were completely annihilated?

As noted earlier, there is some debate as to Achashverosh's overall outlook toward the Jews: did he harbor anti-Semitic tendencies that were simply brought to the fore by Haman's request (or possibly even a virulent anti-Semite himself, who, perhaps for practical or other considerations could not or would not independently issue a genocidal decree against the Jewish people)? Or was he simply apathetic toward them – the Jews being just another group of people over whom he ruled. The Megilah itself doesn't express an explicit opinion on the matter even while various sections and conversations can be read in either direction. *Chazal* seem to waver between these two poles, with some Talmudic and Midrashic comments reading a more vicious and nefarious backdrop to some of Achashverosh's words and actions and other comments reading something more in the direction of apathy.

Recognizing much of this ambiguity, Esther appealed to a different tactic – portraying Haman as disloyal and a threat to Achashverosh's rule. She begs Achashverosh to intervene, not out of pity or mercy for the Jewish people, but rather because Haman wants her dead. Given her continuous attempts to paint Haman as a royal threat, she hoped – and succeeded – in convincing Achashverosh to get rid of Haman. At first glance, Esther clearly succeeded with her plan; Haman was dead. But even while that was clearly Esther's short term goal, her larger objective was clearly to eliminate the threat to the Jewish people, which seemed to have failed quite miserably.

Responding to Esther's pleading, Achashverosh decrees Haman's death and even bequeaths Haman's estate to Esther as a sign of good will. Perhaps as an 'apology gift' for having suspected her of infidelity (*Manot Ha-Levi*) or simply as a means of hoping to make her feel loved instead of threatened, it's clearly a bonus that she wasn't expecting. From Achashverosh's perspective, the problem has been solved. Haman's threat to his sovereignty has been eliminated, Esther's life is secured, and all is good in Shushan.

But interestingly, Achashverosh makes no effort or even inquiry as to the mortal threat against Esther's people. She was quite clear that her life was in jeopardy since the decree was against her entire people, yet Achashverosh appears or at least acts oblivious to them. This seems to further the perspective that, throughout the story, Achashverosh is only interested in his own political gain and survival. Once his kingship is secured, very little else matters to him.

It's also quite clear that despite Haman's death, the original decree against the Jews is still very much in play. So much so, that Esther must now approach the king again and beg and plead with him to reverse it. And when she does, Achashverosh's response is that 'obviously' it cannot be rescinded, because such is the nature of royal decrees in Shushan, once promulgated there is no recourse to retract them. It's pretty clear that Achashverosh recognized that executing Haman would not result in saving the Jewish people. And given that once Haman is executed the only thing he does is grant Esther rights to Haman's estate, it's quite clear that he is well aware that Esther's people (it's a bit unclear if he has yet discovered that she is Jewish) are still in mortal danger.

This whole turn of events seems to take Esther by surprise. It seems quite clear from the text that she anticipated Achashverosh reversing Haman's decree. She was either unaware of the intricacies of the Shushan bureaucracy preventing the rescinding of a royal decree or perhaps assumed that Achashverosh could grant a one-time override of the general rules. It's clear because after her moving soliloquy and compelling argument to Achashverosh that eventually got Haman killed, she then needs to approach Achashverosh a second time to rescind the decree. It was something that she clearly thought would have been automatic or at least quick in the coming. And it was not.

* * *

Esther was unprepared for this. Approaching Achashverosh this second time, she is distraught and pleads, begs, and cries to him to save her people. It's clearly an act of desperation, but in light of the main focus and lesson of the Megilah, there is also something far more fundamental happening. As she does earlier in the Megilah, Esther recognizes that she is in a historically unique position to make a difference. She capitalizes on her access, aware that there is a larger plan afoot, and chooses to be an active player in His grand scheme. From a literary perspective, it's quite fitting: Esther initiates her plan when Mordekhai teaches / reminds her that, from a Jewish perspective, there are no coincidences, and if she was chosen to be the queen, it's because He has a role for her to play.

The final touches of her plan – the actual salvation of the Jews – will also ultimately come about because she takes an initiative, recognizing that given that He has a plan for the Jews, she actively chooses to play a role. As bookends to the entire story of their salvation, the Megilah's message is clear: Hashem has a plan for the world and when we recognize it, we can choose to be part of something transcendent beyond our own individual stories.

# Chapter Thirty-Six

Realizing that her goal was far from accomplished, Esther seizes the moment. She recognizes that Hashem has clearly granted the Jewish people a reprieve; that her initial efforts were fruitful and that, while not achieving a complete salvation for the Jews, things were starting to generally improve. Even while their *tefilot* were not yet completely answered, she recognized that He was clearly listening. Esther, understanding her unique historical and national position, takes charge.

When she approaches Achashverosh now, she does so more confidently than before and without hesitation, realizing that her confidence is only in her awareness of her unique historical position but simultaneously taking in the seriousness of the genocidal decree against her people. Such that even though she is approaching the king anew, the Megilah describes it as וַתּוֹסֶף אֶסְתֵּר – she continued, or added on to their previous discussion. From her perspective, things are not yet finished.

But her situation is somewhat complicated. From Achashverosh's perspective, he has already answered her request by executing Haman and not only that, he even went one step farther by granting Haman's estate to her. She needs to make sure that she doesn't appear ungrateful and find some way to couch her request in a manner that will appeal to Achashverosh.

* * *

Esther decides to frame her request as a natural outgrowth of what Achashverosh has already done. She seems to want to convince him that the next natural step for him to take is to reverse Haman's decrees. On the face of it, Esther isn't terribly sure that Achashverosh has any vested interest in actually saving the Jewish people and therefore she isn't certain of her success.

So in addition to couching what appears to Achashverosh to be a new request (but from her perspective was her original intention all along) as simply an extension of his previous decisions, she also appeals to his emotions. This is the one and only time in the Megilah that Esther cries. She not only adds on to what she previously requested (וַתּוֹסֶף אֶסְתֵּר וַתְּדַבֵּר לִפְנֵי הַמֶּלֶךְ – Esther continued and spoke before the king) but now also falls to his feet, cries, and begs the king (וַתִּפֹּל לִפְנֵי רַגְלָיו וַתֵּבְךְּ וַתִּתְחַנֶּן לוֹ – falling at his feet and weeping, and beseeching him) to reverse Haman's decree.

She prefaces her request with language that would clearly signal to Achashverosh that even while appearing new to him, is really just the natural next step from what he already did. She appeals to him that אִם עַל הַמֶּלֶךְ טוֹב וְאִם מָצָאתִי חֵן לְפָנָיו וְכָשֵׁר הַדָּבָר לִפְנֵי הַמֶּלֶךְ וְטוֹבָה אֲנִי בְּעֵינָיו – If it please Your Majesty and if I have won your favor and the proposal seems right to Your Majesty, and if I am pleasing to you. Two of those four phrases are quoted verbatim from her original request at the party: אִם מָצָאתִי חֵן בְּעֵינֶיךָ הַמֶּלֶךְ וְאִם עַל הַמֶּלֶךְ טוֹב – if I find favor in your eyes, king, and it appears good to the king. By repeating already similar phrases, Esther wants Achashverosh to subconsciously draw a link between the two requests and concluding that just as already granted the first, he'll just as quickly grant this as well.

But she also appeals to emotion. She specifically does not ask for mercy so as not to wipe out an entire people, particularly now that Achashverosh is aware that it's the Jewish people who are being victimized. Instead, she asks for a personal favor. Twice she mentions that she is asking something of him to do for her; that if there is any connection at all, if has any feelings at all for her, he will consider and concede her next request.

While clearly not part of her original plan, Esther realizes that the way in which she makes her request could save or seal the fate of the Jewish people. Even while not granting her everything she had hoped for, Achashverosh not only had Haman executed but also gifted Haman's entire fortune to Esther. This wasn't something she asked for or even likely anticipated. Similar to the entire episode resulting in Haman's execution, it seems spontaneous and reflective of Achashverosh's mood. Previously, Achashverosh had acted quite magnanimously toward Esther – or at least said he would do so. Each time she approached him about attending her parties, he asks what he can do for her, עַד חֲצִי הַמַּלְכוּת וְתֵעָשׂ – even to half the kingdom, it shall be fulfilled.

And even while it's somewhat unclear precisely what Achashverosh had in mind, the phraseology indicates that he was trying to be generous. Esther, for her part, 'merely' requested that he attend her parties.

* * *

When Achashverosh grants Esther all of Haman's fortune – while somewhat unexpected from Esther's perspective – it's not completely out of character for Achashverosh. He was clearly in a giving mood. Up until now he had always offered עַד חֲצִי הַמַּלְכוּת and Esther, wisely, didn't take him up on it. Now it's his chance to show his affection and appreciation for Esther. But Esther is trying to use this opportunity to accomplish far more.

The way in which she frames her request is all about herself with very little about the Jewish people as a whole. Esther is trying to show Achashverosh that while she appreciates his 'gift,' if he really wanted to show his affection or at the very least his care and concern, he could grant her this one 'little' favor.

It's also possible, that Esther had something else in mind as well. After all, the Megilah isn't quite clear on Achashverosh's motivation in gifting her Haman's estate and fortune. While it seems like a nice gesture, the precise nuance behind the move may make a difference. In fact, R. Alkabetz suggests that Achashverosh felt guilty after having previously considered the possibility of infidelity on the part of Esther with Haman. This was her original plan after all – to convince Achashverosh that she was having an affair, which would have likely resulted in both of their deaths. While Esther changed course during its execution, the thoughts, fears, and hesitations that she planted in Achashverosh's mind were still very real. Just because she redirected her efforts didn't make his concerns disappear. But in the end, it was quite clear to Achashverosh that Esther most certainly had no romantic relationship with Haman whatsoever; he was actually her mortal enemy, plotting not only to kill her but her entire people.

* * *

Not having anticipated Achashverosh's overwhelming generosity, it's quite possible that Esther realized and understood his motivation and seeming change of heart. Until now, Achashverosh had consistently responded to Esther by talking a big talk, but as she never took him up on the offer, she could never be sure if it was more than just talk. But realizing that Hashem clearly has a plan in mind, Esther decided that it's now time to find out.

Even while the Megilah does not offer a reason for Achashverosh's sudden largesse, Esther is well aware that her original plan was to convince Achashverosh that she and Haman were having an affair. She is also likely well aware that her plan was quite effective. Achashverosh's actions the previous night indicated that her potential infidelity, particularly with Haman, was clearly on the king's mind. Going into the second party, Achashverosh had more than a hunch that something was going on between Esther and Haman; it kept him up the night before and moved him to belittle and disparage Haman – his closest and most trusted advisor – just hours before he was to attend a private drinking party with the king and queen. Achashverosh wasn't exactly sure what was supposed to happen at the party, but he was pretty sure that he wasn't going to like it and that making sure Haman was well aware of his station within the royal hierarchy could prove an effective means of the king maintaining control over the situation.

Given his heightened suspicions and willingness to act on them, it must have come as quite a shock when Esther revealed that Haman wasn't interested in a romantic relationship with her, but was rather out to kill her and her people. In the midst of responding to this changing reality, it's important to question what happened to Achashverosh's initial suspicions and hesitations.

Even at the time, he realized that he didn't have any hard proof about their relationship; if he was more certain, he would have never attended the second party, let alone offer Esther to grant her any request. These were just thoughts, the speculations of a nervous king. Achashverosh recognized that while he must act cautiously – since his kingship and possibly his life could have depended on it – there was a chance that he simply misread the entire situation. At the end of the story – at least from his perspective – it's clear that he was wrong.

Esther, having choreographed the entire situation, is well aware of what she deliberately misled Achashverosh to believe and that he is likely feeling somewhat regretful or at least somewhat apologetic and embarrassed to have questioned and doubted her loyalty. She realizes that this is why he likely gave her the gift of Haman's estate – to apologize and make up for his incorrect (from his perspective), inappropriate, and frankly offensive assumption about her. Esther, for her part, is not going to correct him. After all, she planned all of this and it clearly worked. She was simply hoping for a slightly different outcome – that Achashverosh would reverse Haman's decree.

When she didn't completely accomplish her goal, she needed to quickly reassess and figure out her next move. Recognizing Achashverosh's gift as indicative of a relative and brief vulnerability in that he feels somewhat guiltily indebted to her, Esther manipulates the opportunity to her advantage. This is why she frames her request as being all about how much she means to the king and plays up her loyalty to him. אִם עַל הַמֶּלֶךְ טוֹב וְאִם מָצָאתִי חֵן לְפָנָיו וְכָשֵׁר הַדָּבָר לִפְנֵי הַמֶּלֶךְ וְטוֹבָה אֲנִי בְּעֵינָיו – if it appears good to the king, and if I find favor in his eyes, and it is appropriate in his opinion, and I am good in his eyes. Since, Esther is intimating, all of those descriptions are true, Achashverosh was completely off base in even considering the possibility of her infidelity. As she is about to make her request, she makes sure to rouse within Achashverosh that same guilt that he just felt on his own.

What makes this particularly interesting is that Achashverosh is once again unaware of what is going on around him. He is unaware that Esther orchestrated this entire story and that it was her intention that he should mistakenly believe that she and Haman were having an affair. But even while Achashverosh now recognizes that his suspicions were misplaced, it's hard to know what, in retrospect, did he think about the various aspects of Esther's plan, such as the multiple parties, the suggestive language, and the parties' very exclusive guest lists.

As the Megilah continuously presents Achashverosh as politically astute and even somewhat contemplative, it's quite possible that in recognizing his error, he perhaps thought that he simply let his anxious, hesitant, and somewhat suspicious overall nature get the better of him. As such, he's willing to read all of Esther's actions far more charitably, as her attempt to stop Haman. Given that Haman's status, allegiance, and alliance with Achashverosh was public knowledge, Achashverosh can understand why Esther didn't just come straight out to him with her request. Achashverosh rationalized that she was hesitant and somewhat nervous about approaching him with serious concerns about his closest and most trusted advisor. While he may not be able to explain every detail of why she did what she did, he understands why she went about this request in a rather roundabout way. It makes sense that she would try to bring all three of them together and it makes sense that she would try to play up their marital relationship. After all, she wanted something of Achashverosh that if she would have asked for outright, he would have almost certainly denied.

* * *

From Achashverosh's perspective however, Esther is completely unaware of his suspicions. All he thinks is that Esther was trying her best to utilize her relationship with the king to grant her request and save her life and the life of her people. He has no idea whatsoever that all of his suspicions were actually part of Esther's plan all along. From his perspective, it wouldn't make any sense that she would try to feign a relationship with Haman; how would that even help? Esther, for her part, recognized that she must be willing to risk her life to get Haman killed and hopefully save the Jewish people, but this wasn't something that Achashverosh even considered.

So when Achashverosh grants Haman's estate to Esther, he doesn't expect her to realize that it's a 'gift of guilt.' He is just being magnanimous, showing his concern for Esther who up until now was worried that her life was at risk. Esther however, understands full well what is transpiring, perhaps even reveling in the recognition that her plan was so convincing that Achashverosh feels that he needs to make up for having believed it. But realizing that the Jewish people were still in danger, Esther capitalizes on the situation to her advantage.

Playing off Achashverosh's guilt – which he thinks Esther is completely unaware of – she pleads with him that if he really cares for her and if she, as the Persian queen, plays a meaningful role, he will grant her another request. For Esther, it wasn't really about love or the depth of their relationship, of which the Megilah doesn't really give much background, but given Achashverosh's penchant for political calculation, likely did not require a solid foundation of marital bliss for him to qualify it as a political success. Instead, Esther was simply manipulating Achashverosh's already existing guilt and possibly some shame in questioning the fidelity of his wife who was actually just trying to save her own life.

Realizing that Achashverosh didn't immediately associate rescinding Haman's decree with executing Haman, Esther understands that this was not going to be a simple request. This is why she frames her petition as a concession that Achashverosh would be making for her and is overly effusive with how Achashverosh granting this request would demonstrate and display his trust and care for his dear wife.

# Chapter Thirty-Seven

Esther's request isn't quite as straightforward as it might seem. She asks Achashverosh to reverse Haman's decree and the king immediately responds that even though he might want to, he can't do that since royal edicts can't be rescinded. Instead, Mordekhai ends up issuing a follow up promulgation that the Jews – the targets of Haman's original decree – should be עֲתִידִים לַיּוֹם הַזֶּה, ready and attuned for that which will happen on that day. Leaving the details of Mordekhai's letter and promulgation aside for the time being, the back and forth between Esther and Achashverosh is difficult enough.

Was Esther unaware that royal proclamations were eternal and could never be rescinded? If so, what exactly was she asking for? If she wasn't aware of this peculiarity, why not? Considering the Mordekhai was an advisor to the king and, more generally, a politically active member of the Shushan aristocracy, it's hard to believe that he wasn't aware of the details of how a bill becomes a Persian law. Was this not that well known? But even if it was a rather unknown detail, more importantly, why would or should Persian law work in such a strange way?

There are clearly bits of information missing from this story which lead the commentators to take different approaches, by 'filling in the blanks' in various ways.

For example, the Megilah consistently portrays Mordekhai as a prominent member of Shushan's governing class and a natural leader who is able to navigate the political machinations of a strange governmental structure and eventually manage to actually save the Jewish people. Mordekhai is consistently presented as a knowledgeable and clever government official, making it hard to believe that he was unaware of the rule that royal decrees cannot be rescinded. At the same time, it's pretty clear that Esther (and by extension Mordekhai with whom she devised her plan) assumed that Haman's decree would die with him.

These seemingly contradictory assumptions led some to conclude that while the non-revokability of royal decrees was well known, this procedural regulation was something that Haman himself had instituted. With Achashverosh executing Haman for treason, it wasn't unreasonable to assume that those regulations that Haman had put in place would immediately expire. If so, it's no longer unreasonable for Esther to request to rescind the decree and letters that Haman has spread throughout the kingdom. This whole approach is somewhat difficult since Daryavesh of Madday, who ruled prior to Koresh, makes reference to such a peculiarity of Persian law (*Daniel* 6:13), predating Haman's rise to power by several years.

Alternatively, others argue that it was well known to both Mordekhai and Esther that Achashverosh could never issue a royal decree taking back Haman's letters and decree. That's simply not how things worked in Shushan. What they were hoping for was that after killing Haman for plotting against the queen and the Jewish people, that he would sympathize with them and at the very least issue a decree granting them the right to defend themselves. When Achashverosh did not do so spontaneously, Esther approaches him with this very request.

Other commentators offer a slight variation on this last approach, suggesting that Achashverosh also recognized the predicament of the Jewish people. He knew that Haman's letters already reached their intended recipients and that there were citizens throughout his kingdom who had plans set to annihilate the Jewish people in about a year's time. There was simply nothing he could do to stop it. He had hoped that by his executing Haman and very publicly granting Haman's estate to Esther, it would clearly demonstrate that he, as the king, does not wish any harm to befall the Jews and in fact is handsomely rewarding them. Achashverosh hoped that his actions would serve as an example that, in truth, he didn't want to kill the Jews.

This last approach is perhaps most rooted in the text. When Esther requests to send a second set of letters with a new decree, Achashverosh responds by noting that he has already executed Haman and granted Esther his estate – a point that while true, without this background, doesn't appear to be terribly relevant. But according to this approach, this was actually part of Achashverosh's own response to the threat against the Jews. He tried to demonstrate that not only did he not harbor any ill will toward them, but that the very person who tried to have them killed was himself put to death by the king and the king went one step further, by granting Haman's estate to the very queen that he was trying to kill. In fact, several commentators point out that to make sure this end was accomplished, Achashverosh asked for this very story to feature at the opening of Mordekhai's letter to the people.

* * *

From a broader perspective however, the biggest challenge facing Mordekhai and Esther is how to proceed. If it wasn't clear originally, now it most certainly was clear that Haman's original decree couldn't be rescinded. The best they could do is send a second decree; but even in doing so, they couldn't actually void the first. One option would have been to write that the first decree was a forgery; that Haman issued it without the king's knowledge or consent. But this would just raise an immediate second problem – why would anybody believe this second decree more than the first? Maybe the second was a forgery and the first was valid? Given the confusion, how could a far flung Persian citizen decipher fact from fiction? Rav Alkabetz in fact argues that this was precisely Achashverosh's idea – to sow confusion in the minds of ordinary citizens so that instead of acting on either of the decrees, they would look to him for guidance and follow his lead. Since Achashverosh had just put Haman to death and granted his estate to Esther, the citizenry would see that the Jews are finding favor in Achashverosh's eyes and they too would act benevolently toward them.

Regardless of the approach one takes to understanding this particular back and forth, it still doesn't guarantee any particular outcome or necessarily spell salvation for the Jews.

# Chapter Thirty-Eight

Perhaps one of the most troubling aspects of this story is why the Jews needed permission in the first place to defend themselves? If Haman were still alive and his decree still actively enforced, what exactly were the Jews planning on doing on that fateful 13th of Adar? If the decree was to kill them off, what would they lose by defending themselves? Even if they had no permission to do so, what's the worst that could happen? Would they be put to death for violating the edict? And since Mordekhai's new decree didn't actually stop anybody from trying to kill the Jews, what did it practically mean that now the Jews had royal permission to defend themselves? Even after Mordekhai's letters, the facts on the ground didn't change much neither for the Jews nor for their enemies.

But even while the motivation and impetus are somewhat clouded, the effect of Mordekhai's letters was quite significant. וְרַבִּים מֵעַמֵּי הָאָרֶץ מִתְיַהֲדִים (And many from among the nations converted to Judaism) as well as מְנַשְּׂאִים אֶת הַיְּהוּדִים (showed deference to the Jews) – not only did many Persians refrain from acting violently toward the Jews, they themselves chose to either convert to Judaism or otherwise come to sincerely respect the Jewish religion and the Jewish people. While there still were a great number of people who fought against the Jews on that fateful day, the reader is left imagining how much more lopsided that battle would have been if not for Mordekhai's letters. Apparently, they had a significant effect.

It's hard to guess the perspective of a common Persian citizen of the time. Considering the lack of fast and efficient communication, it seems fair to assume that most of Achashverosh's subjects were completely unaware of the day to day happenings of Shushan. All they knew was that a few weeks ago they received a message from Haman, Achashverosh's most trusted advisor, to be ready in eleven months' time to exact vengeance, punishment, and violence upon the Jewish people. The Megilah doesn't mention much more content to these letters and it's quite possible that they said little more than simply that, "Be prepared to kill all of your Jewish neighbors on the upcoming 13th of Adar." That they were willing to do so (evidenced by the fact that many of them in fact eventually did so), seemingly without reason or excuse, indicates some basic level of antisemitism just beneath the surface looking for an excuse to be put into practice.

It's hard to imagine that a random Persian citizen in a far flung province would have harbored and cultivated such a strong sense of Persian identity, loyalty, and fealty that if asked to completely annihilate a different sect of the population that he would have so easily complied. This relates somewhat to the earlier theme the Megilah seeks to highlight in describing Haman's vicious plot: antisemitism doesn't need a reason, only an excuse. Haman was well aware of this just-beneath-the-surface feeling among many of his compatriots and leveraged it to his advantage.

Recognizing this reality tremendously complicates the job lying ahead of Mordekhai and Esther in saving the Jewish people. Haman was pandering to a population of people just looking for an excuse to exact vengeance and violence upon the Jewish people. Practically speaking, the only way to completely prevent anything from happening would be for Achashverosh to explicitly revoke the original decree – something that he was practically unable to do. What they therefore needed was for some way for Achashverosh to show the people that, regardless of the impression given by the first letters, he certainly does not wish for the Jews to be killed.

* * *

The challenge was to figure out a way to show that Achashverosh no longer supported the original decree, while at the same time not technically revoking it. With that in mind, the content of the second letters makes a lot more sense. Clearly, even had the second letters not been sent, the Jewish people would have defended themselves; they would have had no reason not to. Having known the date of the anticipated communal attack, they likely would have banded together to defend themselves and their families. Even though seriously outnumbered, they hoped that their valiant effort would at least be able to defend their people and their community, fighting for their very survival. The point of Mordekhai's letters was not to grant them this permission, which they didn't actually need. Instead, it was a demonstration of Achashverosh's preferences and desires.

For those receiving these second letters, it was certainly strange. Since they knew that the original decree couldn't be rescinded, a follow up letter was most certainly not an everyday occurrence. That alone would have garnered these letters sufficient attention that the intended audience would take them quite seriously. To further insure that they had maximum impact, Mordekhai specifically chooses to use the very same messengers that delivered the first letters to deliver this set as well.

The distribution network necessary to deliver a royal decree and message to all 127 provinces was likely elaborate, requiring coordination and skill. In an era before more efficient communication, it also required messengers who were not only familiar with the route, terrain, and area they were to reach, but also necessitated making sure that the intended audience would be receptive to the message. While it was likely far simpler than today to forge a decree, it's safe to assume that there was some protocol in place to authenticate each message and guarantee its royal authorship.

That said, the arrival of a second letter standing in stark contrast to the first, was likely to encounter some resistance. To quell any such mistrust, Mordekhai specifically sent the very same messengers back along the very same routes from which they just returned. He wanted to insure that the recipients in each and every city and village would recognize them from just a little while ago and recognize that these second letters were just as authentic and reliable as the first.

This is why Mordekhai waited until the 23rd of Sivan to send the letters out. While there is some debate as to the precise date that Haman was hanged – the 15th, 16th, or 17th of Nissan – with Esther's plea to send out a second set of letters immediately thereafter, the Megilah doesn't give any context or reason that Mordekhai waited over a month to send out his letters. Doing so immediately would have emphasized how important they were or how certain Achashverosh was about trying his best to everything just short of revoking the original decree. However, doing so would have meant finding a completely new set of messengers since the first set were still out on their mission (reaching the farthest of the 127 provinces presumably took several weeks). While the two messages would have arrived within a week or so of each other, the ensuing confusion would have simply escalated. The two messengers may have even crossed paths on the respective back and forth journeys and, considering that the first messenger was likely completely unaware of Haman's recent demise, wondering what in the world was going on in Shushan. It wouldn't require a high dose of skepticism for a recipient to hesitate and speculate as to how seriously these second letters are meant to be taken.

To avoid all of this confusion, Mordekhai wanted to specifically send the very same messengers who delivered Haman's letters. While the messengers themselves might be somewhat confused as to what happened in Shushan during their absence, when the citizens of the very same cities and villages that they recently visited would greet them a second time, the messengers would be automatically assumed to be carrying an official royal proclamation and carry an aura of trust and authenticity about them. In fact, while the Megilah is quite clear that Mordekhai waited for over a month to send this second letter (even if the commentators quibble as the exact number of days), once he decides to send them, the Megilah repeatedly highlights the speed and rush with which they were sent. הָרָצִים יָצְאוּ מְבֹהָלִים וּדְחוּפִים בִּדְבַר הַמֶּלֶךְ... (the messengers went out in urgent haste at the king's command) – from the story's narrative perspective, a full month already elapsed, and there is no reason given for Mordekhai suddenly speeding things up as the 23rd of Sivan approached. But if the Megilah wasn't describing Mordekhai's rush, but rather that of the messengers', it makes a lot more sense. The messengers who just returned from delivering Haman's letters were commanded to immediately turn back around and do the exact same job they had just spent weeks fulfilling – but this time with Mordekhai's letter in hand. Mordekhai was indeed in a rush to get these letters disseminated far and wide as quickly as possible. And once it was feasible, once the specific messengers he wanted to use arrived back in Shushan, he immediately sent them out once again, with no time to spare.

# Chapter Thirty-Nine

While normally focusing on the differences between the letters, at least superficially, there are many similarities as well. Both are written by the king's second in command, both encourage battling among the king's subjects, and both are sent via an elaborate royal decree-spreading messaging service. Even much of the language surrounding the writing and disseminating of the letters seems similar. That said, it only highlights the potential significance of the small differences.

Haman's letters:

> וַיִּקָּרְאוּ סֹפְרֵי הַמֶּלֶךְ בַּחֹדֶשׁ הָרִאשׁוֹן בִּשְׁלוֹשָׁה עָשָׂר יוֹם בּוֹ וַיִּכָּתֵב כְּכָל אֲשֶׁר צִוָּה הָמָן אֶל אֲחַשְׁדַּרְפְּנֵי הַמֶּלֶךְ וְאֶל הַפַּחוֹת אֲשֶׁר עַל מְדִינָה וּמְדִינָה וְאֶל שָׂרֵי עַם וָעָם מְדִינָה וּמְדִינָה כִּכְתָבָהּ וְעַם וָעָם כִּלְשׁוֹנוֹ בְּשֵׁם הַמֶּלֶךְ אֲחַשְׁוֵרֹשׁ נִכְתָּב וְנֶחְתָּם בְּטַבַּעַת הַמֶּלֶךְ. וְנִשְׁלוֹחַ סְפָרִים בְּיַד הָרָצִים אֶל כָּל מְדִינוֹת הַמֶּלֶךְ לְהַשְׁמִיד לַהֲרֹג וּלְאַבֵּד אֶת כָּל הַיְּהוּדִים מִנַּעַר וְעַד זָקֵן טַף וְנָשִׁים בְּיוֹם אֶחָד בִּשְׁלוֹשָׁה עָשָׂר לְחֹדֶשׁ שְׁנֵים עָשָׂר הוּא חֹדֶשׁ אֲדָר וּשְׁלָלָם לָבוֹז. פַּתְשֶׁגֶן הַכְּתָב לְהִנָּתֵן דָּת בְּכָל מְדִינָה וּמְדִינָה גָּלוּי לְכָל הָעַמִּים לִהְיוֹת עֲתִדִים לַיּוֹם הַזֶּה.

> On the thirteenth day of the first month, the king's scribes were summoned and a decree was issued, as Haman directed, to the king's satraps, to the governors of every province, and to the officials of every people, to every province in its own script and to every people in its own language. The orders were issued in the name of King Achashverosh and sealed with the king's signet. Accordingly, written instructions were dispatched by couriers to all the king's provinces to destroy, massacre, and exterminate all the Jews, young and old, children

> and women, on a single day, on the thirteenth day of the twelfth month—that is, the month of Adar—and to plunder their possessions. The text of the document was to the effect that a law should be proclaimed in every single province; it was to be publicly displayed to all the peoples, so that they might be ready for that day.

Mordekhai's letters:

> וַיִּקָּרְאוּ סֹפְרֵי הַמֶּלֶךְ בָּעֵת הַהִיא בַּחֹדֶשׁ הַשְּׁלִישִׁי הוּא חֹדֶשׁ סִיוָן בִּשְׁלוֹשָׁה וְעֶשְׂרִים בּוֹ וַיִּכָּתֵב כְּכָל אֲשֶׁר צִוָּה מָרְדֳּכַי אֶל הַיְּהוּדִים וְאֶל הָאֲחַשְׁדַּרְפְּנִים וְהַפַּחוֹת וְשָׂרֵי הַמְּדִינוֹת אֲשֶׁר מֵהֹדּוּ וְעַד כּוּשׁ שֶׁבַע וְעֶשְׂרִים וּמֵאָה מְדִינָה מְדִינָה וּמְדִינָה כִּכְתָבָהּ וְעַם וָעָם כִּלְשֹׁנוֹ וְאֶל הַיְּהוּדִים כִּכְתָבָם וְכִלְשׁוֹנָם. וַיִּכְתֹּב בְּשֵׁם הַמֶּלֶךְ אֲחַשְׁוֵרֹשׁ וַיַּחְתֹּם בְּטַבַּעַת הַמֶּלֶךְ וַיִּשְׁלַח סְפָרִים בְּיַד הָרָצִים בַּסּוּסִים רֹכְבֵי הָרֶכֶשׁ הָאֲחַשְׁתְּרָנִים בְּנֵי הָרַמָּכִים. אֲשֶׁר נָתַן הַמֶּלֶךְ לַיְּהוּדִים אֲשֶׁר בְּכָל עִיר וָעִיר לְהִקָּהֵל וְלַעֲמֹד עַל נַפְשָׁם לְהַשְׁמִיד וְלַהֲרֹג וּלְאַבֵּד אֶת כָּל חֵיל עַם וּמְדִינָה הַצָּרִים אֹתָם טַף וְנָשִׁים וּשְׁלָלָם לָבוֹז.

> So the king's scribes were summoned at that time, on the twenty-third day of the third month, that is, the month of Sivan; and letters were written, at Mordekhai's dictation, to the Jews and to the satraps, the governors and the officials of the one hundred and twenty-seven provinces from Hodu to Kush: to every province in its own script and to every people in its own language, and to the Jews in their own script and language. He had them written in the name of King Achashverosh and sealed with the king's signet. Letters were dispatched by mounted couriers, riding steeds used in the king's service, bred of the royal stud, to this effect: The king has permitted the Jews of every city to assemble and fight for their lives; if any people or province attacks them, they may destroy, massacre, and exterminate its armed force together with women and children, and plunder their possessions.

Mordekhai seems to take a more active role in the letter writing – וַיִּכְתֹּב, וַיַּחְתֹּם, וַיִּשְׁלַח, whereas Haman seems to be satisfied in merely seeing that it was done – נִכְתָּב וְנֶחְתָּם, וְנִשְׁלוֹחַ. Perhaps Mordekhai was familiar with *Chazal*'s comparison between Avraham and Bil'am, praising the former and condemning the latter for their respective personal involvement and lack thereof in the minor details of carrying out God's command. Aside from that detail, there is another difference, which, if just presented with Haman's letters, would not have stood out as significant, but in light of the Megilah implicitly presenting a comparison between the two, stands out as far more significant.

Haman's letters are quite clear in their expectation. The recipients are to לְהַשְׁמִיד לַהֲרֹג וּלְאַבֵּד all of the Jewish people on the 13th of Adar. And lest there be any confusion as to whom this applies, it was to be לְהִנָּתֵן דָּת בְּכָל מְדִינָה וּמְדִינָה גָּלוּי לְכָל הָעַמִּים – clearly and unequivocally applying to everybody and anybody within the kingdom. Similarly, Mordekhai's letters are clearly addressed to both the political leadership as well as the local Jews in each village and city. While the clear difference is that Mordekhai's letters grant permission to the Jews to not only defend themselves but exact justice on all those who seek to harm them, there is also a more subtle difference in the formulation, easy to glance over.

Whereas Haman commands לְהַשְׁמִיד לַהֲרֹג וּלְאַבֵּד, Mordekhai is clear to indicate אֲשֶׁר נָתַן הַמֶּלֶךְ לַיְּהוּדִים אֲשֶׁר בְּכָל עִיר וָעִיר לְהִקָּהֵל וְלַעֲמֹד עַל נַפְשָׁם – the permission for the Jews' defense comes directly from the king himself. It's a subtle difference, but one that Mordekhai likely deliberately insisted on making sure was included. These second letters were bound to cause some confusion amongst their readers in the various provinces. Mordekhai wanted to insure that the confusion was only about Achashverosh's motivation in issuing these two seemingly contradictory orders so back to back but that the message of the second letters was unambiguously understood. For whatever reason that the letters didn't explicate, it was to be clear that Achashverosh clearly wanted the Jews saved.

Anybody who read that second letter realized pretty quickly that the Jews didn't actually need royal permission to defend themselves; they most certainly would have done so with or without Achashverosh's agreement. What this letter unequivocally indicated was that Achashverosh is now behind their defense and wants them to succeed. That was the message that Mordekhai wanted to convey.

* * *

While both Haman and Mordekhai carefully planned how to spread their message to each of the 127 provinces, the Megilah gives the strong impression that the citizens of Shushan carried a more distinguished and elevated status than their fellow Persians. At the very opening of the story Achashverosh makes a separate party for them, distinct from the one held for the visiting officials and representatives. At the end of the story, the Jewish battle in Shushan takes a day longer than anywhere else in the Empire – indicating that Shushan and its citizenry were not always on par with the rest of the Empires subjects. After all, they likely interacted with the king himself or his ministers far more frequently and directly than anybody else and were more up to date on palace happenings and political gossip. But that said, it's hard to know how much of what transpired between Esther, Haman, and Achashverosh they were aware of as much of it took place in closed quarters.

In a time before mass communication and organized media, it took time for decisions, stories, and political moves to make the rounds among the populace. This is likely why Haman put in a lot of effort to make his decree quite clear, plastering it everywhere and anywhere to ensure that it would be heeded. So when Mordekhai's second decree finally came out without so much as an explanation as to how to reconcile the obvious differences between the two, the people were left to their own devices to make sense of the whole thing. What was Achashverosh really thinking?

It's also hard to know if the local Shushanites were aware of what exactly happened with Haman. Haman was hanged in his own backyard. After all, that is where he originally erected the tree to hang Mordekhai. The Megilah is quite clear that the tree was בְּבֵית הָמָן (in Haman's home) and not in the public square, where it's far more likely that other royal executions were held. While the tree was most certainly quite tall, presumably Haman's estate was quite large and therefore it's hard to know how many people actually saw Haman hanging or were even aware that it happened.

And even if a few people did see it, or more likely heard about it by word of mouth, the details surrounding his execution were most certainly not that well known. Did it even have anything to do with Haman's original decree? Or was it for some other reason altogether? Was there even any reason for the local Shushanites to associate the two events? Were they even aware that Haman authored the original decree? The commentators debate this point, but the simple reading of the Megilah does not give any hint that Haman's name was associated with the publicly distributed decree. While the people were likely aware of Haman's anti-Semitic tendencies, it seems more likely that they presumed that Haman impressed upon and finally convinced Achashverosh to finally go along with his hateful plot.

Mordekhai's second letters – with all of his efforts to demonstrate that they reflect Achashverosh's true motives and desires – played an important role in alleviating much of this confusion. According to some commentators, Achashverosh even asked Mordekhai to include Haman's execution at Achashverosh's behest at the opening of the letter, so as to make it quite clear that the king did not support Haman or his initial decree. Nonetheless, the facts on the ground were that there were still two valid royal decrees on the table: one declaring that the nations should come together to wipe out the Jewish people and a second decree that the Jews are given official sanction to defend themselves against their enemies.

* * *

To help quell any such hesitations and possible confusion, Mordekhai embarked on a public relations campaign. Immediately after sending the messengers off with his new decree, the Megilah describes,

> וּמָרְדֳּכַי יָצָא מִלִּפְנֵי הַמֶּלֶךְ בִּלְבוּשׁ מַלְכוּת תְּכֵלֶת וָחוּר וַעֲטֶרֶת זָהָב גְּדוֹלָה וְתַכְרִיךְ בּוּץ וְאַרְגָּמָן וְהָעִיר שׁוּשָׁן צָהֲלָה וְשָׂמֵחָה.
>
> Mordekhai left the king wearing royal robes of blue and white, and a magnificent crown of gold and a mantle of fine linen and purple wool. And the city of Shushan was joyous and celebratory.

At first blush, it seems to be a triumphant display, demonstrating Mordekhai's greatness and wisdom in finding a way to thwart Haman's plans. But that's not actually what happened. Even after issuing that second decree, Mordekhai could not be sure that the Jews were completely safe. They now had permission to defend themselves, which was great, but was no guarantee that they would be successful. It would seem that Mordekhai's triumph is completely misplaced when the lives of his countrymen still hang in the balance!

But perhaps it wasn't about triumph at all.

# Chapter Fourty

In describing his celebratory leaving the palace, the Megilah highlights and details the exquisite clothing he was wearing. In juxtaposing that description to the people's reaction, it seems that it's specifically seeing Mordekhai in those clothes that led to וְהָעִיר שׁוּשָׁן צָהֲלָה וְשָׂמֵחָה (the city of Shushan was joyous and celebratory). It's also not the first time that the people of Shushan watched Mordekhai exit the king's palace regaled so beautifully.

Just two months prior, Mordekhai was paraded throughout the streets of Shushan, similarly bedecked in the king's finest attire, riding on the king's horse, and being led by Haman himself. Watching that spectacle, the Jews of Shushan were likely somewhat perplexed as to what exactly was going on. While Haman was loudly proclaiming כָּכָה יֵעָשֶׂה לָאִישׁ אֲשֶׁר הַמֶּלֶךְ חָפֵץ בִּיקָרוֹ (This is what shall be done to a man whom the king wants to honor!), it wasn't really clear at all why the מֶּלֶךְ was חָפֵץ בִּיקָרוֹ at all. Did the people even know that Mordekhai helped foil a secret assassination plot so many years earlier? Even if they did, why would that be a reason for Achashverosh to reward Mordekhai now?

When Mordekhai left the palace that first time, there was no צָהֲלָה וְשָׂמֵחָה – Haman's threat was still very real and the Jews of Shushan were at the tail end of their three-day fast for Esther's success. While it seemed to portend something fortuitous – maybe their *tefillot* were helping? – they could not celebrate while Haman's edict still hung over their heads. The only thing that was clear to them was that Mordekhai clearly found favor in Achashverosh's eyes; the opulent and garish manner of 'rewarding' Mordekhai was clearly the work of Achashverosh.

And so when Mordekhai exited the palace this time, once again royally adorned in the finest of clothing, jewelry, and accoutrements (and according to some commentators, in the very same clothing he wore the first time), it was clear to everybody that he was doing so at the behest or at least with the agreement of Achashverosh. And this is exactly what Mordekhai wanted.

When the people of Shushan heard, read, and saw Mordekhai's letter, they didn't know how to react, since Haman's edict was still technically valid and wasn't (or more accurately, couldn't be) rescinded. As citizens of the capital city, it mattered very much to them to know which version Achashverosh himself supported. So on the very day that Mordekhai's letter was publicly displayed and published, Mordekhai himself emerges from the palace bedecked in the king's finest – he was sending a clear message that he and his letter had Achashverosh's support. This wasn't an act of triumph, but rather an attempt to sway public opinion to recognize that Achashverosh fully supported this second letter and only because of legal technicalities was unable to rescind Haman's earlier decree.

* * *

The Jews of Shushan were undoubtedly relieved when they read Mordekhai's letter which was publicly displayed only hours earlier, but only partially so. As people who lived around the palace long enough, they knew that what really mattered, when all was said and done, was Achashverosh's support. They were well aware that Achashverosh was quite politically astute and made decisions that primarily benefited himself and helped establish his rule and dominion over the Empire. He was the type of dictator to issue statements and edicts for political gain, even if he didn't stand completely behind them. So long as there was some political gain, the people of Shushan knew that Achashverosh would get involved. So when he gave permission for Mordekhai to issue his letter, was that because Achashverosh really backed Mordekhai's position or for some potentially selfish political gain?

That's why when the Jews of Shushan saw Mordekhai's clothing that they immediately צָהֲלָה וְשָׂמֵחָה. It wasn't out of pride (which they surely had) or misplaced triumph, but because this was a very public demonstration to the people of the capital that Achashverosh was fully in support of Mordekhai's agenda.

* * *

Mordekhai's plan was clearly successful. Jews everywhere celebrated the new decree while many מֵעַמֵּי הָאָרֶץ מִתְיַהֲדִים – and even while the commentators argue as to whether that means that they converted, were merely more favorably politically inclined toward the Jews, or something in between – it's pretty clear that the rest of the nations clearly got the message.

Nonetheless, there were still those among the vast Empire, including a fair number of Persians in Shushan, who took the opportunity as it was given to lash out and attack the Jews. With the technicalities of the law on their sides, these enemies were free to attack the Jews with the awareness that the Jews had explicit royal permission to defend themselves and exact justice and vengeance upon their enemies. It's not that Mordekhai's letter didn't accomplish its intended goal. It's pretty clear that throughout the vast Empire, the message was quite clear – Achashverosh not only granted explicit permission for the Jews to defend themselves, but through a variety of means mentioned earlier, it was clear that this decree had Achashverosh's full support.

The Megilah describes how Mordekhai's letters – both their explicit content and implicit demonstration of Achashverosh's full support – reached far and wide.

> וְכָל שָׂרֵי הַמְּדִינוֹת וְהָאֲחַשְׁדַּרְפְּנִים וְהַפַּחוֹת וְעֹשֵׂי הַמְּלָאכָה אֲשֶׁר לַמֶּלֶךְ מְנַשְּׂאִים אֶת הַיְּהוּדִים כִּי נָפַל פַּחַד מָרְדֳּכַי עֲלֵיהֶם. כִּי גָדוֹל מָרְדֳּכַי בְּבֵית הַמֶּלֶךְ וְשָׁמְעוֹ הוֹלֵךְ בְּכָל הַמְּדִינוֹת כִּי הָאִישׁ מָרְדֳּכַי הוֹלֵךְ וְגָדוֹל.
>
> All the officials of the provinces—the satraps, the governors, and the king's stewards—showed deference to the Jews, because the fear of Mordekhai fell upon them.

In fact, the Megilah testifies that when the Jews came together to defend themselves, וְאִישׁ לֹא עָמַד לִפְנֵיהֶם כִּי נָפַל פַּחְדָּם עַל כָּל הָעַמִּים (And nobody stood in their way for their fear was felt by all the nations). And nonetheless, in those two days of fighting in Shushan the Jews killed 800 enemies and in the 127 provinces, in a single day the Jews killed 75,000 people. The Megilah seems to be downplaying the numbers, that this rather staggering number was only a relatively minimal number of enemies. But if after everything that took place, more than 75,000 enemies battled the Jews, the reader is simply left wondering how horrific the carnage would have been without

Mordekhai's letters. If he and Esther hadn't succeeded, if nobody got the message to stand down or recognized that it was Achashverosh's desire that the Jews survive, the Jewish slaughter would have been massive. It's hard to believe that any of them would have actually remained. The point of the body count is to show the complete reversal of roles and fortunes, the dramatic total turn of events that led to אֲשֶׁר יִשְׁלְטוּ הַיְּהוּדִים הֵמָּה בְּשֹׂנְאֵיהֶם.

* * *

Mordekhai's letter granted the Jews permission to battle against those who rose up against them: כָּל חֵיל עַם וּמְדִינָה הַצָּרִים אֹתָם טַף וְנָשִׁים – Any force of any people or province that attacks them together with their children and wives – and all those who were מְבַקְשֵׁי רָעָתָם – Those who sought to harm them.

There is some debate among the commentators if permission was granted to exact revenge against the Jews' enemies more broadly, namely those who had for years harassed and incited violence against them, even if they didn't take up arms on the 13th of Adar. As noted earlier, the very fact that Haman's decree was well received revealed an underbelly of antisemitic swelling among the general Persian population, who were likely not too thrilled that the Jews just received a royal imprimatur to defend themselves. And while the Megilah describes that the Jews killed all those who were מְבַקְשֵׁי רָעָתָם, in its summary of the first-day-of-battle's events, it mentions וַיַּכּוּ הַיְּהוּדִים בְּכָל אֹיְבֵיהֶם (The Jews struck at all their enemies) more generally. However, in deliberate distinction from Haman's intention, Mordekhai mentions nothing about the spoils of war. Haman decreed that the Jews should be killed וּשְׁלָלָם לָבוֹז (and their possessions plundered), whereas Mordekhai doesn't even address the issue.

But even so, the Megilah points out – three times – that וּבַבִּזָּה לֹא שָׁלְחוּ אֶת יָדָם (they [the Jews] did not take any of the spoils of war). The Jewish battle was not one of aggression, but rather of defense and survival. They courageously fought against all those who raised arms against them, and according to some commentators, also those mortal enemies who harbored antisemitic feelings and tendencies but were too fearful to act on that day. But as a clear demonstration that theirs was a battle for their national survival and nothing more, וּבַבִּזָּה לֹא שָׁלְחוּ אֶת יָדָם. Although this was never articulated in Mordekhai's letters and not communicated between the various Jewish populations throughout the sprawling Empire, wherever the Jews battled, וּבַבִּזָּה לֹא שָׁלְחוּ אֶת יָדָם. It didn't need to be said, decreed, or mandated – it was understood that in a spiritually inspired battle for their survival, priorities are of prime importance.

This war wasn't the end of the Jewish settlement in the Persian Empire. It wasn't until Achashverosh's son Daryavesh that royal permission was granted to restart the building of the *Beit ha-Mikdash* in Yerushalayim, at which point only part of the Jewish community returned to Israel; many still remained. Regardless of what the future held, when the Jews fought on that 13th of Adar, they have no plans on leaving once the battle was one. Their Persian neighbors – the vast majority of whom did not rise up against the Jews and were not targeted in the battle – would still be there on the 14th and it was important for the Jews to continue to maintain good relations with them. It's hard to guess what these Persians thought of their Jewish neighbors, particularly in light of multiple edicts and letters, but at the same time, the Megilah makes no mention that any of them stood with the Jews to help defend them against a completely unprovoked and completely racist-driven attack.

After all was said and done, as the 13th of Adar started coming to a close, the Jews were certainly not annihilated, but their status within Persian society was still somewhat uncertain. It's true that some of the locals were מִתְיַהֲדִים out of פַּחַד מָרְדֳּכַי (fear of Mordekhai), but regardless of what that precisely means, it seems clear that the Megilah is indicating that it was certainly not because of respect and admiration for Mordekhai and what he and his people stood for. It's one thing to outwardly accord respect to a rising political leader, particularly as the Megilah notes out of פַּחַד, and something far different to lay aside an inner disdain and even hatred, possibly built up over many years.

Blatant antisemitic attempts at total annihilation do not and cannot occur in a social vacuum. While many of these non-Jewish neighbors did not actively attack or incite violence against the Jewish people, it's hard to believe that they all lived in complete peace and harmony. Antisemitism, even if not necessarily rising to the level of outright murder and violence, was clearly bubbling just beneath the surface. As a calculated move – and without any coordination among the various Jewish communities – they made an active choice to not take any spoils of war, even though, by right, it was theirs for the taking.

The Jews wanted the collective memory of that fateful day to be of a Jewish fight for survival and certainly did not want the picture in people's minds to be that of Jews walking off with riches that they plundered from their enemies. Better forgo that wealth than risk inciting the just-barely-hid antisemitism lurking in their hearts. The unambiguous image of the Jewish victory was one of survival and nothing more; a strategic move that was so innate and natural that although it needed every single person to participate, it didn't need an ounce of coordination.

# Chapter Fourty-One

As the 13th of Adar was coming to a close, Achashverosh, who has clearly been closely monitoring the situation, gives Esther a status report with the updated battle count and death toll. Perhaps realizing that she may have a somewhat different perspective than he as to how to judge success of that day, he reaches out to her once again to see what else he might be able to do for her. As opposed to previously, Esther is forthright with her two specific requests without any prefatory remarks or pleading with Achashverosh to listen to her. She recognizes that in the midst of these battles that he is clearly closely monitoring, Achashverosh would be open to suggestions about how to insure a Jewish survival. Esther asks that the Jews of Shushan be granted permission to continue fighting through the next day, the 15th of Adar, and that Haman's sons be hanged. Achashverosh immediately grants both requests.

Esther doesn't give any particular reason why the the Jews of Shushan actually needed a second day. What would have happened if Achashverosh hadn't granted permission? The other nations' permission to attack the Jews (from Haman's first decree) also expired on the 13th of Adar; they too wouldn't be allowed to engage in combat the next day. Was Esther afraid that the local Shushanites would ignore and violate the expiring decree and continue fighting the Jews the next day? If so, why was her request limited to the Jews of Shushan?

If she was worried that the nations would continue attacking the Jews the next day despite not being given specific permission to do so, it seems more likely that the concern would apply universally throughout the kingdom. Clearly, this was not at issue. Esther assumed that once permission was given to battle on the 13th, then it would end, regardless of outcome, on the 13th. Which only further begs the question, what was so unique about Shushan that required an extra day of fighting? And what does that have to do with hanging the already executed ten sons of Haman?

Esther desperately wanted to secure a Jewish future, not by merely surviving Haman's decree, but by establishing themselves as an official part of Persian society, deserving of respect, even if not appreciation or actual equality. She needed to find some way to demonstrate that this was not simply her desire and aspiration but rather a royally-sanctioned goal. This was particularly important in Shushan, the seat of governmental power and the people who naturally had the greatest influence in the larger political scheme throughout the Empire. These were also her neighbors, people who lived in and around the palace. Esther needed to further insure that, particularly in Shushan more than anywhere else, it was perfectly clear that everything she and Mordekhai did was with Achashverosh's complete support and backing. She therefore looked for some way to demonstrate that was Achashverosh not simply 'going along' with the current plan, but that he put his full force behind it and was involved in orchestrating it. Which is why she asked for the extra day.

Esther wanted there to be a clear royal decree in support of the Jewish cause which had nothing to do with Haman's or Mordekhai's original decrees. Since their decrees themselves sewed confusion and doubt as to Achashverosh's true intentions, she needed something additional and immediate that would clearly demonstrate that Achashverosh's heart was clearly with the Jews. Considering it was already getting late into the day of the 13th of Adar, Esther was looking for something public and striking that would unambiguously demonstrate Achashverosh's allegiances without leaving room for any misinterpretation. Something that would quickly grab everybody in Shushan's attention.

When the people of Shushan woke up early on the morning of the 13th – both Jew and Gentile – they knew that there would be a long, drawn out battle. But come sunset, the fighting had to end. Both Haman's and Mordekhai's decrees were quite specific in giving permission to fight only on the 13th of Adar and not a moment longer. Giving sudden permission to the Jews to continue to defend themselves the next day took the whole city by surprise. It's not something that anybody anticipated or could have even planned for; it was sudden and rash. And that was precisely the point.

It was proof positive that this day-long extension had nothing to do with either of the earlier decrees. Whatever any Shushan citizen surmised was Achashverosh's motives in issuing the contradictory decrees was now put to rest. While just prior it was likely that some in Shushan weren't sure of Achashverosh's true intentions – and the citizens of Shushan specifically recognized that this is really all that mattered in the Persian Empire – now there was no more question. Granting this extension, specifically now as the 13th of Adar was ending, was clear demonstration that Achashverosh most certainly supports the Jewish cause.

This is also why Esther also asked to publicly hang Haman's sons – to clearly connect Haman's plot to that day's battle – and simultaneously demonstrate that Achashverosh held Haman responsible for it and it was this seditious behavior that got him executed.

They were killed as part of the battle in Shushan, either because they rose up against the Jews in the city or were known to be active inciters of violence against the Jews. Haman's sons, more than anybody else throughout the kingdom, were well aware that killing the Jews was clearly not Achashverosh's will or desire. Since they were still technically within the confines of the law, they most certainly took advantage of the opportunity. Haman's hatred of the Jewish people was well known to those around him and those who heard of him; his sons continued to carry both his name and his banner. And even though they no longer ruled over Haman's estate (Achashverosh granted it to Esther), they were still clearly identifiable as Haman's ten sons, which is how the Megilah continues to identify them even after his death some 11 months earlier.

It's quite likely that there was a concerted effort that they be killed, as in fact they were, on that first day of battle. But at the end of that day, Esther asks Achashverosh for permission to hang them publicly. There is more here than simply poetic justice, since while the imagery is similar to the fate of their father, the punishment is not. Haman was executed by hanging; his sons were killed and then posthumously hanged. What's the purpose in hanging his sons and why does Esther frame it as part of her request to allow the Jews of Shushan to continue fighting for another day?

Hanging Haman's already dead sons was clearly designed to specifically be a public spectacle. It was done at Achashverosh's command and presumably with all the pomp and circumstance worthy of a royal hanging. The idea was that anybody watching would quickly recognize that they were being hanged at Achashverosh's behest, by his guards, bearing his seal, and presumably, in a public / royal venue. While the Gemara assumes that Haman's sons were hanged on the same tree that Haman was hanged, with even some commentators indicating that Haman was actually left hanging on that very tree for those 11 months such that he and his sons all hanged together, the simple reading of the Megilah seems to indicate a more public and recognizable venue for the sons' hanging. Considering that they were already dead, it's clear that hanging Haman's sons was intended to make a statement.

Because there may have been some question or confusion as to Haman's role and relevance to the original decree and as to Achashverosh's precise intentions and desires regarding the Jews' survival, Esther wanted to emphatically answer and allay any such concerns. A public display of royal power in punishing those responsible (or at least supportive of the one responsible) for this whole mess would cement Haman's connection to the original decree and clearly show the Shushan citizens that Achashverosh ideally would have called off the entire thing if he could. Since his hands were tied, he did the next best thing by granting formal permission to the Jews to defend themselves.

# Chapter Fourty-Two

For many readers of the Megilah, the story seems to end with the end of the eighth chapter. The fortunes are reversed, the Jews not only survive but even triumph, and all appears good in the land. And yet, the Megilah seems to drone on for another chapter and a half with detail after detail of the actual battle, both in Shushan and in the outer provinces and then concluding with a seemingly repetitive recounting of the establishment of the holiday of Purim. But even while seemingly important, neither aspect really seems to fit in well with the rest of the story. The earlier sections of the Megilah are in fact a story, a narrative of loyalty and trust, seduction and cunning. This last chapter and a half are rather dry.

In fact, the Megilah seems to lead to a conclusion twice, except that in both instances, the Megilah seems to continue with details that, at first glance, don't appear vital to the story. The first instance is right before the detailed discussion of the battle. After Achashverosh gives permission to the Jews to defend themselves, the Megilah could have easily simply concluded with a sentence or two indicating that the Jews battled valiantly, successfully defended themselves, and lived happily ever after. Instead, the Megilah details the reaction of the Jews to Mordekhai's second letters, how the Jews prepared for that day, and finally offering painstaking detail as to how many people were killed in Shushan, in the rest of the kingdom, and the strategies employed to insure a Jewish victory. While these all provide an accurate historical record of what transpired, all of this not only seems stylistically out of place, but doesn't seem to significantly contribute to the Megilah's overall narrative. As should be clear by this point, considering that the Megilah was written quite deliberately and inspired by רוח הקודש, there must be some meaning behind these details.

As is often the case, it's the last scenes of a film or chapters of a book that leave the most indelible mark on the reader. If so, the message contained within these details cannot be tangential to the essential message of the Megilah. Instead, it's specifically in these details – when read in the proper light – that help solidify the Megilah's theme of recognizing the *yad Hashem* in this world, in a meaningful way.

Many of the more mystically-oriented commentaries note that one of the Megilah's most fundamental and underlying themes is indeed captured in one of these details:

וְנַהֲפוֹךְ הוּא אֲשֶׁר יִשְׁלְטוּ הַיְּהוּדִים הֵמָּה בְּשֹׂנְאֵיהֶם.

> The opposite occurred: The Jews conquered and controlled their enemies.

This is not only a story of Jewish survival, but of the utter and complete reversals of fortunes in every sense of the term. The Jews were triumphant and did not just manage to survive by the skin of their teeth. King Achashverosh, who signed off on the initial annihilation plot, reversed course and granted permission to the Jews to stand up to their enemies. The evil and powerful Haman, who plotted so viciously against the Jewish people, ended up hanged together with his entire family, by the hands of a Jewess. The Jews' possessions, which Haman declared should be plundered by their enemies were not only untouched, but Haman's own estate was royally gifted to Mordekhai and Esther. And lastly, Mordekhai, who starts the story as Haman's arch-nemesis whom Haman couldn't even bare the ignominy of seeing as a fellow palace minister, rises up the ranks to surpass Haman (Achashverosh actually transfers the royal signet ring that he originally handed to Haman to Mordekhai) to be the official מִשְׁנֶה לַמֶּלֶךְ (viceroy to the king), a title not bestowed on a Jew in a foreign land since the days of Yosef in Egypt.

The main thrust of the Megilah's message is to seek out and find the *yad Hashem* playing out in the world and in history. The story of the Megilah takes place just on the cusp of the inauguration of the second *Beit ha-Mikdash*, a historical-spiritual period described by the Gemara as "post-miraculous." While it's somewhat debated, the general impression from *Chazal* (see *Yerushalmi Yoma* 1:4) is that the daily or regular miracles that punctuated much of the *Mikdash*-life of the first *Beit ha-Mikdash* were missing from the second. *Chazal* have a tradition that attributes chapter 22 of Tehillim, לַמְנַצֵּחַ עַל אַיֶּלֶת הַשַּׁחַר to Esther, explaining that just as the

אַיֶּלֶת הַשַּׁחַר ends the nighttime period, similarly the story of the Megilah signifies the end of the era of miracles. Maharal (Introduction 2) explains that homiletically speaking, daytime describes the natural order of events, when the causal connection between things is evident and obvious, while the nighttime symbolizes a more miraculous period, when it's harder to tell how or why things take place. The אַיֶּלֶת הַשַּׁחַר therefore appropriately describes the very end of the nighttime, when the first rays of the sun are about to break through and herald the beginning of a new era.

It's for this very reason that Hashem's intervention [or even His name] is never explicitly acknowledged in the Megilah. While it's clearly present, it's never openly acknowledged because that precisely describes this new point in history – seeing the *yad Hashem* in the world requires scratching beneath the surface. Transition periods are often hard to concisely describe, since by their very nature they contain elements and characteristics of both the past and present eras. Presenting an accurate picture and capturing the essence of such a period can be a challenge, particularly in maintaining an appropriate balance between elements of the past and of the future. As the Megilah's story straddles the fence between the epoch of open miracles and one where His hand is more hidden, it finds itself in this very conundrum.

This is the reason for focusing so sharply on the notion of וְנַהֲפוֹךְ הוּא – the Megilah wants to make sure that Hashem's hand is indeed never explicitly revealed throughout the story, but at the same time insure that it's plainly obvious that it is indeed Hashem who is orchestrating the entire story from behind the scenes. The way in which it manages this is not only by listing the very many seeming 'coincidences' within the story, but by highlighting how in so many of these instances there was a complete and total reversal of fortunes. It's not just that things managed to work out, or that the Jews just barely managed to eke out a solution to their problem – which would have been reason for celebration and recognition of Hashem's Hand in historical affairs – but that everything was completely turned on its head.

In describing these complete reversals of fortunes, the Megilah is trying to insure that the reader not only takes note of the many coincidences, but comes to emotionally recognize and eventually internalize that the sheer number and nature of these 'coincidences' are not the result of chance alone, but part of a Divine plan for the Jewish people. Indeed, Hashem's Hand is still hidden and His name absent from the story, albeit in the most obviously present sort of way. And that's precisely the point.

Detailing the preparations for the battle, describing how Mordekhai ascended the palace ranks until reaching a point that Persians wanted to join the Jewish people כִּי נָפַל פַּחַד מָרְדֳּכַי עֲלֵיהֶם, and highlighting the overwhelming Jewish triumph in all of the military arenas are all part of this effort. All of these details are seemingly unnecessary if the goal was simply Jewish survival. The purpose of including these details is to highlight these coincidences and make all of them – both the amount and the nature of each – so abundantly obvious, such that even a casual reader will recognize that at the very least, 'something' must be going on behind the scenes. Even though from a narrative perspective these details don't add all that much to the plot, the Megilah deliberately includes these details so as to drive home its main message in a more exaggerated and real way.

On a deeper level, several commentators note that the complete reversal of אֲשֶׁר יִשְׁלְטוּ הַיְּהוּדִים הֵמָּה בְּשֹׂנְאֵיהֶם is uniquely appropriate as a fitting end to the Mordekhai-Haman / Jewish-Amalek rivalry. When the Torah describes the original battle with Amalek, it concludes with a stark command: תִּמְחֶה אֶת זֵכֶר עֲמָלֵק מִתַּחַת הַשָּׁמָיִם – completely wipe out Amalek from the face of the earth. Jewish survival in Persia would have certainly been a sufficient salvation and may have even heralded the continued effort of rebuilding the second *Beit ha-Mikdash*, but it would not have meant the end of Amalek's presence in this world, including their physical presence as well as their spiritual outlook on life. It's only through the complete reversal of fortunes, of the אֲשֶׁר יִשְׁלְטוּ הַיְּהוּדִים הֵמָּה בְּשֹׂנְאֵיהֶם that the Megilah can conclusively end with the ultimate defeat of Amalek.

# Chapter Fourty-Three

Understanding how the details of the battle, while seemingly trivial, are included to bolster the Megilah's central message, the Megilah once again seems to head for a quick ending. Following the victory, Mordekhai and Esther set out to eternally commemorate these miraculous historical events as a *bona fide* holiday on the Jewish calendar. But instead of just indicating that Mordekhai and Esther initiated such an idea that *Bnei Yisrael* accepted, the Megilah spends a great deal of time describing in exquisite detail how Mordekhai and Esther sent letters to the Jews to encourage adopting the holiday, the nature of which was changed somewhat during these negotiations but was eventually universally accepted. Clearly, the Megilah thinks that it's central lesson is evident, relevant, and important to convey in these details as well.

It's in the course of describing these negotiations that the Megilah explains the unique name for this holiday: Purim – עַל שֵׁם הַפּוּר (on account of the lottery). As noted at the very beginning, the name selection is itself rather strange in specifically choosing to focus on the means by which Haman chose the date to attempt to annihilate the Jews instead of something more positive, or at the very least, something more central to the plot of the story. But even in accepting the theory presented earlier that the name Purim highlights how that which appears random and coincidental is most certainly not so, instead of simply making this observation and explaining the role of the פּוּר to the plot, the Megilah first tries to capture the main thrust of the story in a few short words:

> כִּי הָמָן בֶּן הַמְּדָתָא הָאֲגָגִי צֹרֵר כָּל הַיְּהוּדִים חָשַׁב עַל הַיְּהוּדִים לְאַבְּדָם וְהִפִּל פּוּר הוּא הַגּוֹרָל לְהֻמָּם וּלְאַבְּדָם. וּבְבֹאָהּ לִפְנֵי הַמֶּלֶךְ אָמַר עִם הַסֵּפֶר יָשׁוּב מַחֲשַׁבְתּוֹ הָרָעָה אֲשֶׁר חָשַׁב עַל הַיְּהוּדִים עַל רֹאשׁוֹ וְתָלוּ אֹתוֹ וְאֶת בָּנָיו עַל הָעֵץ. עַל כֵּן קָרְאוּ לַיָּמִים הָאֵלֶּה פוּרִים עַל שֵׁם הַפּוּר

> Because Haman the son of Hamdata the Aggagite, the tormentor of all Jews, planned to destroy the Jews and cast lots (פּוּר) to [determine the date] to destroy them. And with her coming before the king, he said that Haman's plan should be thwarted and he and his children were hanged on a tree. And so they called these days Purim, on account of the פּוּר ...

It's fascinating to note what the Megilah itself sees as the highlights of its own story. Clearly, it must include mention of the lots, since that was the impetus for the naming. It briefly describes the rise and fall of Haman, which itself was miraculous and set the stage for the eventual Jewish victory in battle. And it's also true that this victory was only possible when Achashverosh agreed to 'rescind' [or more accurately, agreed to issue a second decree that would have the practical effect of reversing the ramifications of the first] Haman's original letters. But why the mention of וּבְבֹאָהּ לִפְנֵי הַמֶּלֶךְ? It's indeed true that Achashverosh only agreed to send this second set of letters at Esther's request. But is Esther's coming before the king the most essential detail to highlight?

Perhaps, the point of this entire final section of the Megilah is to show that the Jews indeed learned the message of looking for *yad Hashem* in this world and responded appropriately. This is the same lesson that Esther learned and also put into practice when she had to approach Achashverosh a second time after Haman's execution, so as to reverse the decree. And this is all part of the reason for the naming of the holiday.

* * *

THE MAIN LESSON of the Megilah is recognizing the *yad Hashem* in this world and recounting the heroic ways in which it's appropriate to respond to this recognition. This is what Mordekhai explains to her when she initially hesitates to even approach Achashverosh the first time – וּמִי יוֹדֵעַ אִם לְעֵת כָּזֹאת הִגַּעַתְּ לַמַּלְכוּת. Esther realized that he was right and started seeing the *yad Hashem* in history. She recognized her historically important role in the Jewish story and rose to the occasion by risking her life to put into effect the elaborate plot that eventually brought Haman's downfall.

This is also what Esther took to heart in approaching Achashverosh after Haman was already killed to reverse Haman's decree. As opposed to the first time, Esther now approaches more confidently; more focused and far more forceful. She realizes that even while Haman is no more, the fate of the Jewish people still lies on her shoulders. Esther recognizes that it's all up to her. She just orchestrated Haman's downfall and realized that her plan had worked. Esther was keenly aware of the *yad Hashem* behind her success and that He was showing her that her involvement yielded results.

She is now at a second crossroads, but now she doesn't need any encouragement from Mordekhai as to how to act. She knows what she must do and seizes the moment, recognizing the lesson that Mordekhai taught her, וּמִי יוֹדֵעַ אִם לְעֵת כָּזֹאת הִגַּעַתְּ לַמַּלְכוּת – maybe this is why she is where she is. This is her role in life and a challenge she must conquer. This is why it's also the most passionate of her requests as she realizes this is her mission in life. In fact, to ensure that the reader feels this passion, the Megilah adorns the phrase וּבְבֹאָהּ לִפְנֵי הַמֶּלֶךְ with a *zarka* – an extended musical phrase that extends the word, building to a dramatic crescendo, highlighting the importance and feeling this phrase should evoke. It's not just another piece of the plot line, but a demonstration that Esther absorbed the lesson of the Purim story. **The Megilah is then not just offering a message of seeking out the yad Hashem in this world but also a story of how the main characters of the Megilah did just that and responded appropriately**. This is why the Megilah notes this point on the plot-line, even though only a seeming detail among many, in declaring the official name for the holiday. The Megilah wants the reader to remember its essential lesson.

This also explains the intense focus on the negotiations behind and eventual acceptance of Purim as a national holiday. When the Jewish nation recognizes the *yad Hashem* working on a grand scale, when they more keenly come to appreciate how Hashem choreographs even that which seems normal and natural, and through that experience a national salvation – the appropriate national response is to dedicate a holiday to commemorating those miraculous events. It's a lesson they learned from Esther herself, בְּבֹאָהּ לִפְנֵי הַמֶּלֶךְ.

Recognizing the *yad Hashem* in this world is the first step; what's then necessary is to appropriately respond. On a national level, that means commemorating those events on a communal level. With a historical awareness in mind, Mordekhai, Esther, and the Jews of the time realized that what they had experienced was not only of certain national importance but also of tremendous historical significance. The Jewish people as a whole were saved and, as the Megilah describes it, וְנַהֲפוֹךְ הוּא – with a complete reversal of fortune. The *yad Hashem* was visible to all who simply sought it out and therefore warranted a religious response. The nature, scope, and precise details as to how this response would be practically canonized in history was still in flux, necessitating some back and forth between Mordekhai and the Jewish community. But the idea itself – the eternal commemoration of these days as a cognizant awareness of the *yad Hashem* in history – was something that came naturally to everybody.

It's for that reason that the Megilah spends the good portion of the ninth chapter on this religious response: the days which were selected and how they corresponded to the nature of the miracles experienced; the specific religious ritualistic requirements of the day; and even a discussion and negotiation as to the manner in which the celebration should be held (as a full-fledged *Yom Tov* or a special day with a festive meal). The point of this section of the Megilah is to highlight how the Jews of Shushan and the entire Persian Empire understood the hidden message in the then-current events.

It's therefore completely appropriate for the Megilah to couch the naming of this holiday with a quick summation of the focal point of the story. Purim as a holiday is dedicated to both recognizing the *yad Hashem* in history as well as commemorating those who appropriately responded to it. Beyond just demonstrating to the reader how the *yad Hashem* had played out in history some 2,500 years ago, it's also meant as an inspiration that when we encounter the *yad Hashem*, whether on an individual or communal level, that we too should be prepared to respond.

# Chapter Fourty-Four

The Gemara makes much ado about the various formulations and details included in each of the proclamations issued by Mordekhai and Esther about the establishment of the holiday. There is an entire discussion of how it transitioned from a day of שִׂמְחָה וּמִשְׁתֶּה וְיוֹם טוֹב (celebration, feasts, and a holiday) to one that was limited to שִׂמְחָה וּמִשְׁתֶּה minus the יוֹם טוֹב component. In thinking about these discussions, it's important to realize that Purim was one of the very first *mitzvot derabbanan* and certainly the first obligatory Rabbinically-ordained holiday. It's understandable that this was not a simple process; most firsts aren't.

Mordekhai, as great as he was, was a member of the Persian king's court, intimately involved in Shushan politics, and as the Megilah itself testifies, while certainly popular, only רָצוּי לְרֹב אֶחָיו (popular [accepted] by most of his brethren). There was likely nobody who doubted Mordekhai's leadership abilities or his dedication to the Jewish people. All Jews, throughout Achashverosh's vast kingdom, were overly grateful for his intervention in Haman's plot and saving not only them as individuals, but the Jewish people as a whole. But all that said, for some, all this doesn't necessarily translate into Mordekhai being the right person to start fiddling with religious doctrine.

In fact, from a broader perspective, why exactly did Purim become a Jewish national holiday? Unfortunately, throughout our long history, there have been terrible episodes of death and destruction at the hands of the ruling oppressors. There were also many instances where plots were hatched, plans were laid, and yet, the Jews were saved and survived. This is true of almost all points in our long history. There are a myriad of personal stories of being "in the right place at the right time" to avoid selection, deportation, and death at the hands of the Nazis, communists, and Arab terrorists. There are stories of communities that were spared pillage and pogroms throughout the Middle Ages due to sudden changes of heart or what otherwise appear to be insignificant reasons. And even in Biblical times, *Sefer Melakhim* is replete with instances where the Jewish people were saved, time and time again. As believing Jews, we attribute all of this to *yad Hashem*; nothing is random or coincidental. What then makes the Purim story so unique that it warrants its own holiday?

It's because aside from telling an inspirational story, and teaching fundamental truths about how Hashem runs the world, the story of Purim is a watershed event in the transmission and acceptance of Torah.

In describing the events of *Matan Torah*, the Gemara relates the oft-cited notion that *Bnei Yisrael* were somewhat hesitant about accepting it as is. To 'incentivize' *Bnei Yisrael*, Hashem held *Har Sinai* above them (כפה עליהם הר כגיגית) and offered them a deal: either they accept the Torah or He drops the mountain for them to be buried underneath it. While *Bnei Yisrael* quickly acquiesce to the deal they cannot refuse, the Gemara immediately notes that such a transaction isn't considered valid – מכאן מודעא רבא לאורייתא! Rashi explains that for all eternity, *Bnei Yisrael* couldn't be held liable were they not to keep the *mitzvot* since neither they nor their ancestors ever willingly agreed to do so. This would be the ultimate cop-out: how could Hashem hold us liable for something that we never wanted any part of?

To which the Gemara quickly counters, הדר קבלוה בימי אחשורוש – there was a voluntary acceptance of the Torah during the Purim story. Not merely relying on a Tradition to this effect, *Chazal* see a hint to this in the very last chapter of the Megilah, when *Bnei Yisrael* accept Mordekhai's suggestion to create the holiday of Purim. The Megilah says קִיְּמוּ וְקִבְּלוּ הַיְּהוּדִים עֲלֵיהֶם וְעַל זַרְעָם – Jews fulfilled and accepted that which they had begun to practice (to celebrate and commemorate the miracles). Noting the double language of קִיְּמוּ וְקִבְּלוּ, the Gemara offers an additional level of interpretation: שקבלו כבר – they fulfilled that which they had previously accepted. Whereas approximately 1,000 years earlier *Bnei Yisrael* were pressured to accept the Torah, now they did so out of their own free will.

* * *

ONE OF THE most difficult challenges to this approach is the Biblical narrative itself! Famously, the Torah describes that when presented with the opportunity to receive the Torah, *Bnei Yisrael* shout out in unison:

נַעֲשֶׂה וְנִשְׁמָע – we will do and we will obey. Our Tradition is heavily invested in their having accepted to act even prior to understanding how or why. Regardless of precisely how that dual phrase is translated, נַעֲשֶׂה וְנִשְׁמָע certainly sounds like a voluntary commitment and a national opting-in to the Torah covenant. This story isn't in some obscure, lesser known Midrash, but is arguably the simplest reading of the Torah text itself. What possibly then could this passage in the Gemara mean?

The *Midrash Tanchuma* (*Noach,* near the end) presents the same narrative as the Gemara, albeit with a slight caveat. The Midrash explains that indeed כפה עליהם הר כגיגית and that the covenant of the Torah was coerced upon *Bnei Yisrael*. However, that is only part of the story. When it came to the תורה שבכתב, the written Torah (meaning that which is contained in the text of the חמשה חומשי תורה), *Bnei Yisrael* were more than happy and eager to commit to following its precepts, rules, and regulations. Its terms are easily understood, it has a defined beginning and end, has clear expectations, and is available as a guide to all who seek it out. It's to the תורה שבכתב that *Bnei Yisrael* enthusiastically responded נַעֲשֶׂה וְנִשְׁמָע.

But when it came to the תורה שבעל פה, the oral Torah, they were far less responsive. The תורה שבעל פה represents all that was taught to Moshe at Sinai, but for a variety of reasons, was not included in the text of the Torah. Understanding its precise nature and defining its boundaries has been the essential core topics of Jewish scholars from time immemorial. Beyond just including Traditional definitions of Torah concepts and phrases as well as other seemingly random rules and regulation that are completely divorced from the Torah text, Rambam includes far more than what appears in the text of the Torah alone.

He explains that תורה שבעל פה also includes all of the rules, regulations, and principles that *Chazal* derived through the י"ג מדות שהתורה נדרשת בהם – the officially sanctioned principles of Biblical exegesis. Although these are rules that the rabbis develop, since they are using the Divinely sanctioned principles to derive them from the Divine text, Rambam considers these all to be part and parcel of the תורה שבעל פה.

Accepting this notion leads to an interesting question as to the historical scope of these regulations. While Rambam considers all the rabbincally derived rules and regulations that utilize the י"ג מידות שהתורה נדרשת בהם to discern deeper levels of the Torah's text as in fact Biblical in nature, Netziv (*Kidmat ha-Emek* introduction to his *Ha'amek She'eilah*) points out that this may actually be a matter of Talmudic dispute. But even accepting that they do in fact apply on a Biblical level since they derive from the actual text of the Torah, the Chida (*Simchat ha-Regel*) wonders as to the historical applicability of these laws. If the rabbis of a particular generation utilize one of the י"ג מידות to derive a certain Torah law, does that law apply only from here on in or, considering that we believe that the text of the Torah has not changed since its revelation, does it even apply retroactively? Meaning, was it always a hidden Torah law, just waiting for the right rabbis to figure out how to reveal it, although part of the original intent, or, given the role that the rabbis play in elucidating the law, does it only have practical relevance once that is actually brought to fruition?

Interestingly, Chida assumes that these rules do apply retroactively, and are all part of the original intent of the Torah. For our purposes, this means that the exact parameters, limitations, and extent of the תורה שבעל פה could not have actually been known to *Bnei Yisrael* at the time of *Matan Torah*, as in every generation there possibility of its expansion – and according to the Chida, even its retroactive applicability, even back to the time of *Matan Torah* – always exists.

Rambam even goes so far as to include two additional categories that qualify as תורה שבעל פה, far more broad than the previous one: rabbinic requirements and rabbinic prohibitions. These are rules and regulations that are not even loosely based on the text of the Torah but were entirely invented by the greatest of Jewish sages. While they are often patterned after Torah laws (כל דתקון רבנן כעין דאורייתא תקון), they are completely additional and secondary to them. Rambam seems to be arguing that the corpus of תורה שבעל פה is far more expansive, encompassing all that *Chazal* instituted as means of enhancing our religious lives. Fulfilling these Rabbinic *mitzvot*, and even studying them, becomes an integral part of Torah.

Clearly, the parameters of תורה שבעל פה are far vaster than תורה שבכתב. The level of detail, the meticulously laid out requirements, and the seeming never ending ability for the rabbis to continue to grow the תורה שבעל פה, was too much for *Bnei Yisrael* to handle at the time.

They were committed to Hashem and were ready to commit to him that which they could see in front of them, the תורה שבכתב, but the accepting the תורה שבעל פה required some measure of coercion. It turns out, then, that הדר קבלוה בימי אחשורוש refers specifically to the תורה שבעל פה; whereas it was previously coerced, they now accepted it voluntarily.

# Chapter Fourty-Five

The Megilah's effusive description of the willingness and participation of *Bnei Yisrael* in establishing the holiday of Purim certainly paints the events in a positive and voluntary light. But even while the Megilah's description of establishing the holiday is quite detailed, there appears to be no mention or hint of the entirety of תורה שבעל פה.

But it's more than just a recorded Rabbinic tradition as to the deeper symbolism of the קִיְּמוּ וְקִבְּלוּ in establishing Purim. Maharal points out that Purim was the first of the rabbinic *mitzvot* to attain national support and acceptance. Although he uses somewhat different terminology, taking Rambam's listing of the different components of תורה שבעל פה into consideration, Maharal explains that building upon and adding to תורה שבעל פה presupposes a voluntary and willingness acceptance of all of תורה שבעל פה that preceded it. Establishing the holiday of Purim demonstrates that, certainly by this time, *Bnei Yisrael* have not only completely and willingly accepted the תורה שבעל פה but were willing to be partners in building it.

If then, Rav Hershel Schachter argues, *Megilat Esther* represents *Bnei Yisrael's* acceptance of תורה שבעל פה, it's understandable why some might think it inappropriate to include this story as part of the official canon of תורה שבכתב in Tanakh. In fact, the question seems so compelling that it's hard to understand why it was actually included in the end. Shouldn't the historical introduction to תורה שבעל פה be included as part of the תורה שבעל פה – and if so, be maintained as an oral and not as part of the written Tradition. He suggests that the answer lies in a further look at the events surrounding *Matan Torah*.

At some point during *Matan Torah* (there is some debate as to the precise chronology of events that aren't relevant to the current discussion), Moshe reads for the people from the סֵפֶר הַבְּרִית, lit., the "book of the covenant." It is through accepting that which it said in the סֵפֶר הַבְּרִית that *Bnei Yisrael* accepted the Torah and became obligated in its dictates. It's right after reading from the סֵפֶר הַבְּרִית that Moshe solidifies and actualizes the covenant by sprinkling from the blood of the sacrifices on the nation, symbolizing acceptance. While the Torah does not describe the contents of this סֵפֶר הַבְּרִית, Rashi explains that it was the actual Torah up until that point in history. Meaning, it was the story of *Bnei Yisrael* and the history leading to that auspicious historical moment. The acceptance of the Torah necessitated or at the very least included a recounting of the events leading to the occasion and by describing it as the סֵפֶר הַבְּרִית, the Torah is indicating its importance in the process. The covenant was sealed by recounting the events leading up to it. Rav Schachter argues that *Megilat Esther* fulfilled a similar purpose.

In light of the *Midrash Tanchuma,* the formal voluntary acceptance of the תורה שבעל פה after the miracles of the Purim story also necessitated a סֵפֶר הַבְּרִית – a recounting the events that led up to that momentous occasion. So even while the Megilah recounts the events that led up to the formal acceptance of the תורה שבעל פה as the סֵפֶר הַבְּרִית through which this covenant was sealed, *Chazal* chose to include it in the official canon of Tanakh. As a סֵפֶר הַבְּרִית, it had to be written, even while it described the acceptance of the non-written Tradition, and therefore, as a סֵפֶר, it took its rightful place among the other כתבי הקודש.

Nonetheless, as the transitional document and moment in history, straddling the gap between תורה שבכתב and תורה שבעל פה, even while it is formally part of the תורה שבכתב, there are certain unique features of the Megilah that distinguish it from the other כתבי הקודש. The Gemara notes that the Megilah refers to itself as both a סֵפֶר as well as an אִגֶּרֶת. Generally speaking, a סֵפֶר includes several halakhic properties, such as it must be written on parchment with indelible ink, among other requirements. An אִגֶּרֶת however, does not need to meet such strict standards. For example, a handwritten Megilah is considered kosher even if it is missing a few letters or even words, so long as the majority of the text is intact. When it comes to a *Sefer Torah,* we are far more exact and such a lenient standard is completely unacceptable. Similarly, when it comes to the stitching of the pieces of parchment together, a Megilah is considered kosher with only three stitches while a *Sefer Torah* requires stitching along the entire edge of the parchment. Even while formally part of the כתבי הקודש and the official canon of Tanakh, recognizing its unique status as introducing and formalizing the acceptance of the תורה שבעל פה, these differences exist, reflecting its unique status as straddling the fence between the written and oral Traditions.

* * *

It's no mere coincidence that *Bnei Yisrael* voluntarily accepted the תורה שבעל פה specifically after the miracles of Purim. And even while it's true that the simple reading of the Megilah doesn't seem to discuss the תורה שבעל פה at all and *Chazal* developed this idea based on a careful reading of two repetitive words (קִיְּמוּ וְקִבְּלוּ), it seems clear that they found particular significance and symbolism in the Megilah to support this contention. And it makes good sense.

*Megilat Esther* is the story of how Hashem works behind the scenes, how not everything is always as it appears, and that there is a whole architecture and system coordinating everything behind the scenes. This is also an apt description for the תורה שבעל פה – it also supports and makes sense out of the תורה שבכתב and often provides added necessary meaning and explanation for that which appears challenging or difficult to understand. As a story dedicated to the hidden side of things, it perfectly dovetails with the entire notion of תורה שבעל פה. It was never written down and was transmitted completely orally from father to son, teacher to student. While it was surely taught openly and spoken about in public and in that sense was certainly not hidden, in contrast to the תורה שבכתב which was written and therefore accessible to anyone and everyone, the תורה שבעל פה maintained a more ethereal quality.

The same is true of the *yad Hashem* in history; it was always openly acknowledged but not always felt quite as acutely as during the miracles of Purim. The symbolism is therefore particularly apt, that on the holiday acknowledging the real life relevance of that which sometimes appears hidden is also the holiday commemorating the acceptance of the 'hidden' part of the Torah tradition.

Following the same line of reasoning of *Megilat Esther* highlighting that which is normally hidden, there is a rich *Kabbalistic* tradition as to both the significance of various personalities, events, and actions within the Megilah as well as to a multifaceted appreciation, explanation, and deeper meaning to the holiday of Purim itself.

It's this hidden Torah and Hashem's hidden hand in history that we are charged with uncovering and discovering, both on Purim and throughout the entire year.